Critical acclaim for *Tim: An Ordinary Boy*:

TIM

An Ordinary Boy

Colin and Wendy Parry

CORONET BOOKS
Hodder and Stoughton

Copyright © 1994 by Colin and Wendy Parry

The right of Colin and Wendy Parry to be identified as
the Author of the Work has been asserted by them
in accordance with the Copyright, Designs and Patents
Act 1988.

First published in Great Britain in 1994 by
Hodder & Stoughton
A division of Hodder Headline PLC
First published in paperback in 1995 by Hodder & Stoughton
A Coronet paperback

10 9 8 7 6 5 4 3 2

Parry, Colin
Tim: Ordinary Boy
I. Title II. Parry, Wendy
942.71085092

ISBN 0 340 61790 X

Typeset by Hewer Text Composition Services, Edinburgh
Printed and bound in Great Britain by
Mackays of Chatham plc, Chatham, Kent

Hodder and Stoughton
A division of Hodder Headline PLC
338 Euston Road
London NW1 3BH

This book is dedicated to the memory of our son Tim, who was anything but an ordinary boy

Acknowledgements

Wendy and I wrote our book about Tim and the events that followed his death together. I did the writing, hence the use of the first person throughout, while Wendy checked everything I wrote as well as planning with me what material we should include.

We would like to thank all our family and close friends for their help and support since the day Tim was so seriously injured in the bombing of Bridge Street. Had it not been for their help, we could not have written this book. We drew on their strength, which they offered freely and without preconditions.

As well as to our family and friends, we want to express our special thanks to the following people:

To Brian Masters, for his encouragement in the writing of the book.

To Father John Walsh, for asking the right questions and for saying the right things.

To Paul Matthews, for going way beyond the call of duty and becoming a good friend and confidant.

To Les Lee and Mick Holland, for doing their very best and for caring so very much.

To the staff at Warrington and Walton Neurological Hospitals, for all they did in trying to save Tim and for minimising his and our suffering.

To Norma, for working so tirelessly and without complaint on the manuscript, and to Tracey, for taking over so well at the very end (while Norma was on holiday).

To Albert, for arriving from nowhere and for doing so much.

To Del O'Sullivan and her friends, for showing that ordinary Irish people do care.

To Susan and Arthur McHugh and all other Irish people actively seeking peace – don't stop, keep going.

To Piers and Neil, for being Tim's friends, and for the fact that they will always remember.

To Mel, Gareth and Tina, for loving Tim so much.

Finally, our love and thanks to Dominic and Abbi who have lost and suffered so much but complained so little.

Colin and Wendy

UACHTARÁN NA hÉIREANN
PRESIDENT OF IRELAND

Foreword

This is a remarkable book. It tells how Tim Parry was killed in an explosion in Warrington in March 1993. To the extent that it accounts for the loss of a beloved child in terrible circumstances it is eloquent enough. But it goes further than that. It also describes how the parents of that child set out on a profound moral journey. It tells how they sought out the country and culture which that act of violence had claimed – falsely, of course – to represent.

Some of the most poignant chapters of this book keep track of that journey. They observe Colin and Wendy Parry as they travelled from helpless grief to an unswerving attempt to unravel the old diversities and misunderstandings which cost their son his life. They tell how, with a direct gaze, and with the authority of their own suffering, they asked straight questions and looked for straight answers. I hope that the reader will take from this book, as I have, the image of two people who sought to honour the child they loved and had lost by attempting a demanding act of rapport and empathy which very few could manage under the circumstances.

When I was asked to come to Warrington for the memorial service of Johnathan Ball and Tim Parry I was particularly struck by the wording of the invitation. It asked me to be there 'to represent the true spirit of Ireland'. And when I returned in November 1993 to launch The Warrington Project, I found that those who had framed that phrase had created a spirit of Warrington – a vivid and healing initiative. And I felt honoured – in simple human terms and as a Head of State – to be there at that moment.

The Warrington Project is a direct result of the bombing. It represents the magnanimous energies of a whole community who responded to disaster with thought and purpose and a hope for the future. Through conferences and scholarships it hopes to bring together the youth of these two countries so that an understanding of each other's cultures can be shared from the start.

I do not want to smooth away any of the raw edges or eloquent pain of this story. It tells of the loss of a beloved child in terrible circumstances. It tells of the death of Johnathan Ball on the same occasion. It describes the wounding and maiming of the other people who were also caught in the blast. To suggest any false consolation or meaning for this is the very opposite of my intention.

And yet it would be equally wrong not to recognise the human spirit and courage the Parrys showed in the aftermath of the bombings. It is hard to be anything but optimistic and admiring of the actions of the community in Warrington who reached past their own shock and anguish in a rare act of generosity which touched the feelings and imaginations of so many people in Ireland. And it is important to note that this book – after the terrible event which gave rise to it – puts a primary value on life and diversity and human understanding. And that, after all, is its source and origin: one human life – Tim Parry's – which was deeply cherished and is truly honoured by this remembrance of it. Despite all the temptations to be otherwise, this book proves the beautiful words of the British poet Philip Larkin: 'what will survive of us is love'.

Mary Robinson

Mary Robinson
President of Ireland

Prologue

Saturday, 20 March 1993 was to be the most extraordinary day in our lives and, tragically, it was to be the most extraordinary day in the short life of our son Tim.

It had begun much as any other Saturday. I got up at 8 o'clock to make the breakfast. While Wendy did this during the week, it was my job at weekends. Our children were planning to spend the day with their various friends, while the two of us had arranged to take Wendy's car to be seen by the mechanic who had regularly serviced it when it had belonged to its previous owner, Wendy's father John.

Tim was particularly keen to be up, breakfasted and out that morning. This was most unlike him, for of all our children Tim was almost always the last out of bed, the last dressed and the last to become fully functioning. But not this Saturday. This Saturday he had an urgency and purpose about him, brought about by the fact that he had just about finished the 'no sport – no physical exertion' embargo imposed on him by the surgeon at Warrington Hospital who, on 10 February, just five short weeks earlier, had removed Tim's appendix in an emergency operation.

Unbeknown to me, Wendy had eventually succumbed to constant pressure from Tim to allow him to play in goal for the school's under-13 football team just a few days earlier. (I should explain that Tim had only very occasionally expressed an interest in playing in goal – usually when his club team, Penketh United, were on the wrong side of a hammering. At these times, he would trudge off the pitch telling me how he could have kept a clean sheet!) Quite perceptively he had reasoned that there was more chance of his mum allowing him to play a leisurely, undemanding game in goal than there was of him playing outfield. So, as events turned out, his tactical plan paid off handsomely and he was allowed out of his enforced sport exile to play.

Ironically, had he played badly and let in a netful of goals, he would probably be alive today. Instead, by all accounts he played well and topped his unexpectedly good performance by saving a penalty. As you can imagine, this all served to create the unwavering conviction that he was England's, or better still, Everton's, future goalkeeper.

On the morning of that fateful day, I remember vividly taking the mickey out of Tim, as he told me of his plans to go into town with his friends to buy a replica pair of Neville Southall's (Everton's Welsh International goalkeeper's) shorts. I said to him that he had several pairs of football shorts, but, as the parents of all young boys these days will know only too well, just any old shorts will not do; they had to be Neville Southall's shorts with the specially padded side strip on the legs.

I put my arm around his shoulders and gave him a squeeze and a kiss on the cheek, not knowing that this was to be the last time I would ever see Tim as I knew him, and the last time I would ever hear his voice or to see his magical smile. He left the house to call on his friends, Piers and Neil, before he set off on his urgent mission. Ironically neither he nor his mother and I knew that he did not even have enough money to buy the shorts he wanted. They cost £19, as we were to discover subsequently when we bought a pair for him to be buried in – and Tim had only £11 with him.

Meanwhile, Dominic and Abbi left to call on their friends and Wendy and I set off to her parents' house in Manchester.

The problems with Wendy's car were duly diagnosed and it was left at the mechanic's to be fixed. Wendy's dad drove us back to Great Sankey and we arrived at about 1.00 p.m.

As we got out of John's car, our next-door neighbour, Paula, asked whether we had heard anything about the bombs that had gone off in the town centre. We had not been listening to the car radio on our return journey, but had been nattering away about the car and its maintenance history, and so we knew nothing of the bombings.

Not surprisingly, there was no immediate panic, though naturally there was a feeling of unease, knowing as we did that all three of our children had planned to go into town.

Wendy made phone calls to account for our children. Abbi was at her friend Katie's house. The two girls had tried to get into town, not knowing about the bombs, and they had been turned back by the police. Next, Wendy tried to locate Dominic. Although he was not with his friend Johnny, Johnny's mother said that they had not long left the house and were just up the street. As Tim had left for town first that morning, we left tracing him until last, expecting him to be at Piers's house, having completed his shopping expedition. When Wendy phoned Piers's house she was answered by his grandmother, who tearfully explained that Piers had been 'hurt' in the bombing and that Yvonne, Piers's mother, had been taken to Warrington Hospital by her next-door neighbour, Christine.

While Wendy was being told this, I could see by her face, and could tell by her voice, that there was cause for great concern. When she replaced the phone, she simply stated that Piers was hurt and that his grandmother had no information about Tim. I told Wendy to get in the car, while John set off home, telling us to let

him know when Tim returned so that he could stop
worrying.

I admit that my earlier unease had now turned to real
concern, though I kept telling Wendy that Tim would be
unhurt and was probably on his way home as we sped
towards the hospital.

It was a beautiful sunny spring day. All along the main
road into town, crowds of people were walking away from
the centre, and I remember the scene being reminiscent
of refugees fleeing a war zone. People's hurried walks,
and their looks of real fear, increased my growing, but
unspoken, worry.

When we arrived at the hospital, we had to push our way
through the large numbers of people who were standing,
sitting or just simply milling about.

This was the prelude to three of the longest, and certainly
the most painful, hours of our lives.

1

Parents with more than one child will always tell you that though they love them all equally, they love them differently, and this was certainly true of us with our children.

From his baby years onward, Tim had always been a laughing, happy and contented boy. Obviously, he had his 'moments', as every child does, but I can recall little about them now.

One of the many differences between Tim and his older brother Dominic, and his younger sister Abigail (to use her full name, which we never do), was that Tim was accident-prone. I recall particularly well how on May Day 1989 Tim split his chin wide open, after fooling around with Abbi in the bathroom. Both of them had wanted to be first to use the bathroom and a pushing fight had begun. Abbi, though younger than Tim, was heavier and she stood her ground when Tim pushed her, making Tim lose his balance, so that he fell on to the sharp corner of the bath and sliced a one-inch gash in his chin.

The ear-piercing screams we could hear from Abbi and the yelling from Tim had me taking the stairs three at a time. When I managed to calm them down for just long enough to find out what had happened, Tim tilted his head back slowly and I was nearly sick at the sight of the gash opening wider and wider. Surprisingly, there was almost no blood at all from such a deep wound.

Tim was eventually patched up at Warrington General and life settled back into its normal pattern. However, if there was ever anything predictable about Tim, it was his unpredictability. On the very next Bank Holiday, he fell off his bike and managed to cut his chin open again, only this time the cut went the opposite way. As a result he had a crossed scar on the point of his chin which made it appear longer and more pronounced than it had before his accidents.

It was about this time that I remember saying to Wendy that I did not think Tim would go his 'full term', by which I meant I did not think he would live a long life. I admit that, having said it, I quickly discounted such a fatalistic and awful prophecy. How well I remembered these thoughts when Tim lay mortally injured in his hospital bed.

Dwelling on Tim's accident history would give the impression that he brought himself and his parents nothing but pain and worry, so I turn instead to his Day Book to recapture the many happy, amusing and very personal memories I recorded of Tim throughout his life.

I kept diaries, which I entitled Day Books, for each of our children, so that when they were old enough to sit down and relive their past, they could enjoy recreating the images and memories that are so easily lost as we get older. Obviously, it would never have occurred to me in a million years that we would be drawing upon the memories of Tim's life before he even reached his teenage years. That we have been forced to do so is deeply painful, but at least as we read those entries across his twelve delightful years we can drift back to a happier time which we can share with you. In this way, Tim lives again not just for us, but I hope for you too. It is through these recorded memories that our Ordinary Boy will reach out and touch your hearts and, I hope, make you smile as well as cry.

1 September 1980

Welcome to the world, Dear Timmy
To our beautiful second child, and second son, who
arrived at 1.25 p.m. on Monday, 1 September 1980.
You weighed in at 7 lbs 14 ozs, just one ounce lighter
than your brother Dominic, and you were 48 cms to
Dominic's 51 cms, though I must say that I haven't
a clue what length this is in feet and inches!

The day began with me looking after Dominic
because your mum was taken into hospital to be
induced. This was decided by the ante-natal clinic
because you were two days overdue.

It is notable that Tim began life late, and he continued in
this vein for the rest of his short life.

8 September 1980

Dear Timmy
I went to the Hospital Registrar today to legally name
you and collect your birth certificate. On the day you
were born, but before you arrived, your mum had the
nurse write the name 'Andrew' on a white marker
board in the delivery room. When I walked in the
room and saw this, I objected, partly on the grounds
that I was not especially fond of the name Andrew, but
mainly because I had a vision of you being called 'Andy
Parry', which to me sounded awfully like 'Andy Pandy'.

So, in something of a panic, I blurted out the name
Tim, which had been the name of the lodger of our dear
friend and neighbour, Pat. He was a young man of whom
we had become quite fond, whilst he lived next door.

Needless to say, even the choice of 'Tim' was not
straightforward because 'Tim', as you now know, is

short for Timothy, another name of which I'm not terribly fond. In the end, Timothy Andrew is the name with which you were registered, but I can tell you now that you will never be called Timothy or Andrew by me, only Tim, Timmy or Timbo. I dare say, as you get older, you will become unhappy at being called Timmy and Timbo, but whilst you are a little fella, I think these are right!

The day of Tim's christening.

19 December 1980

Dear Timmy
Today you were involved in your second public duty (the first being your birth, of course). You were christened in St Matthew's Church, Highfield, Wigan, by a curate named George Thomas.

This curate, who also christened Dominic, used to go to the same youth club I went to in Bootle, 19 years ago when I was (sweet) 16.

George was, and still is, a good true blue Evertonian just like you are going to be, and as soon as you are old enough, which will be in 4 or 5 years' time perhaps, I will start to take you and Dominic to see the 'blues' playing at Goodison, much as my dad did when I was just 6 years old, back in 1952!

Tim's first birthday and Granddad burns the sausages.

1 September 1981

Dear Timmy
Today is your first birthday and various family members have gathered to pay homage to the little

chubby one. Your Granddad John brought his home-made barbecue, built from what looked very like big pieces of Meccano, and he stripped to the waist with just a plastic apron to protect his chest from the spitting food. He laboured long and hard to produce a couple of burned sausages which we ate eagerly after waiting for what had seemed an eternity.

12 October 1981

Dear Timmy
To add to your older, and noisier, brother, your mum and I have produced a nice little sister for you. She is to be called Abigail, though I don't suppose that at 1 year, 1 month and 12 days old, you will be particularly impressed or interested in this news, but I hope that in the months and years to come, you, Abigail and Dominic will all grow to be great friends.

Certainly now that we have a daughter, we will not be adding to the family any further. I just hope that all the horror stories people tell us about having three children do not come true, and in particular, that the middle child of three always feels the odd one out and develops some kind of persecution complex as your mum did (so she tells us!).

Christmas 1981

Dear Timmy
Christmas is a wonderful time for all young children, though with all three of you being so very young, you are not really terribly discerning yet. Abbi lay in her carry cot with some new cuddly toys, you

seemed more interested in the boxes and wrapping paper that your presents came in than you were in the presents themselves. Dominic at 3 years and a bit was certainly in his element playing with everything, but especially with those things which made the most noise. The sight of you all lying around or playing around the Christmas tree was worth waiting for though, my son.

5 June 1982

Dear Tim
Rotten luck, Timbo, in the middle of the best heatwave we've had for a couple of years, you have to go and get chickenpox and, oh boy, you've certainly got it! It's hard to see the skin between your spots. They're in your hair, under your feet and near your eyes.

On Sunday morning, I took you to the hospital, just to be sure it was only chickenpox. You were very well behaved until the doctor made you lie down, and then you let him hear what a fine pair of lungs you've got.

Having our house in Wigan extended to accommodate the rapidly increasing family brought with it some incidents that you would expect with two young boys.

Monday, 28 June 1982

Dear Tim
You and Dominic have been helping the builders, who dug out the footings and poured in the wet concrete today. You fell into the wet concrete, not once but twice. On the second occasion, we

considered letting the wet concrete set on you so that we could put you in the garden as a garden gnome, complete with fishing rod, but because we love you, Mum washed you down.

So far as your relationship with your brother Dominic is concerned, you've been standing up to him more recently, so that your fighting and squabbling are more frequent than they used to be. You love to pinch one another until you are both screaming and crying – what a pair you are!

Further adventures with the house extension.

Saturday, 28 August 1982

Dear Tim
Yesterday you left your boot-prints in the wet concrete on the new kitchen floor. If future civilisations unearth our late 20th-century dwelling, they may discover your fossilised boot-print and wonder what strange creature could have left it. Answer – 'a Timbo!'

Lately, you have developed a predisposition to play with dangerous items, like six-inch nails, axes, saws, hammers, chisels, etc., etc., so that I now have to walk about behind you like your gaoler!

Dad's thirty-sixth birthday.

27 November 1982

Dear Tim
Dad's birthday and the most lasting present I have to show the world is a badly swollen, sore nose, and guess who inflicted it? You! You, Nic and I were

wrestling on the lounge floor when you decided to squeeze my nose – not with your little fingers, which may have brought tears to my eyes anyway, but with your razor-sharp little fingernails, digging as deeply into my tender flesh as possible. There was no way I could dislodge your fingers without risking the loss of the end of my nose, so I had to wait until you released your vice-like grip. Eventually, to my eternal relief, you did, though whether due to tiredness or some deeply hidden love, compassion and sympathy for your dad, I do not know.

Just when I thought my punishment was over, Nic dropped from goodness knows where, knees first, on to my unprotected chest. So, for my birthday presents from my two boys, I got the breath knocked out of me, and an extremely tender nose. I retired to my corner to nurse my injuries. Obviously, I should take out special personal insurance before grappling with you two hooligans again.

7 December 1982

Dear Tim
Bad news, old son! As you have been laid low with a dreadful cough and heavy cold for a couple of days now, Mum and I took you and Abbi (this is the first time little sister Abbi gets a mention in Tim's Day Book – she is now 10 months old) to the doctor's surgery and he diagnosed tonsillitis and whooping cough. Thankfully, the whooping cough is mild because we had all three of you vaccinated. You've not eaten for two days and you're looking decidedly fed up and gloomy, but then who can blame you, poor chap! You did eat one tiny piece of toast for breakfast, but promptly vomited it into

your lap, whilst Nic looked on in horror as he ate his Rice Krispies. God willing, you will have recovered in time to enjoy Christmas.

8 January 1983

Dear Tim
Happy New Year, son. Christmas has come and gone again, and you had a good time after all, with no lingering ailments to bother you. So far as presents from Father Christmas are concerned, your favourite was an indoor tent. We put it up in your room but unfortunately, it took up so much space we had to take it down again and ask Nic if he would mind us putting it in his room instead. Needless to say, he didn't mind at all.

My next entry is some months later and concerns Tim's talent for avoiding parental retribution. In fact this was the first recorded reference to the skill Tim developed into a fine art later in life, whereby he could escape punishment by employing his natural charms in very effective ways.

25 April 1983

Dear Tim
There are two things I want to record in your Day Book today. I must admit, the first is amusing and it concerns your behaviour when confronted by Mum's anger or mine. You've taken to running off to whichever human being in the vicinity looks the friendliest – any adult will do – and you shower them with affection, telling them how much you love them. I find it most amusing to see you at 2 1/2 years old employing your diplomatic skills to such good

effect – I think you may well have all of the qualities needed to become a very polished politician when you reach manhood.

The second item I recorded on this day concerned Tim's predisposition even at this very early stage of his life to inflict serious damage upon himself. This is an early manifestation of the accident-prone side to his nature which I mentioned at the beginning of this chapter.

You have become really clumsy of late. You trip or stumble over real or imaginary obstacles. On Sunday, whilst out playing with the other young ones, you tripped over a scooter and fell flat on your face on the road. The result was that you scratched the skin off your nose and top lip, as well as gathering a mouthful of grit. Now, two days later, you have a fine collection of scabs which you are busily trying to pull off. I've decided that the distribution of your body weight in relation to your little legs is the problem – you're top-heavy, my old son!

My next entry is on Tim's third birthday, and again he is not in the best of health. Neither is he at all sure how he is supposed to behave at friends' parties.

1 September 1983

Dear Tim
Happy birthday, big fella, but I'm sorry to report that you have a very bad cough which makes it sound like you've been smoking cigarettes for the past 3 years.

On a happier note, let's see what you got by way of presents. Well, you got a machine-gun which makes a terrible racket, but since Mum and I bought it for you, we can't really complain. You also got an aeroplane, a helicopter, cricket bat, ball and stumps and money from your Granddad Eric.

Earlier this week, you went to your first birthday party at Clare's house, but apparently you left to come back home as soon as Clare's mum sat you all down to eat. Thankfully, the party was only two houses away, and you didn't get lost. You haven't quite got the hang of partying yet, son!

From here on, the gaps between my entries in Tim's Day Book start to become bigger, but the next entries are typical of the humour young children provide without realising they are doing so.

3 February 1984

Dear Tim
Sitting at breakfast today, you told Mum that you had 'seen pictures in your eyes when you were asleep.'

For Tim's benefit, when he came to read this entry in future years, I explained that this statement was the charming reference of a three-year-old to the process of dreaming.

Further on in this day's entry, I recorded that Abbi had managed to push Tim into a wardrobe and then lock it. Tim had eventually been released when Wendy had vaguely heard a distant voice calling her, and Abbi had told Wendy, in her best English, that 'Timmy wardrobe'. Upon discovering where Tim had been incarcerated, Wendy unlocked the wardrobe, and Tim burst out clutching his hands tightly over his eyes until they adjusted to the light.

The next entry is on Tim's fourth birthday and reveals how birthdays had become a carefully managed affair.

1 September 1984

Dear Tim
You're 4 years old, my son, and I have to report, sadly, that you are continuing to lose your baby-like chubbiness which made you different from Dominic and Abbi – they never really had a chubby phase and so were never quite as cuddly as you.

Your face lit up when we unveiled your BMX bicycle in the lounge. We also gave Dominic his BMX, and Abbi her doll and doll's house at the same time. This was to avoid any jealousy between the three of you.

I should point out that Dominic and Abbi share a common birthday, 12 October, only three years apart. Wendy and I felt rather sorry for Tim on Dominic's and Abbi's previous birthday in 1983, as they unwrapped their presents and Tim was the odd one out. So we saved some of Tim's presents to give him on their birthday, and now, having started the practice, we felt under some obligation to repeat the process, but this time in favour of Nic and Abbi. Being nearly six years old, Dominic remembered what we had done for Tim on his and Abbi's birthday and he expected us to do the same for him and Abbi on Tim's birthday.

In any event, Wendy and I thought that with Tim getting a major present like a new BMX bike, which was all the rage back in 1984 before mountain bikes took over, Dominic would be really put out. Quite frankly, we did not relish the sibling rivalry we knew we would have to live with for the six weeks until Dominic's birthday, so we took the easy way out, and gave him his BMX bike too!

Consequently, for a few years, birthdays were to be within a six-week time zone starting on 1 September and ending on 12 October. No wonder the children were never quite sure of their birth-dates until they were a little older!

And so to the next Christmas.

Boxing Day 1984

Dear Timbo
Quite apart from wanting to record your delight at getting your first proper wristwatch from Father Christmas, I wanted to keep, for posterity, another of your 'gems'. At dinner yesterday, and whilst under the usual relentless pressure from me to eat your food, you turned, looked at me and asked whether, when you were grown up, you too would have 'stripes' like me. For a moment or two, I really had no idea what you were talking about, but, seeing my confusion, you pointed to your forehead to show me where the stripes were! Yes, my amusing little man, you too will have lines and wrinkles one day, but they are many, many years away yet.

My next entry in the Day Book begins with another health scare.

22 June 1985

Dear Tim
You gave us quite a shock this week, young man. On Monday morning, your urine looked the colour

of brown paint and so Mum took you to the doctor's surgery. He advised Mum to take you to the hospital straight away, and he ordered an ambulance to take you, Mum and Abbi.

As it turned out, you were kept in hospital for three days under observation to allow them to carry out a variety of tests. They never did tell us what had caused the blood, for that was what it was, to get into your urine, but once they were satisfied that you had stabilised, they let you come home.

The one bright spot of your stay in Wigan Royal Infirmary was the arrival of a bright-eyed, pretty 6-year-old girl called Karen McDonald. She was in the next bed to you and when we came to visit on your second night, we found you sitting next to Karen on her bed whilst she read to you. I couldn't help but notice that there was a distinct look of love in your eyes, as you announced to us all, Karen too, that you were going to marry her. Sadly, however, Karen was discharged before you were and that has seemingly brought to a sudden end your first 'love', but never mind, pal, I'm sure that with your charm and rakish good looks, it's just the first of many, many more to come in the years ahead.

As I turn the page, I discover that the next entry is yet another hospital trip.

5 August 1985

Dear Tim
Your misfortunes continue, my son. As you, Nic and I were all wrestling on the floor last night, I managed to fall on your foot with my knee. You

let out a piercing scream which nearly deafened me and I picked you up and rubbed it better for several minutes. You stopped crying and said the pain had stopped and so I relaxed, thinking the worst was over, but no, two days later you were still limping and so I took you to the hospital for an X-ray. The result? I had fractured a small bone in the second toe of your right foot, so now you have got to attend the 'Fracture Clinic' as well as waiting for the results of your latest kidney X-rays. I've come to the conclusion that we might as well move into Wigan Infirmary. Oh, I almost forgot to mention the fact that we have now got two kittens – twin brothers, aged 8 weeks. They are lovely little things. They're black with white paws and little white bits on their faces. We had a family meeting and various names were suggested, and in the end we all agreed to Mum's suggestion of 'Bill' and 'Ben'. Like all kittens, they run around at an incredible pace, and chase everything, including their own tails, much to everyone's amusement. The three of you hold them so tightly that they almost suffocate.

My next entry is for one of the big milestones in Tim's young life – his first day at 'proper' school.

30 August 1985

Dear Timbo

School has arrived at last for you, although it is mornings only for the first few weeks. Being born on 1 September will always mean that you are the oldest in your school year and this is something you will just have to get used to, but I know that it's hard. During this past year at Nursery, it was really tough for you knowing that all the other children of your age group were already at school and you have been stuck with the 'little ones'.

So far as school itself is concerned, you seem to have mixed feelings. To begin with, you took to it like a duck to water; your writing was good and your reading was steady if not spectacular. More recently, though, you have become a little hostile to the idea of going in the morning, and Mum has had to threaten you with execution once or twice to get you to go in.

Your Granddad Eric has now moved from Liverpool to Wigan and has moved into a house very close to the school. This means that quite often he takes you and collects you for the afternoon in order to give Mum a well-earned break.

You and Dominic have started swimming lessons at Wigan Pool. You are to have ten lessons each, and my hope is that you will be an Olympic swimmer in a few weeks' time!

By the way, we celebrated your 5th birthday with a party for all your friends at McDonald's.

There follows quite a long gap before my next entry, which was made, it seems, just to record another of those innocent yet amusing things that young children say.

17 April 1986

Dear Tim
Whilst watching an episode of an awful TV pro-gramme called *The Colbys*, you suddenly remarked about a man and his wife, 'They're not married, they're not the same size!' I asked what you meant by this, and you replied, 'They're not the same

size.' But why does that matter, I enquired, to which you replied that they would not be able to kiss each other!

Next, another birthday entry.

1 September 1986

Dear Tim

Happy 6th birthday, Sunshine! Today you got your most earnest wish – one of the new Everton football shirts, and how very smart and proud you looked too.

We had a small family gathering at Granddad Eric's house. My cousins, Brenda and Joan, and Joan's husband Roy along with Aunty Em (Brenda and Joan's mum), Granddad John and Nanna Betty were there. Granddad and Nanna have not seen my family since Mum and I married in May 1977.

What a shame it is that my mum, your Nanna Lucy, couldn't have met you all. Still, perhaps she can see you and her other grandchildren from up in Heaven. God bless her, she was a lovely mum to me.

There follows another hospital trip – what else?

April 1987

Dear Timbo

Your second time in hospital, my son. This time it's to have your tonsils removed and your nose cauterised to stop it bleeding so easily and so frequently. Hopefully, you will be as fit as a butcher's dog, like Dominic has been since he had his tonsils taken out.

PS: I enclose a couple of passionate love letters from Sarah who lives up the road. There's also a lovely photograph of you both kissing – you look a little coy, but maybe it's best to play hard to get.

The next entry in Tim's book is a brief record of his first foreign holiday.

1 August 1987

Dear Timbo
We have just returned from two weeks in sunny Spain. You, like Nic and Abbi, are a lovely colour. Typical of you, however – you gave us a real scare when, but for Mum reacting quickly and pulling you out, you might have drowned in the hotel pool. It really did affect your confidence, not surprisingly, and for almost the whole of the rest of the holiday, you stayed in the children's pool.

By the time I next wrote in Tim's book, we had moved home from Wigan to Warrington.

June 1988

Dear Tim
Seven months ago in November last year, we moved to Warrington, to a house which is rather bigger than the previous one. It has a splendid conservatory which we are already enjoying in this early part of the summer.

There was a very sad footnote, however, to our moving from Wigan. We asked Pat, our next-door neighbour, to mind Bill and Ben whilst we had to move in temporarily with your grandparents (Mum,

Dom, Abbi and you with Mum's parents, and me with my dad).

Poor Bill was run over by a passing car and the driver left him dying on the footpath, outside our old house. Pat discovered him just before he died from his injuries.

I came over to your Nanna's house and told Mum the sad news first, and then I took the three of you upstairs to tell you. Well, son, I knew you would be upset, but nothing could have prepared me for your reaction. You absolutely broke your heart crying and sobbing in my arms for several minutes, whilst Dom and Abbi were standing there with their bottom lips trembling. They both contained their feelings and remained quite calm, and Dominic was soon asking me a lot of questions as Dominic always does, about how and where it happened, etc., etc. Meanwhile, you were inconsolable for quite a while. I did expect you to be the most openly upset, but I had not prepared myself for just how much. Your tears and heartbreak affected me so much that the tears streamed down my face too. My heart really ached for you, Timbo, it really did. I had never ever seen you so upset in your life, and God willing, it will be a very, very long time before anything ever upsets you like this again. We will have to keep an eye on Ben and hope that he too does not go and do anything silly.

Tim's eighth birthday.

1 September 1988

Dear Tim
Happy 8th birthday, Timbo. You really are quite the young man now. You are very slim and quite

tall and certainly handsome – even allowing for fatherly bias!

Your birthday party was held at the Sankey Forum Leisure Centre/Pool. You and your friends were allowed one hour in the pool followed by another hour in the Play Room where there was lots of lemonade, cakes, etc., and very noisy games. You got a skateboard amongst other things, and I am very impressed at how you stay on it and do clever turns. I can't stay on it for more than a second or two, so I'll stick to roller skates – more my generation!

Uncle Phil and Aunty Karen came all the way down from Dumfries to see you. Wasn't that good of them?

The children see their first New Year in at a friend's party.

2 January 1989

Dear Timbo

On New Year's Eve, we all went over to Alan and Cathy's house to see the New Year in. We stayed until the wee small hours of the morning and crawled home tired and a little tipsy (Mum and I, not you kids) at about 2.00 a.m.

You and Dom along with Alan's two boys, Kieran and Drew, became a little too boisterous on a few occasions, and to cap it all, someone managed to damage Kieran's violin – I wonder who! How's that for outstaying your welcome? I just hope it is easily fixed.

The next entry in Tim's book concerns his first recognised sporting achievement.

22 August 1989

Dear Tim
The local sports centre has activities for school-children to provide them with organised games during the school holidays and today you defeated four other kids your own age to win a junior squash competition. You have been told that you will be awarded a squash racquet on your birthday, so we shall see!

On your birthday, the promised squash racquet turned into a voucher for McDonald's. What a let down! Still, you were bought some really good presents which made up for your disappointment over the racquet. Mum and I bought you a keyboard which can do just about everything, apart from make the beds. Nanna bought you a tracksuit and your Granddad Eric bought you your first squash shoes. I've been taking you to play squash for the past 6 months and you are coming along pretty well. Obviously, at 9 years old, you don't have the power or the stamina yet, but your hand–eye co-ordination is very good, though I must point out you do get a bit 'ratty' with me if I make you run around too much.

Here we go again – another New Year and another hospital visit.

21 January 1990

Dear Tim
I do not believe it! The New Year is just three weeks old and we've been back to Warrington Hospital again. This time, you fell on to the edge of a chair whilst playing at your friend Andrew's house, and

you bit into your lip, opening up a half-inch gash. A large German lady doctor, who was really good to you, put some dissolving stitches into your lip. She said that they would dissolve after 10 days. They actually dissolved after 1½ hours, so back we went and this time she used a proper stitch. I can't help fearing that at this rate you are going to be disfigured for life.

On a happier note, you have joined the local Cub Scouts group, and you were invested after your fourth visit. You have also started playing football for Penketh United's under-10 team, and in the first three games you've played, which were all friendlies, you have scored in each game. I filmed you scoring a real 'beauty' with the new video camera. You took on three or four opponents, before coolly slotting the ball past the keeper – I was most impressed, son!

During the course of 1990, Tim switched from Cub Scouts to Sea Scouts, instead of moving up to the Scouts. I think this was due largely to Dominic putting Tim off the Scouts by telling him that the scoutmaster spent most of the one evening per week when they gathered yelling at everyone.

2 December 1990

Dear Tim
You have just returned from your first weekend away from home without your mum and I. You were with the Sea Scouts in Bowness-on-Windermere, sailing a variety of boats. Dressed in your navy blue sweater, your white sailor's cap and your dark trousers, you look very smart indeed. I'm sure Granddad Eric will want your photograph in uniform to remind him of

all the years he spent in the Royal Navy, first as a young rating and then an able seaman and eventually, rising through the ranks during the war, to chief petty officer.

A rare entry next on our fourteenth wedding anniversary.

28 May 1991

Dear Tim
Yesterday evening you came home in tears because you had fallen off your skateboard and banged your chest, such as it is, and in doing so, you bent your wrist back. You thought it was broken and so this morning I took you to your second home – Warrington General Hospital, where they X-rayed your wrist. For a change, it was good news – no break, just a badly bruised 'growth plate'. You have to wear a strong support bandage and must return to the clinic in 10 days.

It really is amazing how you nearly always hurt yourself on or very near Bank Holidays. I've decided that the only sensible thing to do is to strap you into your bed for a few days either side of Bank Holidays.

By the way, you were bought your first mountain bike for Christmas, but you weren't best pleased when you noticed something Mum and I failed to spot – that it was a girl's model. The shop were happy to exchange it when they re-opened after the Christmas break. Another of your Christmas presents was a half-set of golf clubs, and I promised you I would arrange half a dozen lessons from a professional. The first two that I arranged, I had to cancel because on the first occasion you were

sick and by the second you had hurt your wrist. In
the meantime, I asked a colleague at work, Andrew
Bacon, who just happens to be a member at Royal
Birkdale Golf Club, to get your clubs reduced in size
a little. This has now been done, and they await your
return to good health.

The catalogue of entries in Tim's book concerning his
health continues . . .

12 June 1991

Dear Tim
At your school eye-test a couple of days ago, you
were classed as having problems with your 'colour
vision'. In my day this was called 'colour blindness',
but I gather that this is no longer in favour as a
descriptive term. It seems that you suffer from a
comparatively common condition amongst the male
of the species, in that you cannot distinguish between
red and green.

Tim spent a busy and challenging week camping in
Windermere with the Sea Scouts.

11 August 1991

Dear Tim
A few weeks before going on annual camp, you
pestered the life out of Mum to buy your 11th
birthday present – a wet suit – early. We could see
it made sense for you to have it before, rather than
after, the camp and so we agreed. Camp comprised
canoeing, sailing, swimming and making your own
camp. Judging by the colour of you and most of

your clothes, we came to realise that you slept rough most nights and stayed away from soap for most of the week.

Our camping holiday in France during the summer of 1991 was an exceptionally happy holiday and a memorable one.

19–30 August 1991

Dear Tim

We have just returned from our annual family holiday – our first ever in France, and a quite unexpected thing happened – you found yourself a girlfriend! Well, nothing unusual about that, you may think, but when I remind you that this particular girlfriend was 18 years old, you may begin to understand our surprise!

As a change from Spain and cramped hotel rooms, we decided to try a campsite in St Jean de Mont, in the Vendée region of western France. We stayed in a large tent, which we all, apart from your mum, found to be quite all right. Mum didn't like it because there was never enough room to hang clothes up, and we all had to share communal toilets, showers and so on.

We met some really smashing families, such as the Ellises from Peterborough. Dave and Brenda Ellis and their two kids, Rob and Jacqui, spent a lot of time with us, and there were lots of laughs and barbecues. I must admit that Rob amused me a great deal with some of his daft antics, and Dom, Rob and you got along together very well – you were all a good match – you're all crazy!

In the next tent to ours was a young family from Oldham, and staying with them was an 18-year-old girl called Tina Smith. It was Tina with whom, I think, you fell in love. All of you enjoyed Tina's company, and she clearly enjoyed meeting all of you too, but there was something special about Tina for you, my son, and it wasn't just that you liked her red trainers, and that she often let you wear them.

It was as if you were no longer just eleven years old, Tim, you seemed more like a young man of 18 yourself. I watched you and Tina talking quietly together and laughing together too, and it was lovely to see two young people with a wide age gap getting along together so naturally.

We went, on a couple of occasions, to the Aquapark just a few miles away, and had great fun on all the slides. Our particular favourite was to sit in the big tyres and travel, usually upside down in my case, through a series of rapids, before being becalmed in small whirlpools, where you sometimes just went round in circles waiting for someone else's tyre to push you back into the rapids. Great fun!

In the evenings, you, Dom and Abbi, along with Rob and Jacqui, generally played around the bar which had games and a disco. There were never any arguments between you. Every fifteen minutes or so you would all come around to the tent or to Dave and Brenda's caravan on the scrounge for more money.

The evening is my favourite time on holiday. Everyone has showered and changed into clean clothes and there's time to relax with friends in the warm evening sun. You kids get rid of your final reserves of energy running around, then you all fall into bed for a well-earned rest before doing it all again the next day.

Meanwhile back to Tina. You were so fond of her red trainers that she promised to buy you a pair for

your birthday, and she was as good as her word. Her
kindness to you was very touching, and, I think, her
love for you was very real. It would be good if you
were able to maintain contact in the future, Tim, we
shall see . . .
Much love,
Dad

At this point I have reproduced Tina's own words to
describe the nature of the friendship and closeness she
developed with each of our children, but particularly
with Tim.

Memories of 'My Little Love'

It was in the middle of the first week of my holiday
in France. We had finished tea and went to the bar,
as usual, for the rest of the evening. Carla and Louis
were playing on the mini-roundabout, so I went to
check on them. As I got closer, I realised that they
had made a couple of new friends, Abbi and Jacqui.
It didn't take us long to begin chatting, and I took
some photographs. Next, Tim, Dom and their friend
Rob appeared.

They asked me my name, my age and where I was
from. Whenever I talked, they laughed at my accent
and tried to copy it. Dom informed me that we were
in the tent next to him.

Tim then got on to the subject of football, talking
about Oldham Athletic and Joe Royle. It was obvious
then how much he loved the sport. After this evening,
Tim spent a lot of time talking to me.

A day or so later, Tim came into our tent, where
he spotted a pair of my trainers, next to my bed.

They were red suede boots that I wore only when travelling. He loved them, and asked me what size they were, and then he tried them on. After that, I think he only took them off when he was in the pool or in bed. Dom and Rob used to laugh at him because they looked too big on him, but he didn't care, he still wore them.

When I realised just how much he liked them, I told him that I would buy him a pair for his birthday when we got home. I don't think anybody believed that I would, but I stuck to my word, as promised.

As the days went on, Tim made it quite obvious that he liked me in a different, special sort of way. He told me he was going to tell his friends at home that he had a girlfriend who lived in Oldham. He sometimes asked to wear my plain gold ring that I have on my little finger. He also promised me that when he passed his driving test, he would come and pick me up in his car and take me to Warrington.

When Tim was on his own, he was totally different. I remember one particular afternoon I had gone to sit in the bar next to the pool. I could see Tim with Dom and Rob playing in the water. He didn't see me at first, but as soon as he spotted me he got out and came dashing round to sit with me. We sat there for ages just talking. Now and again we were joined by somebody else, but it was mainly just Tim and me.

In the evenings, we would all hang around in our little group. Quite a lot of photos were taken and I've noticed that in the ones with Tim and me, he is either sitting on my knee or holding my hand. I used to call him 'my little love', which embarrassed him a little.

Towards the end of the holiday, I think most of the people on the site knew Tim, Dom and Rob for their cheek or for making them laugh. They were certainly known for pulling down their swimming trunks at the top of the water slide to make them go faster.

The day I was least looking forward to finally arrived. It was time to travel home to England. There were still a couple of hours left before leaving, but it was raining hard. I was in the tent on my own when Tim and Dom came to keep me company. I remember feeling sad as we had to say our goodbyes, but I kept reminding myself that you were all just down the motorway and I could visit now and again. I gave Abbi and Dom a quick 'peck', and then gave Tim a big hug. Again, he was a little embarrassed. Then I waved you all goodbye.

I sent Tim his new red trainers for his birthday, and he phoned to thank me. I also received a letter from Colin thanking me for my kindness.

Tina's words express so well the innocent young love that Tim felt for her and she for him. They shared some good times together, and it's clear that although Tim was not quite eleven years old and Tina was eighteen, there was a bond between them. Tim felt grown-up being treated so well by Tina, and for that experience we will always remember her. I am quite sure that Tina was Tim's first real love and she felt a special affection for him.

This was our first camping holiday and our first holiday in France. The children made good friends and so did Wendy and I, as we discovered the delights of rural France, where the food and wine were excellent and cheap. Dominic and Rob, Abbi and Rob's sister, Jacqui, Tim and Tina – each of them had great holiday fun together without there ever being any arguments. Wendy and I hit it off well with Dave and Brenda, Rob and Jacqui's parents, and we enjoyed several barbecues together on the long, warm summer evenings.

I remember particularly well at one barbecue how Rob and Dom wanted Tim to do his 'wolf whistle' at two girls who were approaching. Tim had been giving very loud demonstrations of his prowess in this ancient male skill earlier in the day, but now, when the two older boys wanted to hear it most, he suddenly became totally uncooperative. Dave was busy with barbecuing the langoustines, Brenda was pouring the local red wine, Wendy was relaxing, and I was videoing the two families together. As the girls got closer, and then passed by in front of us, Tim had still not positioned his fingers quite right in his mouth to blow the wolf whistle which was by now being frantically called for by Rob and Dom. As you can appreciate, his tardiness was tantamount to torture for his older brother and his demented friend! Finally, Tim acceded to their screeched demands and did his duty, but the girls were so far in the distance that somehow it didn't really matter any more.

We now look back wistfully on such carefree pleasant memories with a deep yearning. If there were only some powerful force to bring them all back again . . .

There is a long gap before my next entry in Tim's book, which recaps on some of the preceding eleven months.

12 July 1992

Dear Timbo

Quite a while since my last entry, son. Let's see what I should record. To begin with, on the school front, you are in your last year at junior school and, frankly, you have not been performing well. Last parents' evening we had quite an uncomfortable time being told that you and your current best friend, Barry Laker, are being kept apart to stop you terrorising the younger ones in the class.

I must say that I am looking forward to you starting at the high school where, hopefully, the teachers may be able to locate your dormant brain and kick-start it again.

I am pleased to report that you have stayed with the Sea Scouts, and your annual camp is coming up soon.

Physically, you have grown quite tall and you are a good-looking boy, but you can spoil yourself by being very sullen and silent these days – quite unlike Dom, who is extremely noisy.

You and Dom are not exactly the best of friends at the moment. You irritate him by winding him up to the point where he belts you and then he generally gets into trouble for hitting you. I never had brothers or sisters and so I'm afraid I don't like you arguing and fighting each other because it is not something I ever experienced.

Last Saturday you took a girl, named Kirsty, to the cinema to see *Batman 2*. I'm afraid that as I drove you both there I was really annoying you by ribbing you about 'snogging in the back row at the pictures'. I suppose I'd have been just as embarrassed had my dad done the same to me – so you had every right to tick me off about it!

Anyway, Tim, high school beckons. You're a bright boy provided you're motivated – again like any other kid, so let's hope you rise to the challenge.

Next, a few months after starting high school, and after Christmas too.

7 January 1993

Dear Tim
Your 12th birthday, Christmas and your start at high school have all passed since I last wrote in your book.

So far as school is concerned, you seem to have settled in reasonably well. Obviously, having your older brother there helps in a number of ways. Physically, like Abbi, you are changing noticeably. Your face is becoming the face of a young man. Coinciding with this change, the number of girls calling at the house for you seems countless. You are constantly telling me about the number of girlfriends you have, usually all Dom's age.

Turning back to Christmas for a moment, you were really overcome with tears of joy at getting what you had wanted so much – an electric guitar – and you have already arranged with Andy next door for him to give you lessons once a week. Watch out Eric Clapton!

My next entry in Tim's book is the penultimate one and records our final health fright before his life was to end so prematurely.

10 February 1993

Dear Tim
This entry comes unusually soon after the last one – but big news, my boy. You have had your appendix removed tonight at 8.30 p.m.

Though we hadn't realised it at the time, your appendix had become badly inflamed yesterday and had caused you to vomit several times, including during the night.

Mum and I assumed you had eaten something which disagreed with you, or had picked up a stomach bug at school, and so you were kept off school today.

Foolishly, Mum and I left you at home alone to

get over it as you had stopped being sick, although the pain was still there. I rang you at midday and it took you ages to answer the phone. When I asked had I woken you, you replied that it had taken you so long to get to the phone because you had crawled. The pain was so acute, you could not stand up straight.

This frightened me, and I rang Mum and told her to take you to hospital straight away. Your temperature was very high and after the operation to remove your appendix, the doctor told us that it had been a nasty situation which had required very prompt action indeed.

By the time we left the hospital, you had come round from the anaesthetic and the nurses were a great crowd and good-humoured. We knew you were in good hands, and they would spoil you rotten!

Thank goodness we did not wait any longer to get you to the hospital.

My final entry in Tim's Day Book is dated 20 March 1993, the day the IRA bombed the town centre shopping area, Bridge Street.

Young Johnathan Ball was killed and fifty-six people were injured, some very seriously. The most seriously injured was our beloved son Tim.

2

Inside the main entrance of the hospital, an information desk had been set up to deal with enquiries from anxious relatives and friends. It seemed to me that there were as many as a hundred people, sitting, standing or pacing about. To deal with them there were three ladies, each holding clip-boards with lists of names.

I pushed my way through and asked one of the ladies whether she had a boy named Tim Parry on the list. I fully expected her to say she did and that he was being treated for shock or minor injuries. So sure was I that she would say this that I did not know what to do or think when she said there was no one with that name on the list. I said to Wendy with a confidence that belied my real feelings that Tim must have set off for home and that he was probably there even as we were making our enquiries.

As we turned away from the desk, Wendy and I were approached by a neighbour, Chris Monteith, who lived about ten houses further up our street. She had driven Yvonne Waters, the mother of Tim's friend Piers, to the hospital.

Wendy had met Chris previously, but I had not, though we were soon exchanging what little information we had. Chris was able to tell us that although Piers had been treated for quite minor injuries, Yvonne was very shaken and upset, and was still with her son. Chris had no news at all about Tim.

I was becoming increasingly unsettled and aware of a feeling of growing foreboding building inside me. I did not say anything of this to Wendy, partly so as not to increase the unspoken worries I knew she must have, but also because I felt that to express my worries openly might in some way have tempted providence.

Looking back, I can recall very clearly how my mind was full of conflicting thoughts. I felt quite incapable of any coherent or logical thought process at the time. My mind was a disjointed mixture of anxiety and increasing panic at the absence of any news or information about Tim.

Yvonne appeared and tearfully explained about Piers's injuries which, mercifully, were only slight. Apparently, the bomb had blasted his jeans on to his legs with so much force that they had chafed his skin. Otherwise, Piers was suffering mostly from shock.

Yvonne finished telling us about Piers and, as tactfully as possible, Wendy and I then asked her whether he knew anything about Tim or his whereabouts.

What she told us next gave us some cause for hope. She explained how Piers recalled seeing a boy he thought was Tim sitting up against a shop wall in Bridge Street. Piers had believed it to be Tim because the boy had dark blond hair and was dressed in clothes that looked like those Tim had been wearing that morning.

Yvonne informed us that the police had taken Piers's clothes away for forensic examination, and she asked whether Chris would go home and bring some new clothes back for Piers to travel home in. Wendy and I agreed that she should go back with Chris to see if Tim had arrived home. I was feeling quietly optimistic at this point, taking my cue from Piers's remarks to Yvonne.

During the time that Wendy was away from the hospital, a young priest, who I later learned was called Alan Devaney, befriended me. I explained to him why I was there and told him of the mixture of hope and fear I was feeling. He decided that he would take a walk around the

Accident and Emergency section of the hospital to make some enquiries of his own about Tim.

Over the next hour or so, he returned several times to let me know how his enquiries were proceeding. He had no news to report. This served to encourage me further and my spirits continued to pick up. I was increasingly sure that Wendy would return at any moment to tell me that Tim was being looked after by a neighbour and that we could go home and make sure he was not too badly shaken up.

While I was on my own, I felt quite useless doing nothing but standing around. Occasionally, I exchanged brief comments with one or two of the by now familiar faces who had been waiting for as long as I had. Partly to create the illusion of doing something purposeful, I would wander out of the hospital and go around to the Accident and Emergency entrance area. I was never sure where it was best to be. The enquiry room staff had no news of Tim; Wendy and Chris had been gone for what seemed to be an eternity; Alan was gone for lengthy periods; and I was just standing around. So I established a pattern whereby I would spend several minutes in the Accident and Emergency area, and then return to the incident/enquiry room. I had passed the point where there seemed any purpose in asking the staff for any news, especially as the numbers milling around were dwindling noticeably as the minutes and hours went by. Strange though it may seem, I had actually begun to feel slightly embarrassed each time I repeated my enquiry. This feeling was not caused by any lack of response or sympathy on the part of the staff, but rather more by my realisation that they would tell me if any news was to reach them and that for me to keep asking them the same question was pointless.

My state of mind was so unsettled, though I kept telling myself that Tim was surely at home and being comforted

by his mum, and that it was just a case of holding on to
my sanity a little while longer until the news that I was so
desperate for came through.

When Wendy and Chris did eventually return, only to
tell me that there was no sign of Tim at home, my optimism
evaporated and my heart sank. I explained how a priest
had been searching the hospital but he too had nothing to
report.

For Chris's sake, Wendy and I tried to maintain our
normal composure, and the conversation, largely thanks
to Chris, carried on in as optimistic a vein as possible. I
recall thanking Chris for staying on and telling her she
could go home and see to her own young family and that
we would be all right, but she would have none of it. She
stayed with us, providing tea for Wendy and coffee for
me at regular intervals. Considering that I had never even
met Chris before, I felt, as I suppose happens to people
at times of great stress, that I had known her all my life.
I remember complimenting her on her support and her
warm smile which was certainly much more than either
Wendy or I could muster.

I would guess that it was about 4.00 p.m. when Alan
returned. I introduced him to Wendy and Chris, and,
addressing his next remarks to both Wendy and me, he
said, 'Can you recall what Tim was wearing when he left
the house this morning?' Wendy told him that Tim had
been dressed in his Joe Bloggs jeans, with the brand name
printed down the side seams, and his navy blue Adidas
sweatshirt.

Alan placed his arm gently around my shoulders as he
had done several times that afternoon, and I remember
thinking how ironic it was that a Roman Catholic priest
should have gone to all this trouble when I was Church
of England, and also how strange it felt to have a man so
much younger than me putting his arm around me in this

friendly way. These thoughts were à propos of nothing in particular, but they struck me forcibly as I sensed a crucial moment approaching.

Alan asked whether Tim had been wearing a watch with a wide canvas strap. Wendy told him that he was wearing such a watch, and Alan then said, 'I think he's the boy in surgery.' Wendy turned away and said, 'Oh my God', and I noticed that everyone in the room turned to look at us.

Alan must have seen this too, and he asked us to accompany him into a side room. I thought to myself that Tim must have been the boy I had heard earlier references to. Not long after arriving at the hospital, I heard that a very young child had been killed and that a young man was in surgery. Some time during the afternoon I also overheard one of the staff saying that the young man was thought to be sixteen years old.

Now my mind was trying frantically to unscramble these apparently contradictory pieces of information. If the boy, who had been in surgery for at least three or four hours, was sixteen years old, it could not be Tim, he was only twelve. Yet Alan had said he thought it was Tim in surgery, in which case I hoped that Tim was in surgery for less serious reasons than the sixteen-year-old.

We went into the side room and sat down for what may have been only a minute or two, although I could not say for sure, because time had been suspended and the whole situation was unreal. Chris was sitting with her arm around Wendy, and I was staring out of the window, when a doctor entered the room.

Even before he spoke, it was obvious that the news he was about to give us was bad, but nothing in life could have ever prepared us for the news we were about to hear.

He sat down and opened a brown envelope from which spilled my St Christopher chain which Tim had been wearing for some time, and his blood-stained watch-strap.

He asked whether we could confirm that these were Tim's belongings. We both said, 'Yes, they are.' The doctor then spoke the words that cut through my heart and soul like a hot dagger. He said that Tim had been in surgery since he had been brought into the hospital, that he had very severe head and facial injuries, and that although he was extremely strong and was putting up a brave fight, he thought it unlikely that he would survive the night. I heard Wendy say, 'Oh no!'

I could not believe what I was hearing. This was our Timbo he was talking about. How could such a random act of violence take our beautiful son from us?

I vaguely heard the doctor saying that Tim had lost a lot of blood and that he would have to leave us to return to the theatre to continue trying to stop the bleeding. He gently patted my hand as he was about to leave the room. He stood up and said how terribly sorry he was to have to give us such desperate news. As he turned to leave, I saw that his shoes were covered in blood . . . our son's blood.

To unravel my emotions and unscramble my thoughts at that time is very difficult. Both Wendy and I were crying but, while crying, I was trying to reason what Tim's chances of survival might be. At the same time, anger and bitterness surged through me, that it could be our son who had suffered such a hideous fate. Over and over, the thought returned that he had only gone shopping for football shorts, and how could such a fate befall an innocent young boy out on such a carefree jaunt with his friends?

I could barely comprehend the magnitude of what we had been told. It was the unthinkable that is every parent's worst nightmare. And yet this was no road traffic accident; it was not death following a short or a protracted illness. No, this was a fit, young, good-looking, sports-mad, happy-go-lucky boy, loved totally by his parents, who happened to go shopping in Warrington on the Saturday that an evil, callous, inhuman creature chose to calmly place a bomb that resulted in injuries to our son that were so extensive that it was unlikely he would survive the night.

I could not compose myself sufficiently to talk cogently to Wendy or anybody else. In any event, Chris had left the room briefly to tell Yvonne and Piers, who had now been discharged from the ward where he had been treated. They both came into the room with Chris, and they were both crying and sobbing freely. Seeing them, I tried to comfort them but without any success, and their tears merely caused my own to start over again. A nurse took Wendy outside to get some air as she had begun to feel sick. They were only gone for a few moments – it had got quite cold now that it was late afternoon.

A social worker brought a telephone into the room and said I could phone anyone I needed to. The same social worker was taken by the police to Wigan to collect my father. I had decided that there should be someone with him when I told him the awful news. He has a heart condition and I did not want to bring on an attack.

Next, I rang Wendy's parents and John, her father, answered. When I told him the news, he broke down and kept sobbing the same words as Wendy had called out just minutes earlier: 'Oh no, not Tim.' As he repeated the phrase over and over, I could hear Betty saying to him, 'What is it, John, what's happened to Timmy?', and 'John, tell me what's happened to Timmy.' Then I heard John trying to explain what I'd told him, but his voice kept faltering until he finally made Betty understand how serious the position was. I handed the phone to Wendy, as I could no longer talk and cry at the same time, and the need to cry was overwhelming. Wendy advised her father to wait a little while before travelling back to Warrington because he was in no fit state to drive so soon after hearing the news.

Prior to hearing from me, John had phoned Wendy's sister, Carol, and told her about the bomb in Warrington and how Wendy and I had dashed off to the hospital to find Tim. At the time, Carol thought her dad was overdramatising events. Later, when John phoned Carol again from our house before we arrived home from the hospital, Carol had been unable to grasp the awful news, and she and her husband Terry spent the whole evening in floods of tears. Over the next week, Carol and Terry were to be towers of strength as they helped us to shoulder our tragic burden.

Before we left the hospital, Wendy and I asked to see Barry Taylor, the surgeon who had given us the terrible news. He listened as Wendy told him that we both urgently felt the need to be with Tim; he said this was not possible until Tim was taken out of the theatre and into Intensive Care.

A short time later, a nurse advised us that Tim was on his way to Intensive Care and that she would take us to see him soon. Just then, Wendy said to the nurse, 'Tim has not lost anything, has he?' I remember that the nurse looked very unsure about how to deal with this direct and, I guess, unexpected question, but then she made her mind up and replied, 'Yes, Tim has lost an eye . . .' I cut her off and told her to say no more, as I could not bear to hear that Tim had suffered even more than this terrible injury. To know that he had been hurt so badly made me feel sick and desperate. To imagine his handsome face so disfigured and damaged that he had lost his eye and God only knew what else was too much to bear.

The nurse led us from the side room and we took the lift up two floors to the Intensive Care unit, where we sat down outside in the waiting room. There, we talked quietly about going in to see Tim.

The terrible fear of seeing him lying motionless, severely injured and connected to a machine breathing for him, required more strength and courage than either of us had at that moment, and so we decided to leave Intensive Care without going in. Our sense of guilt was eased a little by what we were told by the nurse. She said that Tim was in no pain as he was very heavily sedated and that he could not possibly be aware of anything. This was the first reassuring thing we had heard, and we knew that Tim would not have known we were present even if we had summoned up the courage to go in to see him. The nurse said that she thought we had made the right decision, and that if there was any change in Tim's condition the hospital would phone us straight away.

At about 5.30 p.m., Wendy and I left the hospital to return home, but not before thanking as many of the people who had been so kind and helpful as we could. We particularly thanked Chris Monteith, who I said would be a friend for ever for being so brave by staying with us throughout that dreadful, traumatic afternoon. She took Yvonne and Piers home and we all trudged away from the hospital.

By the time Wendy and I arrived home, Dominic and Abbi were there, along with Wendy's parents and my father. John had told Dom and Abbi the terrible news. As we entered the house, there was almost total silence. It was quite eerie. The family were all in the lounge, and when we walked in they all stood up and one by one we held each other close, crying and not knowing what to say beyond the basic things that I expect most people must say when confronted with a totally unexpected and terrifying ordeal.

Someone went to put the kettle on to make tea and

coffee. I can't remember who it was, but I know it was not me, for as everyone else was sipping their hot drink I turned to the drinks cupboard. There was no hesitation as I took the whisky bottle and poured myself a generous measure. It seemed the obvious and right thing to do, even though I have never been a whisky drinker. The hot, harsh, burning sensation as I drank the spirit was appropriate to my mood.

Wendy had a sherry which, just like me with the whisky, was a drink she never normally touched. As the evening wore on, we steadily drank the whisky and sherry until, I suppose, we must have been quite drunk, though I confess I did not feel any of the cheerful sensations I normally associate with 'having had a few'. On the contrary, the anger that had been building up in me all day found vent.

I found it quite impossible to make polite or reasonable conversation with either of Wendy's parents or my father, and in normal circumstances I am sure that they would have judged my behaviour towards them to have been unforgivably rude. Though I never asked them, I suppose they must have all made allowances for me.

Meanwhile, everyone stayed in the lounge, apart from me. The television was on and they were all looking at the screen, but I don't think any of them gave a moment's thought to what was actually showing.

When the main evening news broadcasts came on, I returned to the lounge to hear the coverage being given to the Warrington bombing. Various commentators spoke of the panic and devastation felt by the public who had been out shopping on this bright, ordinary Saturday before Mothers' Day. The death of young Johnathan Ball and the injuries to others, as yet unnamed, were mentioned. We all sat impassively listening to these reports, almost as if we were not directly affected. It was very strange indeed to undergo this curious phenomenon – almost like an out-of-body experience in the sense of standing outside myself, yet being able to observe myself individually and also as part of the family group.

Family dynamics led to sporadic outbursts of grief and uncontrollable sobbing by one or other of us, and this rapidly had a forest-fire effect on the rest of us. Abbi in particular was desperate and cried to the point of total exhaustion. In the middle of the evening, Wendy took Abbi to bed and told her to pray as she had never prayed before and ask God that Tim might survive.

Throughout the evening, I expected the telephone to ring and for the Intensive Care staff to summon us urgently to return. Maybe it was some kind of thought association that made me begin to telephone everyone in the family address book. I began at the letter A and worked my way through. I suppose I must have spent a minimum of two hours on the phone, the length of each conversation inevitably depending on the reaction of the person who heard the news. Some reacted with almost total silence as if they had been rendered unable to respond, whereas others nervously chatted to me, telling me not to give up hope.

Those who managed to find the composure to engage me in some sort of dialogue were able to stem the flow of my tears, while others, who hovered between silence and mumbling the sympathetic responses that spill out semi-automatically, had to deal with my raving and ranting and sobbing. In truth, I do not know precisely what I said to anyone once I had got beyond saying 'Have you heard about the bombs in Warrington today?', followed by 'Well, I have some very bad news to give you. Our son Tim has sustained serious head and facial injuries, and the doctors have told us that he is not likely to live through the night.' I remember saying this over and over again, almost as if it were a pre-recorded message. It was what was said after these remarks I do not recall, owing to a combination of my highest-ever whisky intake and my almost total emotional overload.

Several times, Wendy popped into the hall where I was phoning, to check that I was still sane. Looking back, it must have been worrying to observe my handling of this crisis, because in truth I was not handling it at all. I had succumbed to abject grief, mixed with blind rage and topped up with a considerable amount of whisky.

I had broken off from phoning to recharge my glass when the instinctive impulse to write in Tim's Day Book hit me. I have read this entry again today for the first time since I made it on Saturday, 20 March 1993, and it is reproduced word for word below:

Tim, My Darling Son
Today, I fear, is the end of your all too short and beautiful young life.

Your body has been broken by a maniac's bomb – a maniac with no heart, no soul, no humanity. He has severed your life from you in a most desperate and fearful way.

You may be going to lose your battle for life, but you will live for ever in all our hearts and memories.

No madman can take you away from us. To my dying day, Tim, I will think of you and remember the many times you made us laugh, drove us mad, made me shout at you, and made Dom and Abbi blame you for some piece of mischief.

You left a huge footprint in our lives, son, and there's no consoling us. You will, I hope, be with my mum soon and, who knows, there may be a better existence free of pain and suffering up in Heaven.

God Bless you, Tim, and may he care for you
for ever.

We will meet again

Dad X

That was to be my last-ever entry in Tim's Day Book.

The evening ended with everyone staying at the house,
thanks to some rearranging of beds and bedrooms to
accommodate everyone. The only bedroom not slept in
was Tim's, as there was an implicit understanding that no
one would sleep in Tim's bed and it would remain as he
had left it the previous evening. His pyjama-top was still
under his pillow and there it stayed.

This night was to be the longest and most agonising
night of our lives. We all went to our various resting
places, knowing there could be no rest, no relaxation and
no escape from this awful new reality which had smashed
itself into our peaceful and contented lives. The shattering
of Tim's life had shattered all our lives, and the night was
to prove for Wendy and me an interminable maelstrom of
pain and guilt as our son lay unconscious and broken on
a life-support machine.

Would he survive the night? We feared not. How could
we sleep with our minds full of such sorrow and guilt?

We lay awake throughout the night trying to comfort
one another but finding only constant pain and grief. I
tossed and turned and wept and then lay still, and then
the pattern repeated itself.

At one point in the early hours of the morning, torchlight
beams shone in through the bedroom window and we
thought we heard the garden gate being opened. We
both checked with the other that we had not imagined it,
for reality and illusion that night did not seem to be very
far apart. However, we were both certain that lights had

been visible and that the gate had been tried. We wondered who it could have been, thinking it most likely that it was either the police or the press. I got as far as looking out of the bedroom window but could see nobody. I could not bring myself to dress and go downstairs and into the back garden when I was already incapable of thinking clearly or behaving rationally.

The long night gradually turned into Sunday morning. There had been no phone calls during the night from the hospital, so our son had made it through the night. God had blessed him and given him the courage and spirit to fight on for at least another day.

3

Sunday, 21 March – Mothers' Day 1993

Dominic and Abbi took Wendy's Mothers' Day card into her while she was still in bed. On opening the card, Wendy burst into tears as the pain of reading Tim's name, written by Abbi, seared through her. Not knowing what to do or say, Dominic and Abbi quietly left the bedroom as Wendy sobbed. I tried to comfort her, but found myself sobbing along with her.

Eventually our tears subsided, and we stared at one another silently, acknowledging that today would be a heart-rending day and might possibly be the day that Tim would not survive.

I left Wendy so that she could wash and dress for breakfast, and as I reached the foot of the stairs I could see the Sunday papers lying on the mat inside the front door. Kneeling down to pick them up, I never, for one moment, expected to see pictures of Tim all over the front pages. I stared at them with a mixture of incredulity and horror, knowing immediately that the unnamed person lying prostrate in Bridge Street, adjacent to a shattered bin, was our son. The full magnitude of our situation hit me again like a thunderbolt, as well as the realisation that we were going to go through all this grief in public.

I stared at the pictures of Tim, transfixed, for several minutes. Then I removed the front pages of the papers and hid them so that Wendy would not see them. I knew

that she would be unable to look at them without it causing
her even greater pain than she was already experiencing.

I remember wondering how someone could have stood
there calmly taking photographs of our son instead of doing
something to help him. Thoughts of the Hillsborough tragedy flooded into my mind, for I recalled thinking the same
thing then, seeing so many young people photographed
trapped against the fence by the thousands of spectators
behind them. The photographers at Hillsborough, like
the one on Bridge Street, had presumably felt that taking
photographs was a higher priority than offering help to the
victims before them.

Some weeks later, we were to meet the local newspaper
photographer who had taken all the shots of Tim in Bridge
Street. He was in a state of nervous anxiety as he explained
his actions, emphasising that the money he had made by
selling his prints all over the country and beyond was to
be given to the Victims Appeal Fund.

Despite this explanation which was meant to placate
me, I found it difficult to avoid showing him my extreme
distaste for his actions. Naturally, the rational part of me
understood his journalistic instinct to take pictures that
would be seen around the world, but this was greatly
outweighed by my parental indignation at the fact that,
as he took photographs, my son was at his feet barely
clinging to his life.

Meanwhile we all sat down to breakfast that morning,
but no one really had any appetite. Wendy's mother Betty
had risen first and had toasted most of a loaf, only for it
to be left uneaten. The family's turbulent emotions were
evident at the breakfast table. Betty burst into tears several
times and ran out of the dining room and into the kitchen.
John followed to comfort her. My father sat motionless at
the table, staring blankly ahead, lost in his own thoughts.
Dominic and Abbi were the only ones to eat any of the

toast mountain, but even they could not control their raw emotions – Dominic became very upset and had to leave the table just as Abbi had the previous evening.

Wendy came downstairs and began to stir us into action. She arranged for my father to be taken home and for Dom and Abbi to go with their grandparents to Manchester, from where we would collect them later that day after visiting the hospital. We tidied up the house, and set off.

At the hospital, Wendy and I walked from the car park towards the main entrance. As we approached, we saw Wendy's sister Carol, her husband Terry and their daughters Clare and Nicola in the distance. Carol turned and saw us approaching, and as she did so, she broke into a run. When she reached us, she and Wendy threw their arms around one another. Carol was crying and this started Wendy crying too. Clare and Nicola were also in tears when they reached us. Terry and I shook hands and I thanked him for being with us at this time.

Slowly, we walked towards the entrance where the press were gathered. We walked past them and into the hospital without being approached by any of the journalists. We were greeted by members of the hospital staff, who took us to a side room where they gave us tea. They then notified the Intensive Care staff that we had arrived, to prepare them for our visit.

We were taken to the top floor and into the hospital chapel where the chaplain, Philip Mears, greeted us. Philip was extremely sympathetic and he made us all very welcome by providing more tea and coffee. He spoke to us all in turn; his manner was very helpful and had a reassuring effect on us. When I had finished my coffee, I quietly slipped from the chapel to find a moment alone, to gather my thoughts. Several times I paced the corridor from the chapel to the room where Tim was as I considered whether or not to see Tim, I didn't know whether I would

be strong enough. My fear was very basic. Would I break
down or would I hold up? After several minutes, I walked
slowly down the corridor towards the room, my trepidation
increasing with every step I took. Gingerly, I opened the
door, afraid that my eyes would fall immediately on Tim
and that the sight that would greet me would send me
reeling backwards. My fear, however, was groundless, as
all I could see was a series of cubicles with curtains, some
of them drawn, some not.

A nurse came towards me and told me that Tim was
peaceful and in the end cubicle on the right-hand side.
She said I could go and see him, but I did not respond
immediately as my fear of how the sight of him would
affect me paralysed my legs. I told myself to be calm,
to breathe deeply and to do what was right for Tim. So
I stood at the drawn curtain, hesitating again momentarily
before I pulled the curtain to one side and stepped in.

Tim lay on his back completely motionless except for
the rhythmic breathing of the ventilator. I stared for
many seconds, without breaking my gaze, at his head.
To describe the sight even now causes intense and deep
pain. His head was completely covered in bandages, with
only one side of his mouth left exposed for a tube to draw
off the blood and saliva from his mouth and throat. I
presumed that this was to prevent him choking as he
breathed, though I confess that the amount of rational
thinking I did as I stood over him was virtually nil. All
my thoughts were swamped with the monumental grief
that had overtaken me on seeing our beautiful, vibrant,
fun-loving son so desperately injured.

I did not know the extent of Tim's injuries beneath the
mass of bandages, but I knew it was the path to madness to
allow my mind to dwell on such thoughts. Consequently,
controlling my mind at this time of utter desolation was
an extremely difficult but necessary battle, I knew that I

was not sufficiently resilient to know or to wonder how he might look beneath those bandages.

I looked down the bed, but every other part of Tim was beneath the covers. I was about to leave when the nurse entered the cubicle, and I asked her about his legs and arms. Tim had well-shaped legs, and it suddenly became important for me to know of any injuries to them. She told me that his legs, arms and body had shrapnel wounds, but were not seriously damaged. She asked me whether I wanted her to remove the covers to let me see his upper body and then his legs. I said, 'Yes, I want to see how he is.' His legs were bandaged from mid-thigh to mid-calf, but I looked at Tim's feet with the picked toes and cracked skin. The times Wendy and I had told him to stop picking not only his toes but the skin on his feet were too numerous to count. Only a year or two earlier, I had taken Tim to see a specialist in Liverpool's Rodney Street (Liverpool's equivalent to Harley Street in London) because he had terribly dry and cracked skin. His mother and I blamed modern trainers for this, but all children of his generation wear them so we were resigned to allowing Tim to wear them too.

So I stood there looking at those feet I knew so well, with the familiar-shaped toes, just like my own. It had always been a family joke that at the time each of our children was born I not only counted their fingers and toes, I also looked at the shape and size of their toes. They had all been cursed, Wendy would say, with their dad's feet.

I reached down and held Tim's toes. They were as warm as toast. Tears welled up in my eyes and I felt my chest become very tight as I struggled to contain an overwhelming urge to grab hold of Tim, lift him off the bed and cradle him to me so that my strength and willpower would pass into him and help him pull back from the brink.

I gradually calmed down and gently replaced the covers. Then I left the cubicle to walk back slowly to the chapel. There, I took Wendy to one side and told her that Tim was not as bad as she feared and encouraged her to come back with me to be with him. Wendy gradually gathered herself until she was ready to go. When we arrived at the cubicle, I held her hand tightly and squeezed it to signal that we should enter, but she said, 'No, I can't go in.'

She turned and walked away, and I followed her back towards the chapel. I drew up alongside her and took her hand once again, I told her that Tim needed us there. We must do it for him. She stopped and then slowly turned around and together we returned to the cubicle, and this time we went inside. Wendy stood about three feet away from the bed and, much as I had done some ten minutes earlier, she stared down at Tim and took in the full enormity of seeing her golden-haired son so grievously injured.

We stood in silence. Then the nurse re-entered the cubicle. Wendy asked her if Tim still had his legs, at which point the covers were removed again. I knew, even though no words were exchanged between us, that Wendy was feeling as broken and empty as I was. Words do not come easily at moments such as this, for they require conscious thought, and your subconscious mind is pushing and pulling you in so many directions simultaneously that your conscious thoughts can find no expression.

Again, I struggled to suppress and override the thoughts trying to enter my mind, attempting to force me to consider the magnitude of Tim's injuries. This was proving to be a terrible see-saw battle, made worse by the additional feeling that trying to suppress these questions was in fact nothing more than a selfish act of pain-avoidance on my part. Frankly, the realisation was beginning to take shape that thought-control was going to become an increasingly important form of personal discipline. Without it, I knew that I would be consumed by grief, anger and guilt.

Wendy and I returned to the chapel where Terry and Carol had organised an array of biscuits and chocolate bars for us all, and more tea and coffee. We ate a little and told them about Tim and how he looked. At this point, Terry and Carol asked whether it was all right for them to go and see Tim. We said of course it was. Clare and Nicola stayed with Wendy and me for the next few minutes.

When they returned, the look of sadness and pain in their faces spoke volumes.

We picked up the wrappers from our biscuits and chocolate bars and bade our farewells. Thanking Philip Mears, the chaplain, for his kindness and hospitality, we set off to return home.

As we stepped outside the hospital doors, several journalists broke away from the group gathered there and came across to Wendy and me. Questions rained down upon us: how was Tim and what did we feel about what had happened? One by one the questions were answered, only for the next journalist, who had been unable to get close first time round, to ask the same or a very similar question. The whole process, including television interviews, took perhaps ten minutes.

As we were easing away from the group, one particular journalist, whom I later discovered to be Bob Graham from *Today*, asked if he could have a photograph of Tim. Ironically, the last photograph I had ever taken of Tim was the one that Wendy had placed by his bed (and this was her idea) so that the medical staff could see how Tim looked before the bombing. Terry offered to bring one back to the hospital from home. The other journalists seemed relieved that Bob had been the first to ask the question.

I was to discover later that there is a fierce competitive edge to the relationship between individual journalists

and newspapers, and that Bob Graham is one of those
journalists who is seen by many of the others as a bit of
a maverick, good at his job, but doing things his own way.
This did not always seem to endear him to the others, but
over the coming days and weeks we received several calls
from Bob, often just to ask how we were, as opposed to
asking for comments to print. In fact, it was Bob who
convinced me that, while the press had a job to do, they
were human and that they too had been deeply affected
by the bombing outrage in Warrington.

Back at the house Carol, Terry, their children, Wendy
and I attempted a conversation, but not for very long as
they had to go home and we had to travel to Manchester
to collect Dom and Abbi.

Wendy and I spent most of the journey lost in our own
private thoughts, coping with the heart-rending images of
Tim's heavily bandaged head. There were questions we
wanted to ask one another but chose not to, because
the pain of answering them would have outweighed any
possible benefit.

When we arrived at Wendy's parents', John, Betty and
the children were pensive, obviously awaiting news of
Tim. We told them that he was fighting hard, but that we
had no clear knowledge of his injuries nor of his chances
of surviving another night. The mood remained sombre
and conversation tended to come in short, unconnected
bursts. I felt sure that we all had a million and one things
we could have said but didn't, because you can never be
sure how your words will sound to others at a time like
this, even more so because your emotions are so mixed
up that all your usual control is absent and you have no
defence against the wrong word or the wrong look.

After we had all picked at the meal Betty had made for
us, we turned on the television news, and Wendy and I
were to see ourselves on the screen for the first time.

It was a curious sensation seeing and hearing myself speaking about Tim and the critical state that he was in, and finding myself with tears in my eyes as I listened to my own words. It was all the more upsetting to see Wendy crying at my side during the interview.

Both BBC and ITV had shown the same interview but from different angles, and in the straight-on shots I could see how much impact the thirty hours we had endured had had upon us both. No sleep and virtually no food made us look drawn and tired out.

We set off for home again, and it was a repeat of the earlier journey. Usually Dom nattered away during routine car journeys with incessant questions about everything under the sun. This time, I don't recall him uttering anything more than the odd monosyllabic reply to my occasional question.

Wendy and I explained to Dominic and Abbi that we were going to find a chemist's shop, when we got back to Great Sankey. We called at the local police station to enquire where we would find the emergency chemist's. The two officers on duty listened carefully as I explained who I was and what I wanted. They contacted a pharmacist who agreed to be called out, and then I set about finding the shop. I should explain that I am a completely useless navigator, and even in a town the size of Warrington, where I have lived for nearly six years, I regularly fail to find the place I am searching for. Fortunately, Wendy is a much better navigator than I am and she had a pretty clear idea where the shop was. As it turned out, we arrived before the pharmacist.

We told him that we had not had a minute's sleep the previous night and that we could not face another night of purgatory. He understood and gave us a supply of sleeping pills. Wendy and I agreed that we did not want to develop

a dependence upon them, but for one night there seemed
to be really no alternative.

Within minutes of getting home, we sent the kids off to
bed and we soon followed. The label on the outside of the
pill bottle said that it could take up to half an hour for the
user to become drowsy; I doubt if it took more than ten
minutes before we both fell into a deep sleep.

Monday, 22 March

Despite the sleeping tablet, I awoke at the time my body
clock has become accustomed to over the years – 6.30
a.m. However, rather than immediately getting out of bed,
which is my normal pattern, I clambered forward along
the bed to switch on the breakfast television programme.
I tapped the sound mute button on the remote control
handset, so that I could telephone the hospital to find out
how Tim was.

The nurse who took my call told me that there was no
change at all in Tim's condition, but that a decision would
be taken by the surgeons quite soon on whether or not
Tim was strong enough to be transferred from Warrington
General to the Neurosurgical Unit at Liverpool's Walton
Hospital. She told me that by nine o'clock, which was when
we expected to arrive, it was likely that the doctors would
have made up their minds.

I had intended to let Wendy sleep on, but the television
was about to show an interview with John Britton, the
Headmaster of Great Sankey High School. This is the
school that Dominic and Tim both attended, and I knew
that Wendy would want to hear it, so I woke her up.

The questions put to John ranged from how he had
first heard the news of the bombing and that Tim was

among the casualties, to how he would address the pupils later that morning. I thought that he gave very thoughtful replies to all of the questions and I was impressed by his composure.

The previous evening, before we had all gone to bed, Wendy and I had put it to Dom and Abbi that, subject to their agreement, we would be happier if they went to school rather than being kept at home. They both agreed, but I took Dom in my car that morning because I feared that a television crew might be outside the school, waiting to interview him. I knew that he would find such an interview very difficult.

As we approached the school gates I saw, to my relief, that there were no cameras, and I was able to send Dom into school without any interference. He had declined my earlier suggestion that I go into school with him. He seemed calm and steady and I told him just to try to concentrate on his school work.

Half an hour or so later, I took Abbi to the junior school. As we walked up the path to the school's entrance, two of Abbi's closest friends, Gemma and Katie, were waiting outside for her. As we approached them, they both burst into tears, so I pulled them to me and held them closely, stroking their hair. Quietly I told them that Tim would not have wanted them to be so upset, but he would want them to keep an eye on Abbi for him. Gemma and Katie began to calm down Abbi, who had begun to cry for the first time since Saturday night. Part of me was relieved that Abbi had cried again, because I was worried that since the intense emotion and tears of Saturday evening, she had built a protective barrier around herself and was suppressing her tears and pain. Though this was no different to the rest of the family, Abbi was the most vulnerable simply because she was the youngest.

While the three girls were in a tight huddle, I stepped

inside the school entrance and met the headmistress,
Mrs Steel, in the corridor outside her office. She invited
me inside and asked how Tim was.

I knew that Mrs Steel's interest and concern were
absolutely genuine, but our relationship had never been
easy and this inhibited me from being too voluble in my
explanations; there was an awkwardness borne out of
earlier differences of opinion she and I had aired over
Tim. She said that she and her staff would keep a careful
eye on Abbi and I had no doubt whatsoever that she would
do just that.

It was close to nine o'clock when Wendy and I arrived
at the hospital. We made our way to the Intensive Care
Unit, and as we turned the corner to go inside, I noticed
a tall, grey-haired man sitting very still in the waiting area
outside. At that point it did not occur to me that he had
anything to do with me or my family. I was not to know
then that he would become a very important man in our
lives over the next days and weeks.

Wendy and I sat down in the waiting room inside the
Unit. After just a few minutes, Barry Taylor came into
the room to talk to us. He gave us the encouraging news
that in tests he had carried out on Tim there had been
signs of some basic brain activity. He told us that he would
never have predicted that Tim would survive this long when
he had first had to treat him on Saturday afternoon. He
confirmed what I had heard him say in an interview on
breakfast television earlier that morning, following the
interview with John Britton. He had used the words
'battlefield injuries' in describing the injuries that Tim had
sustained; it was for this reason that he had not expected
Tim to survive Saturday night. To have survived until now,
and also to show brain activity, was a sure sign that Tim
was a great fighter, he told us. He then explained that Tim
needed to be transferred to Walton Hospital so that he

could undergo a brain scan. (I should explain that this could not be performed at Warrington General, because a public appeal for funds to help buy a scanner for £1m had reached only £500,000. Significantly, in the wake of the Warrington bombing, public donations poured into the hospital, and in January 1994 a brain scanner was delivered and installed at Warrington General.) Barry wished us both well as he left the room to go and prepare Tim for the transfer.

Moments later, Philip Mears, the hospital chaplain, entered the room with the tall, grey-haired gentleman we had seen sitting outside earlier. Philip introduced us to the Reverend Gordon McKibben, the vicar of St Mary's parish church in Great Sankey.

Gordon's first words were delivered with a very distinct, though pleasant, Ulster accent. He said, 'I'm Irish; do you mind talking to me?' I assured him that where he came from had no bearing on how we would get along together. He seemed relieved, though he displayed a certain amount of nervous unease which was to be evident throughout the coming weeks.

He then asked whether he could say a prayer for us all. We agreed, and as he began, Philip took hold of Wendy's hand and held it while Gordon conducted his prayer. I felt an immediate warmth towards Gordon whose nervousness made him vulnerable and, I must say, it endeared him to me. He was a straightforward man of God, who did not attempt to crowd us or exert any particular influence over us at any time. He was simply there for us, and I will always be grateful to him for that.

Meanwhile, in the ward outside, there was a real sense of urgency about everyone involved in preparing Tim's transfer. As his bed was wheeled past the waiting room, Wendy and I hurriedly said our goodbyes and thanks to everyone in the vicinity, including Philip and Gordon.

We proceeded to the main entrance, where a Mersey

Regional ambulance was backed right up to the door
awaiting Tim's arrival. We returned to the car and spent
several minutes staring at the door from which Tim would
appear. It struck me as strange that Tim had left the
Intensive Care Unit before we had and yet several minutes
had now passed since Wendy and I got into the car and
there was still no sign of him.

Then, just as before, there was a sudden flurry of
activity. Medical staff appeared at the ambulance and
began the task of getting Tim into the vehicle as quickly
as they could without causing him any stress. We got out
of the car to see what was happening. Wendy pointed out
that one of the doctors in the team responsible for the
transfer had operated on Tim just a few weeks earlier,
removing his appendix. Just a moment or so later, he was
close enough for Wendy to ask him if he remembered the
operation. He looked tired and very drawn indeed as he
replied that he did remember.

We returned to the car, where one or two members of
the press asked us for comments, but there was little we
could say. Television cameras were again in evidence as
Tim was placed in the ambulance and we all drove away.

We had been told to follow the ambulance, and were
warned that it would have a heavy police escort all the
way to Liverpool. I did not expect it to be so difficult
keeping in touch with the convoy, but within a mile of
the hospital, we were already separated from the police
car at the rear. Traffic was moving over to let the convoy
through, but closing up again so that I could not maintain
contact. Before we got on the M62 westbound, I had lost
sight of them altogether, but at least the motorway traffic
was moving quickly, so I was able to increase my speed
and rejoin the convoy further ahead.

As we left the M62 to join the M57, the two police cars
that had escorted the ambulance from Warrington Hospital

peeled off to be replaced by two more police cars and two police motorcycles. I think it was at this point that I remarked to Wendy that had Tim been conscious, he would have enjoyed the great excitement of this high-speed journey.

The motorcyclists and police-car drivers criss-crossed the motorway lanes with great skill and panache, making sure that no vehicles got in the way of the ambulance.

Soon after we joined the M57, one of the police motorcyclists became aware of our car keeping pace with the convoy, and he waved a cautionary hand at us on a couple of occasions indicating that we should back off. Failing to shake us off and obviously not realising why we were shadowing the convoy, he glared at us in disbelief. It occurred to me that he very probably thought that we were members of the press.

The high-speed action continued and was needed most when we left the M57 and joined the East Lancashire Road. This is an extremely busy dual carriageway which connects Liverpool and Manchester. The skilful way in which the police vehicles controlled traffic-light junctions and road intersections in order to prevent any hold-ups was impressive.

The ambulance, police vehicles and our car all pulled up outside the main entrance to the Neurological Unit at Liverpool's Walton Hospital. As Wendy and I got out of our car, the police motorcyclist who had been so irritated by us on the journey recognised who we were and immediately said how sorry he was for not realising sooner.

We were greeted at the door by Wendy Rabett, Assistant to the Chief Executive of the Neuro Unit. She took us up to the waiting room where we were introduced to her assistant, Stephanie Harrison. Among the people who were to make a lasting impression upon me and my family

during the coming days, Stephanie was to be up there with
the best of them for her help, her humour and her sheer
hard work throughout Tim's stay at Walton.

Quite soon after we arrived, Carol and Terry appeared,
and their company and support were to prove, as they had
the day before, invaluable.

Stephanie quickly set about establishing a pattern which
involved making sure that we had a steady supply of tea
and coffee, and explaining what was happening to Tim.
She told us that Mr Miles, the consultant, had been called
to Warrington General on Saturday afternoon to give an
initial diagnosis of Tim's injuries and his prospects. This
was the first time we had been told this, and I was a little
perplexed, not because I was in any way troubled by the
information, but simply because no one had bothered to
tell us before now. Stephanie informed us that Mr Miles
would come to see us just as soon as Tim had been through
the brain scanner and the results were known.

As we waited for Mr Miles, Stephanie told us some of the
history and the work of the Neuro Unit. It was depressing
to hear of the high number of children brought to Walton
as a result of road traffic accidents. In the room where we
waited, there was a large noticeboard full of photographs
of young children who had passed through the Unit, but
Stephanie emphasised, reassuringly, the great recovery
record that the Unit boasted.

Stephanie is a blonde married woman in her mid-forties,
and is full of energy. She is what we 'Scouse' natives of
Liverpool affectionately call a 'Woolleyback', because she
was born in Wigan, the town where each of our three
children had been born and raised until 1987, when
we had moved some fifteen miles down the road to
Warrington. Whenever the conversation flagged or the
mood in the waiting room became heavy, Stephanie would
pick it up with her natural, easy conversational style. She

was an instant best friend and was to remain so over the coming days.

Eventually Mr Miles joined us and we all sat down. He and I were directly opposite one another. I waited nervously for him to begin, for his words would have as great a significance as any ever uttered to me before in my life.

He said, 'Tim is very seriously ill. His head took the full impact of the bomb blast, and his brain is severely enlarged. You must understand that I am not in the business of giving people false hope and I prefer to tell you plainly that I estimate Tim's chances of survival at no greater than twenty to thirty per cent. There is, therefore, some hope, but I repeat that it is unlikely he will survive.'

For several seconds, I tried extremely hard to absorb the words I had just listened to so intently. There was cause for hope because he had said so. Understandably, my mind edited out the desperate prospect that he would not survive, and instead it latched on to the word 'hope' like a drowning man to a piece of driftwood.

Mr Miles asked if we had any questions, and I then put to him what I can only describe as a checklist. I said, 'If Tim survives, will he be able to see?' The response was that Tim had lost his right eye, and they did not yet know whether his left eye was still attached to his brain. If it was still connected, then there was a good chance that he would have some sight in this eye.

Terrible though this was to hear, it was delivered in a very matter-of-fact tone. I pressed on, asking, 'If Tim survives, will he be able to hear?' This was answered in a similar way to my first question; Mr Miles stated that it was unlikely that Tim would have any hearing ability remaining in his right ear, but it was probable that his left ear would still function to some degree.

Next I asked Mr Miles, 'If Tim survives, will he be able to speak?' This time the reply was rather more straightforward. 'Yes, I believe he will,' he said.

Then I asked him whether Tim would be able to walk, and again Mr Miles stated with some confidence that he believed he would.

I then summarised the answers to my questions to be sure that none of us had misunderstood. I said, 'So, what you're telling us is that if Tim lives, he may have sight in his one remaining eye, he may hear in his left ear, he will be able to speak and he will be able to walk. Is that about right?'

'Yes, that's about right,' said Mr Miles. He then went on to explain how very keen the reconstruction team were to be allowed to start working with Tim, for the longer it was delayed, the greater the risk of infection and meningitis. Before we could ask when such work might begin, he told us perfectly plainly that Tim had to show he could breathe without the aid of the ventilator.

This vital next step could not be rushed and could only be attempted when all the conditions were right. He explained that it was a matter of critical judgement between, on the one hand, acting soon enough to prevent infection, and yet not so soon as to cause severe trauma to Tim. He would keep us fully in the picture throughout, he said. Before departing, he told us that he would need to change the dressings covering Tim's head, to clean him up so that the risk of infection was minimised.

Wendy, Carol, Terry and I sat silently for a few minutes after everyone else had left the room. I could not speak for the others, but in my heart was the beginning of real hope that our beloved son was going to beat his terrible injuries and survive to live a different kind of life, but still to be with us, among his loving family and friends. I must admit I was ill prepared for the very different view that Wendy held.

After listening to what I had said, she stated in a tearful voice that it would be better for Tim's sake if he were not to survive. She could not see how Tim could accept such a greatly diminished quality of life afflicted by appalling, disfiguring injuries when he had been such a handsome, vibrant boy. She felt that this was more than Tim or she could bear.

I told her that I understood this well enough, but that regardless of his injuries, I wanted him back, that we would make a life for him. It was our duty to our son. I also emphasised how many wonderful things reconstructive surgery could achieve with modern technology.

Perhaps sensing that our views were diametrically opposed, Terry and Carol suggested that we go and get something to eat, away from the hospital. This made sense, and Stephanie, who had left us so that we could reflect upon what Mr Miles had said, returned and recommended that we try the pub opposite the hospital where they served excellent Cornish pasties.

During our pub lunch, I set about trying to make Wendy change her initial feelings about the extent of Tim's injuries and the kind of life he could lead following extensive medical and surgical attention. In this regard, I felt that Carol and Terry's views were helpful to my cause. They too felt that if Tim pulled through, he could eventually live a life of some quality.

I must say that I did understand Wendy's feelings very well, even though I did not share them. She could not see how Tim could come to terms with the damage he had sustained to his face. Tim had been privileged to be born a handsome boy, and of late he had become quite obviously aware of his charms where girls were concerned. This was a source of both pride and concern to us. Pride because all parents want their children to be attractive and appealing and we were no exception in this; but also concern that at just twelve years of age he was already having groups of girls calling at the house to see him, and I in particular was keen that his school work should come first.

Wendy posed the difficult question of how Tim would be able to enjoy life when he would see his brother and sister and all his close friends doing the things he always enjoyed doing when he would probably no longer be able to do them himself. She believed this would make the rest of his life not only deeply frustrating, but very unhappy.

I understood this point of view, but emphasised to Wendy that Tim was too important a member of the family for us to give up hope on him. I reminded her that if he was able to see, hear and walk, then that was as much, and more, than many other unfortunate people have. I said that with the love of us all, Tim would have a good quality of life, and frankly, the thought of life without him was unbearable.

As I spoke, I could sense Wendy accepting what I was saying. In fact, as I finished, she made something of a volte face by declaring that she would give up her job to care for Tim for as long as it would take. With all the zeal of a convert, Wendy became very positive indeed about what we would do for Tim.

I was pleased and very relieved that Wendy and I were now united in our determination that Tim would not just survive his terrible injuries, but would recover his former life to a considerable extent.

We all returned to the hospital in good spirits, convinced that our boy was going to make it. Indeed, I took Wendy's change of heart to be a sign that he would. We spent a few more hours at the hospital before returning home in time for Dominic and Abbi's return from school.

Dom and Abbi told us that their day at school had been all right, though Dom said that many of the children had spent the day in tears. This was particularly the case with the girls, he said. The school had arranged for counselling services to be provided for anyone who felt they needed help and support. Both our children felt that it had been the right decision for them to be in school.

We told them about our day and explained the nature and extent of Tim's injuries, but then we stressed how there was cause for hope. I think that this was also the first time that I actually expressed openly what I had been thinking when Mr Miles had said that Tim's chances were twenty to thirty per cent. I reasoned that Mr Miles was bound to be erring on the conservative side, for fear of raising our hopes too much, and that really Tim's chances of survival were somewhat higher than the twenty to thirty per cent we had been told. With all the certainty and confidence of a man with renewed hope, I said that Tim's chances were probably nearer to forty or fifty per cent, and that with the power of our combined love and will to fight being transmitted to Tim, he was going to shorten those odds even more and he would pull through.

Tuesday, 23 March

An early telephone call to the hospital resulted in the comforting message that Tim had spent a peaceful night and there was no change in his condition.

Dom and Abbi declined my offer to drive them both to school, and so once they had both left the house Wendy and I set off for Walton. We arrived at about 9.30 a.m. to find that a car-parking space at the rear of the building had been cordoned off for us. This was arranged by the hospital staff to avoid us being besieged by the reporters and TV crews who it seemed were now permanently camped outside the hospital.

Soon after we arrived in the waiting room, Stephanie

and the chief executive, David Cain, came in to see us.
David asked if there was anything we particularly wanted
arranging, to which I replied that Tim and I would be
especially pleased if someone would contact Everton
Football Club to see whether they could send anything
at all that we could give to Tim when he finally regained
consciousness. I felt that a memento from his team would
mean so much to Tim. Stephanie said that she would be
happy to take on this task herself.

Wendy and I went into Tim's private room. The confus-
ing array of tubes criss-crossing him and the fact that his
original bandages were still covering his face were deeply
upsetting. After some two and a half days the dressings
were filthy and beginning to smell. I asked the sister in
charge, Sydney May, a delightful Irish woman whom we
also came to know well, what could be done about them.
Sydney told us that it was likely that the dressings would
be replaced that day, and she suggested that when Mr Miles
arrived she would ask him to come and explain matters to
us direct.

I noticed that quite apart from Tim's skin temperature
being extremely warm, the smell of the bomb's blast was
very strong, particularly close up. As you might expect, I
am not at all knowledgeable about the subject of bombs,
of how they are made or how they work, but I shall never
ever forget the smell that Tim's skin retained. I can only
describe it as a burned smell, as if the fine facial hair that
youngsters of Tim's age still have had been completely
singed by the heat generated in the blast which had
propelled the fragmented pieces of the waste bin into his
face and caused him such severe head and brain injuries.

We left after a short while so as not to interfere with the
nursing staff's routine monitoring of Tim's condition, and
returned to the waiting room where we sat with Stephanie
and had a hot drink. While we were chatting, Stephanie

received a message telling her that some of the Everton players had come to the hospital straight from a training session. We were touched and delighted by the speed will which the club had responded to our request.

Stephanie asked us what we wanted to do, and I replied that I would like the players to be brought up to the waiting room. This was quickly arranged, and in walked Tim's favourite player, Peter Beardsley, along with team captain Dave Watson and midfield player Ian Snodin. Dave Watson presented Wendy and me with an autographed ball and his own autographed No. 5 shirt. I remember that I shook each of their hands and Wendy kissed them. She remarked afterwards on Peter Beardsley's soft skin! I asked the players if they would agree to being photographed presenting the items they had brought for Tim to Wendy and myself as, for Tim, this would be the next best thing to meeting the players himself. They were happy to do so, and the photographs were taken by one of the press photographers in the hospital library. Sadly, I never received any copies of them from the press.

We greatly appreciated the visit from the Everton players and I told them how much it would mean to Tim to have the shirt and ball presented to him when he was better. The players were genuinely concerned for him, and when they left they said that if we wanted anything else we just had to let them know.

After returning to the waiting room, Wendy and I were informed that Tim had been taken to the theatre to have his old dressings replaced with new ones. We were advised that this could take an hour. In fact, it was two and a half hours before Tim was brought back to his room and we were allowed to see him.

We were shocked by the sight that greeted us. The new dressings on Tim's face only covered the right side, down to his mouth. For the first time since Saturday, we could see the left side of Tim's face, where the injuries were far less severe. Even so, to see his left eye hideously swollen, deep purple in colour and completely closed, was a very upsetting experience. Tim's nose was undamaged, though it too was very swollen. We could also see that he had lost teeth on the right side of his mouth. All of this was a shock to us, but perhaps, apart from his swollen eye, the most disturbing feature of all was the size of his left cheek, which was grossly swollen. The overall effect of his visible injuries made him unrecognisable from the sunny, smiling lad he had been on Saturday morning.

I found myself staring at my son, taking in every detail of his face but trying yet again not to allow my mind and my imagination to drift to the injuries we could not see. It was noticeable when I got very close to Tim's face that the bomb-blast smell had remained on him. It had, in fact, become a strangely familiar part of him now in a macabre way.

I began talking to Tim. I got as close as I could to his left ear and quietly implored and begged him, pleaded with him to fight the best fight of his life and pull through. I told him that I knew he could hear me and that he was going to make it. I told him that my will and my strength were passing from me into him to help him to make it back to us. I asked him to give me some kind of sign that he could hear me, but needless to say none was forthcoming. That did not stop me from repeating over and over my urgent pleadings for him to fight, fight and fight again. I wanted him back, I told him, I wanted to hold him, care for him and give him a good life. A couple of times, the tears fell as my strength was replaced by intense sadness and a heavy heart at the sight of our motionless, grievously injured son, lying there before me so completely changed by the callous brutality of evil men who knew no limit to the horrors they were prepared to perpetrate against innocent children and adults. My spirits flagged on several occasions, but then the fighting talk would come back and I would renew my endless litany of begging and pleading.

Wendy encouraged me to return to the waiting room and to have a break, as I suspect my behaviour must have seemed to her to be dangerously close to being obsessive. I was aware of what I was doing, that I was repeating my imploring to Tim over and over, but I thought I was doing it quietly enough for Wendy not to hear me, as I did not want her to be alarmed about my state of mind on top of her anxieties for Tim.

We reflected on what we had seen as we sat drinking our tea and coffee, and then David Cain entered the room with Stephanie. David asked whether we wanted to speak to the press and TV people who were still assembled in large numbers. I looked at Wendy who said, 'It's up to you.' I turned to David and said, 'Yes, we'll see them together.' David said that he had put all the press and TV people in the library and he would lead us down there if we were ready. We picked up our coats and followed him down.

A table with a couple of microphones had been set up at the far end of the room, which seemed as if it were full of reporters, cameras and hand-held tape recorders. I sat down with Wendy on my left and David on my right. David announced that we were ready to answer any questions but that he did not want it to be disorderly. As I recall, the press conference comprised mainly me telling everyone about the change of dressings and how much more we had seen of Tim's face. I told them that we knew we had a vastly different Tim but that if, God willing, we got him back, we would make a new life for him.

The people who asked questions did so in a very polite and professional manner and there was no jostling for position; we were told afterwards that the TV people had agreed to pool their film so that we were not confronted with a battery of cameras.

The day ended with our mood reflecting the fact that our hopes had been given a boost over the past two days, though we did not underestimate the size of the mountain that Tim had to scale.

Back home, during the evening, GMTV contacted me to arrange an early-morning live link-up from Warrington, for their morning television programme.

Wednesday, 24 March

At 7.10 a.m. Wendy and I were interviewed from the Village Hotel in Warrington via a live link-up to the London studio. We were questioned about our hopes for the day and we confirmed that this was to be the crucial day when the painkilling drugs that Tim had been receiving since Saturday would be reduced in order to see whether the reintroduction of pain would lead to brain activity. We knew that this procedure was already under way and that the results would be known by the time we arrived at the hospital in an hour or so.

We concluded the interview and set off for Walton Hospital, arriving at about 8.30 a.m. For most of the journey we had travelled in silence. I speculated endlessly to myself on how the critical tests on Tim had gone, always coming up with the same outcome – that he was going to make it. Today would mark the beginning of Tim's return to us.

As we approached the entrance from the hospital's rear car park, Stephanie came out to meet us. We asked her immediately for news and she told us that there had been no response from Tim . . . yet! Our hearts sank as Stephanie must have known they would. She quickly pointed out that not everybody responds in the same way or at the same time, so there was still time. But she was honest enough to say that the signs were not good. I didn't know whether all hope had gone or not. I just didn't know what to think. We had been led to believe that the results would be known within an hour of the drugs being reduced, and yet here we were some two and a half hours after the procedure had been started with Tim not responding at all, and yet Stephanie was telling us not to give up hope!

The next few hours were spent mostly in silent prayer, willing Tim to feel pain. How strange a remark that seems, and yet it was what we wished for above all else in the world.

We were not allowed to be with Tim at all while the tests were under way, so we sat quietly in the waiting room with me occasionally pacing the room. This is something I often do when I am trying to clear my head, and at this vital time I wanted, above all else, to transmit the strongest thoughts I possibly could to Tim, telepathically.

Something I have come to acknowledge after going through this terrible ordeal is that I no longer sneer at any theory that is outside the accepted wisdom of mainstream thinking. This does not mean that I have become a mystic, or that I practise new and strange rites of any kind, merely that I do not dismiss the unorthodox out of hand as I did previously. In particular, that week I began to believe, because I needed to, that telepathic communication with my son was achievable, and I worked at it harder than anything else. Of course the rational part of me still dismisses this notion, but that rational part of me is no longer always the dominant part of my consciousness. It is frequently challenged by a new open-mindedness based on the knowledge that my previous thinking was stereotyped and one-dimensional.

Despite the sombre and reflective mood that Wendy and
I were both in, the morning seemed to move on quickly,
and at about 11.00 a.m. Terry and Carol arrived. We had
not expected them but their arrival was welcome, as they
brought their own brand of cheeriness with them, even
though they immediately understood the gravity of Tim's
situation.

An hour or so later, Mr Miles entered the room, and
we all stood up as if to attention. He bade us to sit, and I
knew from the look in his eyes and the expression on his
face that we were about to hear the unthinkable.

'I'm so very sorry to have to tell you that Tim has not
shown any response whatsoever. This is bad news, I'm
afraid, as there should have been a reaction long before
now. We will continue to monitor the situation most closely
for any sign of brain activity, but you must be prepared for
the worst.'

No one knew what to say in response to this shocking
and awful news. I was stunned to be hearing it officially
from the consultant in charge. This meant it was the end, no
matter that it was still mathematically a remote possibility
for Tim's brain to respond. Mr Miles realised how hard this
news had hit us and he added that Tim's chances had always
been slim, but that until all hope was gone the tests would
continue. Before leaving, he added the final and possibly
the gloomiest comment of all, by cautioning us that it was
possible that Tim's heart might not withstand the stress
associated with the drug reduction. He said it was possible
that Tim might not survive the night.

He left the room and Stephanie set about comforting
Wendy and me with a consoling arm around the shoulders.
'Do you want a cup of tea or coffee?' she asked. I think it
was Terry who answered 'Yes' for all of us.

Stephanie left and at that exact moment the most intense
anger, bitterness and pain raced through every part of me

and I openly shouted a whole host of expletives. This outpouring of bile was coming from the accumulated emotions that had been bottled up inside me for the past four days.

My anger was directed not just at the evil creature or creatures who had planted the bomb that had fatally injured our son, but at the injustice of Tim losing such a promising young life. I kept thinking over and over again that our beautiful son had had only twelve short years out of a life expectancy of seventy-plus years. My rage was also born out of the fact that I would never hear him again, that he and I would never embrace one another again – all the simple but infinitely pleasurable things you do with your child had been ripped away in a moment of hideous cruelty by an unknown, faceless monster who cared nothing for the fate of our darling son Tim.

I was so consumed by my boiling rage that I was completely unaware of Stephanie's return. She came up to me and held my shoulders and told me that it was right to release all my anger, that it was doing me no good to hold it all in and that she had been worried about where the pain had been going since we arrived on Monday.

Strangely enough, having someone encourage me to carry on the way I was had the opposite effect upon me. It calmed me down and made me somewhat embarrassed about the things I knew I had said out loud in front of Wendy, Carol and Terry. Sensing my awkwardness, Terry and Carol both reassured me that they were not in any way offended but understood exactly how I must feel.

After we had drunk our tea and coffee, we all agreed that Wendy should go to collect Dominic and Abbi so that they were aware of the precarious position Tim was now in. Terry and Carol drove Wendy first to Abbi's school. Abbi was brought into Mrs Steel's office where Wendy told her she would like Abbi to come back to the hospital to see

Tim, but Abbi was quite adamant that she would not. She
said that she would see Tim when 'he was better'. Wendy
asked her again, but there was no moving Abbi, and so
Wendy did not think it appropriate to push her. She told
Abbi to go to her friend Vicki's house after school and to
wait there until we came home.

Next, Terry and Carol took Wendy to the High School
where Dom was summoned to Mr Britton's office. Wendy
went through the same process with Dom that she had with
Abbi, adding that there was little hope left now. Dominic,
in Wendy's opinion, was too frightened at the prospect of
seeing Tim and again she did not think it right to push
him against his will to come to the hospital. Wendy asked
Dominic to go with Abbi to Vicki's house after school and
wait there until we collected them.

During the time that Wendy was away from the hospital,
Stephanie told me that the two paramedic ambulance men
who had been the first medical personnel on the scene in
Bridge Street following the explosions, were outside and
wanted to meet me and, if I was agreeable, to spend a few
moments with Tim. I said to show them in and shook both
their hands warmly, to thank them so much for the care
and help they had given to Tim. I said to them that they
must have seen some awful things that day and I hoped
that such memories would not stay with them for too long.
I told both of them that they were more than welcome to
spend a few moments with Tim, subject to the nursing sister
agreeing, for I had only just left the room after spending
a further thirty minutes caressing Tim's fingers, and his
swollen cheek. Once again, I had spent most of my time
imploring him to respond to the tests and to confound
everyone even at this late stage. It was terribly frustrating
not being able to get hold of Tim – all the tubes made it
quite impossible to do so. I looked the length of his body,
noting that he really had become very tall for his age, and

I winced at the sight of the black shrapnel burns on his upper arms and chest. Both his shoulders and both his wrists were broken, and for the first time I noticed that his right shoulder was very swollen. I also knew that both his legs had sustained nasty injuries. All in all, our son had been badly broken.

I had just about regained some composure when the paramedics arrived. I knocked on the door of Tim's room and the two young nurses, Margaret Colfer and Sue Comer, who had tended Tim so lovingly for the past few days, indicated we could come in. I moved to one side and both of the paramedics stood at the foot of Tim's bed with their heads bowed; they were entirely motionless and silent. The older one turned to me after a couple of minutes to thank me as he withdrew from the room, but his younger colleague asked me if he could stay for a little while longer on his own. I said that he could, and his colleague and I returned to the waiting room. He told me how the bombing incident had affected his partner really badly but said that they both greatly appreciated the privilege of being given their few moments with Tim.

A short while after the paramedics had gone, Mr Miles's senior registrar, Paul Eldridge, came in to talk to me. His being younger and less formal than Mr Miles meant that we could have a frank and more relaxed conversation.

I was told for the first time about the nature of the tests carried out on Tim during the course of the day, and I was surprised at how simple they were. For example, one of them involved dropping cold liquid into Tim's ear to see if there was any brain reaction. Paul explained to me how desperately disappointing it had been that none of the tests had produced any response at all.

He also told me in clear layman's terms how the one organ in the body that has no room in which to swell to any extent is the brain. The skull, which encases the brain in order to protect it, is essentially a box, and just like a box, it is not flexible so will not expand to accommodate the enlarged brain. Tim had sustained the full bomb blast to his head and his brain had swollen, causing great pressure within his skull. I was grateful to him for taking the time to tell me things I had not realised previously.

As we finished our conversation, Wendy, Carol and Terry returned without our children. I was perplexed that neither had wanted to come to see Tim. In fact, I hadn't realised that Wendy was merely going to ask them; I thought she had gone to collect them in view of the hopeless position we now faced.

While Terry chatted to Paul Eldridge, Wendy and I agreed on what now had to be done. We rang Wendy's parents and my father, to tell them that the tests had failed and that we wanted them to see Tim this evening as it was possible that his heart would not withstand the shock of the drug reduction, and that he might die during the night. John said he would ask Wendy's brother Phil to collect him, Betty and my father and bring them all to Walton together. Phil and his wife Karen still lived in Hartlepool, though Phil's job had now taken him to Staffordshire. As a result, Phil had been lodging with his parents while his house was up for sale in the North-East.

It was perhaps 8.00 p.m. by the time Phil and his party arrived. Everyone greeted each other with heavy hearts. Betty looked very drawn and tired and all of John's normal ebullience was gone. My father was very quiet when he arrived, but he then embraced me and cried freely. Disbelief that we were facing this dreadful heartbreaking situation was the prevailing mood among us all.

Wendy and I took her parents in to see Tim for the first time since he had been injured. John broke down in tears on seeing him, whereas Betty stood silently watching him. She was to tell Wendy later that she felt at that moment

Tim at three months.

Tim at eight months.

Tim at ten months. He was affectionately known as 'egghead' because his face was fat and his hat accentuated his round head.

Above left: Tim at two-and-a-half years.

Above: 'I've got the stick, so where's the lolly?' Tim is in our old street in Wigan. Aged three in 1983.

Left: Dominic, Tim and Abbi with snowman in our back garden. Wigan, 1984.

Above: On holiday,
with rabbits,
Tenby, 1985.

Left: Tim with
Abbi. On the same
family holiday,
Tenby, 1985.

Below: Tim with
Dom on the beach,
Cornwall, 1984.

Right: Tim on his sixth birthday at his grandad Eric's house in Wigan. He's wearing his favourite present, his new Everton Football Club shirt. Note the look of pride.

Left: Tim with Abbi in grandad John's and grandma Betty's garden in Manchester, 1987.

Right: Tim with Abbi and Colin, outside our holiday apartment in Estepona, Costa Del Sol, 1987. Tim did not want to be photographed.

that Tim had already gone. After several minutes, Wendy's
parents left the room and my father and Phil came in. They
too cried openly for Tim. On every occasion that someone
else wept, I always started to cry with them. These were
among the most harrowing moments in the week, all of us
paying our silent farewells to a deeply loved son, nephew
and grandson.

We re-assembled in the waiting room, and everyone met
Stephanie. As she had been doing all week, she organised
hot drinks. It was agreed that Phil would take our parents
home and then go straight back to Hartlepool and return
early on Thursday morning with Karen and their children,
Penny and Alice. Betty was very concerned at the amount
of driving Phil would be doing, but he insisted he would
be fine and would take no risks.

It was approaching 9.00 p.m. when Wendy was told that
Father John Walsh was outside asking for permission to
come in to see her. Wendy looked at me for my reaction,
and I asked her who Father Walsh was and what he would
be doing here. Wendy explained that Father Walsh had
been the parish priest in the part of Warrington that
included St Gregory's School, where Wendy had worked
as one of the catering staff. She asked me how I felt about
him coming in. I replied that if she wanted him to come
through, then I had no objections.

This was my first meeting with John. He was no
more than thirty-two or thirty-three years of age in my
estimation, and he had a youthful charm and openness
which were to endear him to us over the coming weeks.
He expressed his deep sympathy to us all and told us how
shocked and horrified he had been when the bombing
occurred, and how he had been even more devastated
to learn on Monday from one of Wendy's ex-colleagues
at St Greg's that it was one of the women he had known
in the canteen whose son had been so appallingly injured.

After several minutes and introductions all round, Wendy
asked whether John wanted to see Tim, to which John said,
'Yes, that's why I came.'

We both took John through to Tim's room and Wendy
stood at the end of the bed holding Father John's hand. He
then asked us both whether he could say a prayer for Tim.
We said that he could, and he spoke very movingly.

Six days later, on the day before Tim's funeral, Father
John called at the house to see us and recounted how in
the week before the bombing incident he had prayed to
God for someone to help him settle into his parish in
the Litherland area of Liverpool. This was quite a testing
appointment for John after his time in Warrington, and
it was against this background that he had asked God
for help. He told us that as he uttered his prayer at the
hospital the night before Tim died, it became very clear
to him that Tim was to be his 'helper'. I remember very
well that this gave Wendy and me much comfort. It was
just one of many simple things that Father John said which
re-established my faith in God. I am not a Roman Catholic,
for I was christened into the Church of England. At no
point in my life had I been a regular church-goer, apart
from when I was a young boy in my pre-teens when it was
the norm to attend Sunday school and the evening service.
Father John was instrumental in re-awakening my need to
have a faith, which in truth I had never lost, but which had
been very deeply buried for a long number of years.

When all of our private moments were done, we went
our separate ways, the family agreeing that they would
return the next morning. John, my father-in-law, promised
to collect my father and bring him to the hospital.

Wendy and I called at Vicki's house, where her parents
Kim and Dave were looking after Dom and Abbi. We
told Kim and Dave that all hope was gone and that Tim
might not even survive the night. They were both deeply

upset on hearing this news and told us that they would do anything at all to help us. We thanked them and drove home, reflecting on how much kindness we were meeting from so many people.

The house felt so cold and uninviting when we entered that none of us removed our coats. I called Dominic and Abbi and asked them to sit down on the settee. I knelt in front of them to explain how that night was Tim's last night of life and that the following day the machine sustaining his breathing would be switched off and that he would then die. I told them that it was unthinkable for them to lose their brother and not to see him, touch him and bid him goodbye before he died. I talked to them very seriously and very fully because it was so important that they understood completely the magnitude of what Tim and our family were facing. I did not know what to expect from them both, but as it turned out I had nothing to fear; they reacted positively, saying that they did understand and that they wanted to be with their brother before he died. I was truly proud of them both and told them so. They had stood up to this awful period in their lives with great courage and a maturity beyond their years. I told them that had it been one of them in Tim's position, Tim would have wanted to be with them, and they agreed with me. We all cuddled and hugged one another and prayed briefly for Tim to survive yet another night against all the odds.

Thursday, March 25

As I had done on each of the previous mornings, I made an early-morning call to the hospital. The nurse on duty told me that Tim had spent a peaceful night and that there had been no change at all in his condition.

As the week had passed, we had been receiving increasingly large amounts of mail each day from all over Great
Britain, Ireland – north and south. We had also been sent
beautiful bouquets of flowers from well-wishers. Wendy
decided that we should take some of the flowers to the
hospital on this final morning.

As I drove into the same rear car park I had used all
that week, I noticed a TV film crew filming us getting
out of the car, unloading flowers from the car boot and
walking from the car to the entrance. Up until this time,
all filming had been indoors in the Press Room.

It was 8.30 a.m. when we entered the hospital, and
soon after we arrived Mr Miles came to see us. He
confirmed that nothing further could be done for Tim
and that we must now give serious thought to switching
off the ventilator which was breathing for Tim. I told him
we were awaiting the arrival of various members of the
family and that we wanted them all to have the chance to
say their final farewells to Tim. This he understood, but
he still pressed me for an idea of the rough time. I told
him that I couldn't be sure, as Phil was travelling from the
North-East, but I thought perhaps 9.30 to 10.00 o'clock. I
was rather irritated at the fact that pressure was being put
on us to switch off the machine at a time like this.

Once Mr Miles had left, Wendy and I took Dominic and
Abbi in to see Tim for the first time since the bombing.
We told them both to be brave and to remember that it
was their brother. They both looked worried and nervous
about what they would see when they entered the room.
Once inside, they were uneasy and unsure of what to do,
so I suggested that they each take hold of one of Tim's
hands, or at least his finger-ends, while I said a prayer
from us all to Tim. I have no recollection of the exact
words I spoke, but they came from the bottom of all our
hearts. My voice choked and faltered several times as the

tears filled my eyes. Wendy, Dominic and Abbi were all tearful as well, as we stood around our motionless son and brother so near now to death. What a bitter, bitter fate to befall so terrific a boy. How in God's name could this atrocity be allowed to take place in a so-called civilised and democratic society in 1993?

Every one of us was in total turmoil, and for Wendy and me to be asked to count down the last minutes of our child's life, feeling so utterly helpless because there was not a thing in the whole world we could do for him, created a feeling of utter impotence and powerlessness.

We asked both of our children to say their goodbyes to Tim. This they did, and as we took them out of the room I said to them that one day they would meet Tim again in a better place.

All our close family arrived: Carol and Terry and their daughters, Clare and Nicola, John and Betty, and my father were there too. Only Philip and Karen had not arrived by 9.30 a.m. By now, we were becoming a little concerned, because even though the drive from Hartlepool to Liverpool can take two and a half to three hours, we knew they were bound to have left early in the morning and we had expected them to have arrived by this time.

In the meantime, everyone spent time either individually or collectively with Tim in a succession of visits to his room.

One visitor I did not expect to come to the hospital that morning was my work colleague and friend David Hughes. I was told that David was in a separate room and would like to see me. When I entered the room I said, 'Hello, David, what are you doing here?' He replied that he had just had to come to express, on behalf of himself and his wife, Margaret, how very, very upset they both were about Tim. We shook hands warmly and then we embraced in the time-honoured way that men do, with our arms around one another's shoulders. Because of the circumstances, this was a spontaneous action and neither of us felt any embarrassment or awkwardness whatsoever.

Pulling away, I asked David if he would like to see Tim, whom he had met a couple of years previously when Wendy and I entertained Margaret and David to dinner at our home. I was not sure what answer he would give, but he said, 'Yes, I would like that, so long as you really don't mind.'

'Of course I don't mind. I wouldn't have mentioned it otherwise, now would I?' I said.

I took David into the room, where Wendy and he embraced closely, before David stood at the foot of Tim's bed looking at him very intently but without speaking. I could see that David was extremely moved by this experience and, knowing him as I do, I realised that he was imagining the horror of what we were going through. His relationship with his own son, Mark, was one that he and I had spoken of often, the way friends do. I knew how losing Mark would affect him and he was well aware of how my losing Tim was affecting me.

David emphasised that if there was anything he could do I just had to ask, and with that, and another handshake and embrace, he left the hospital. I know without ever having asked him since that the experience of seeing Tim so near to death is something he will never forget.

Mr Miles returned to check on whether we were ready to authorise the switching-off of the machine. Wendy and I told him that we were not, as we were still awaiting Phil and Karen's arrival. He chose this meeting to advise us that when the ventilator was switched off the reaction from Tim could and probably would be very alarming. He described how his body could go into spasm and jerk about, perhaps even moving so violently that a leap clear of the bed was possible.

Frankly, this description of how Tim might react so alarmed Wendy that she decided she could not remain in the room at the moment the machine was switched off. But I told Mr Miles that, even though Tim might touch the ceiling, I was staying with him . . . to the very end.

I understand why the medical profession need to adopt a blunt and methodical approach, but at this point Mr Miles's manner and attitude irritated me considerably. He showed no obvious compassion, and after all we had been through his brusqueness was hard to cope with. I dare say he thought he was being responsible in pointing out how Tim might react, but he described the possible scenario in such a graphic way that Wendy was terrified of staying in the room. She regrets and will always regret her decision, but in the circumstances I think she had no choice.

I had decided that I would ask the nursing staff to move all the tubes attached to Tim to the far side of the bed and then move him over from the centre of the bed to the far side. This would give me space to lie down on the near side of the bed next to Tim and to hold him closely, as I had so desperately wanted to do all that week.

I was greatly relieved when the nurses agreed to my request. They asked me to allow them five or ten minutes to rearrange everything in the room. I sought Wendy's assurance that she did not object to my request, and I asked whether she too wanted to be next to Tim. She assured me that she did not object to my doing this, but could not do so herself.

The slightly built Irish nurse, Margaret Colfer, told me I could go in. Tim was lying along the far side of the bed with the clear space I had requested. Margaret and Sue Comer showed no inclination to leave the room, so I politely but firmly told them that I wanted to be on my own with Tim. They understood and withdrew quietly. I removed my leather jacket and gently got on to the bed and lay down next to our son. For the first time since early Saturday morning I was able to make proper contact with him, and I put my left arm across his chest with the fingers of my left hand around the upper part of his right arm. I put my lips to his swollen cheek and kissed him many times. I then kissed him many more times on his lips. While I was so close to him, I bade Tim my lasting and loving farewells. As I did so, I sobbed openly, with every fibre of my body aching agonisingly for this son of ours to rest in peace free from pain for all eternity. I told him I did not know what I was going to do without him, that the gap he would leave in his family's life would be huge and yawning.

After perhaps five minutes, Nurse Colfer knocked gently on the door, opened it slightly and asked if they could come back into the room. I asked for a few moments more to recover my composure. Getting off the bed was agonising because I knew this was to be the last time I would hold my son properly, until the next life.

I returned to the waiting room where the family was assembled, but there was still no sign of Phil and Karen and it was now 10.30 a.m. We were all becoming worried. By 11.00 a.m. they had still not arrived and both Wendy and I felt that we could not delay the switching-off of the machine any longer.

I sat in a chair on the near side of the bed with just Nurse Colfer remaining in the room with me. This was after Mr Miles and another doctor had removed all the tubes and other pieces of equipment. I held Tim's left hand and touched his cheek with my other hand as his breathing reduced. I was astounded by how quickly the rhythmic rise and fall of his chest stopped. However, what astounded and shocked me most was just how quickly his facial skin colour changed from a healthy pink to blue. His lips became dark blue in what could have been no more than two to three minutes. Thankfully, there were no spasms whatsoever, and Tim died gently with great dignity with his dad holding him to the end.

There are no words I can find here to describe these last moments in our son's life. His life simply ebbed away, his chest became flat; in fact, it appeared sunken. He was gone.

After several minutes of just sitting and staring at our son's still body, I rose to my feet unsteadily and looked at Tim for a while longer, only this time from my standing position. He lay there motionless and at peace, but my emotions were anything but motionless and at peace. I tried very hard truly to comprehend that Tim was dead and that after just twelve years his life was over. Could this have been pre-ordained by some higher force? Was it always intended that Tim's allocation of life would be just twelve short years? How in God's name could a fine boy with no health problems, apart from all his self-inflicted injuries over the years, be gone from us so suddenly? How could life be so terribly cruel and unjust? What had Tim, or any of us, done to have this happen to us? In less than one week, our lives had been changed beyond recognition and for ever. We now must face a future as a family of four and not five. Dom and Abbi had been robbed of their brother and Wendy and I robbed of our family joker. Who knows, maybe the world was robbed of a future Seb Coe, Nick Faldo or Paul Gascoigne.

The following poem was sent to us by many hundreds of people; it is very moving and very loving:

GOD'S LOAN (Anon.)

'I'll lend you, for a little time, a child of mine,'
   He said,
'For you to love the while he lives and mourn for when
   he's dead.
It may be six or seven months, or twenty years,
   or three,
But will you, 'til I call him back, take care of him
   for me?
He'll bring his charms to gladden you and, should his
   stay be brief,
You'll have his lovely memories as solace for your grief.

'I cannot promise he will stay, since all from earth
   return,
But there are lessons taught down there I want my child
   to learn.
I've looked this wide world over in my search for
   teachers true,
And from the throngs that crowd life's lanes, I have
   selected you.
Now will you give him all your love, don't think the
   labour vain,
Nor hate me when I come to call to take him back again?'

I fancied that I heard you say, 'Dear Lord, Thy will
   be done,
For all the joy Thy child shall bring, the risk of grief
   we'll run.
We'll shelter him with tenderness, we'll love him while
   we may,
And for the happiness we've known, forever grateful stay.
But should the angels call for him much sooner than
   we've planned,
We'll brave the bitter grief that comes and try to
   understand.'

So many thoughts raced around my head as I backed away from Tim and towards the door. Just backing away from him felt like betrayal, as if leaving his defenceless body alone and unattended was a form of desertion.

I had noted that the exact time Tim had stopped breathing was 11.20 a.m. I quietly left the room with Nurse Colfer remaining. I then went to find Wendy to reassure her that Tim had gone very quietly. I had hoped that this would settle Wendy, but instead she was racked with guilt because, as she said, if Tim had left his body at the moment of his death, he would have seen that she was not in the room with him. The thought that the spirit or the soul does actually leave the body, as many who have had 'out of body' experiences have testified, upset Wendy terribly. She was very angry with herself for allowing Mr Miles to frighten her into staying out of the room.

I tried again to reassure her and told her that if Tim was aware of all that was happening at the time, then he would have known why she was not there and she must not feel guilty about it.

As Wendy began to calm down, Phil and Karen arrived, and we had the awful task of telling them that Tim's machine had been switched off just fifteen minutes earlier. We took them both through to see Tim, who by now was becoming cool to the touch and distinctly blue. Karen, who had always had a particularly close and loving relationship with each of our children, burst into tears and embraced her darling Tim, sobbing, 'Oh, Timmy, Timmy, Timmy, I love you so much.' Her grief was so overwhelming that I was in floods of tears myself, as were Wendy and Phil. Karen was completely beside herself with grief; there was no consoling her. It was particularly hard on her because this was the first time she had seen Tim since the bombing, and since she and Phil had looked after Tim during the

week following his appendix removal. It was obvious that
that week had really cemented what had always been a
loving and affectionate relationship, and to see Karen bent
over him, stroking his face and telling him how much she
loved him and would always love him, was very, very
moving indeed.

Gradually, everyone moved back to the waiting room,
where all thirteen of us tried to comfort one another at
this traumatic moment in all our lives.

Stephanie slipped in to tell Wendy and me that Inspector
Paul Matthews from the Cheshire Police was outside and
would like to talk to us. Neither of us could think what
a police inspector would want with us at such a time,
but we went out and introduced ourselves to him. He
explained that he had been asked to travel to Walton
from Warrington to do anything at all that we required,
whether helping control the media, or getting us to and fro
without disruption. Literally anything at all. We thanked
him and brought him into the room where all the family
was introduced to him. Paul was to be another of the small
band of marvellous people we came to know so well during
the course of our tragedy.

David Cain, the chief executive, took Wendy and me to
one side and asked whether we wished to speak to the press
as we had done previously. Wendy seemed unsure, but I
said, 'Yes, I'd like to, but only if Wendy is with me.' She
agreed for my sake, and we went down to the library.

I remember this particular press conference well because
the assembled media gathered in the room allowed me to
tell them, without any interruption, what we had just gone
through. I do not actually remember any questions being
put to me, though it is possible that some were. I took
my time and described how Tim's valiant fight for life had
been lost and how he slipped away quietly. I found myself
saying that this was most unlike him, and how it would

not have surprised me at all had he sat up right at the end and said 'Geronimo'. This ended up being very extensively quoted in all the following day's papers. Countless people have since told me, and this includes so-called 'hardened' journalists, that what I said at the conference moved them to tears. I must say that I find this very gratifying, because if describing the unjust and totally unexpected death of your son through terrorism is not a moving experience, then God help us all.

I think it must have been from that point on that the kernel of the idea of keeping Tim's face and name in the memory and consciousness of as many people as possible formed in my mind. Here was an appealing and, if I may say so, a handsome young man, whose life had been snuffed out in an instant. Was he to be just one more statistic in the long line of killings arising out of the Northern Ireland problem? Not if I had anything to do with it he wouldn't.

After perhaps fifteen or twenty minutes, we concluded the press conference, thanked everyone and set off towards the car park to return home. As we approached our car, we stopped to thank everyone at Walton who had been so wonderfully kind to us, and at that precise moment Stephanie burst into tears. She had been so solid all week, but now it was all over her guard came down and she cried her heart out. We both embraced her tightly and thanked her from the heart for her great support and friendship while carrying out the tough job she and all the nursing and medical staff had to perform.

A few minutes before we all left the hospital, David Cain, Paul Matthews and I discussed what would happen to Tim's body from here on. David told me that Tim would be transferred to the hospital mortuary and from there to the funeral director's early the next week, probably on Tuesday. Paul confirmed that he would make all the arrangements for the appointment of a funeral director and that we need not worry at all about such matters. Although thoughts of funeral arrangements had not occurred to me at all, it was comforting to know that we would be spared the additional distress of this on top of losing Tim.

Back at the house, everyone found a seat or just flopped down on the floor. I got the whisky and poured myself a generous measure, while everyone else apart from my dad opted for tea, coffee or a soft drink.

During the next couple of hours, several friends called at the house to express their sympathy, having heard of Tim's death on the radio and TV news bulletins.

Rather curiously, my mood at this time was one of complete calm. I felt at ease with everyone and everything. To this day, I do not know whether this unexpected feeling of being at ease came from within me or whether Tim's release from all his pain and suffering, perhaps even Tim himself, was controlling my emotions. From wherever this calmness came, with it came the absolute certainty that Tim had gone to Heaven.

That evening, we watched the major news programmes, all of which featured our son's death as the leading news item. At the point in the press conference when I had wept, I cried again. I realised then just how powerful a communication medium television is.

4

Friday, 26 March

This may sound trite, but one of the first thoughts to enter my head when I awoke that morning was that this was the first day of the rest of our lives without Tim. I had no idea how we would adjust to this new family reality, but I silently pledged to myself that our other children, Dominic and Abbi, would not have their lives ruined.

It was also the day when little Johnathan Ball was to be buried. Johnathan's father, Wilf Ball, had telephoned me on Tuesday to say how much he was praying for Tim's recovery and also to invite Wendy and me to Johnathan's funeral.

We had yet to meet Wilf, and we were rather surprised to have received an invitation when we knew it was to be a family occasion. We accepted the invitation but then on Wednesday, when we knew that Tim was not going to survive, I called Wilf back to explain that we would be unable to be with him and Marie, Johnathan's mother, after all. I was, however, able to extend our invitation to him to attend Tim's funeral, though at the time I issued the invitation I did not know when this would be.

When Dominic and Abbi had left for school, I drove to the local newsagent and bought several morning papers, as I had been doing throughout the week. A quick glance through them confirmed my growing impression that the press was treating my family's tragedy with considerable care and compassion, although we had been caused some

pain by one or two headlines. As time went on, and we
got to know several journalists quite well, they told us that
headline-writing was a separate function and not under
their control. They understood our concern and seemed,
generally, to share it.

Soon after I had finished flicking through the papers, we
received a telephone call from Barry Lickess, press officer
for the Cheshire Constabulary. Barry told us that Senator
Gordon Wilson was in Warrington to attend Johnathan's
funeral, and had expressed, 'through channels', a desire
to meet Wendy and me. We were happy to agree to this
visit, as Gordon Wilson was a man we admired greatly.

My mind went back to November 1987, to the Remembrance Day bombing of Enniskillen when eleven people
were killed, including Gordon's daughter Marie. I could
vividly recall being reduced to tears as I drove to work listening to Gordon's heartbreaking account of how Marie's
last words were 'Daddy, I love you very much.' At the
time, I could not comprehend how any man could show
such immense dignity in the face of such a terrible loss.
Perhaps the reader will understand how it made me feel
when people told me that my words to the media shortly
after Tim died had affected them as Gordon's words had
affected me some five and a half years earlier.

By mid-morning, the postlady had delivered the morning's many bundles of post to us. This was to be the pattern
for many more mornings to come, and in fact on two
successive mornings in the days following Tim's funeral
she simply handed me the sack, saying she would collect
it the next day. The other pattern that became established
on that day, and which continued for the next three weeks,
was the mid-morning arrival of Paul Matthews.

With his apparent fondness for my coffee and his
light-hearted banter, he became a very close friend not
only to Wendy and me but to our children and many

members of our family as well as the friends who called regularly.

Wendy and I had wanted to visit Bridge Street for some time to see the huge number of floral tributes which had been laid at the scene of the bombing, and when we told Paul that this was what we planned to do, he volunteered to take us in the police car. We accepted his offer because he could stop at the top of Bridge Street near the mobile police incident unit, which saved us the problem of parking some distance away and walking across town.

Wendy collected two flower arrangements, and we set off for the town centre. Upon our arrival, Paul stepped inside the incident unit to let his colleagues know that we were there, and then emerged with another officer who was introduced to us before the four of us began walking down Bridge Street towards the sea of flowers.

A large number of people were gathered around the area, either laying flowers of their own, or simply reading the messages on those already there. As Wendy and I approached with the two police officers, people moved aside to let us close to the area where Tim and Johnathan had been fatally injured. Naturally, we knew people were looking at us, and whenever I made eye contact with anyone, I smiled. The smile was generally returned, though not always, but I told myself that this was because the individuals concerned were simply unsure of how they should react.

Wendy and I laid our flowers and then stepped back and stood with our heads bowed for a minute in silent prayer for our son who had fallen at this place six days before. The moment was an emotional one, but as I said to Wendy afterwards, my wish was for everyone apart from the two of us to withdraw and leave us alone with our own thoughts and memories. We did not get the opportunity then and we never have since that day. However, one day we will

stand there alone and we will remember the events of that
awful Saturday in March.

Having turned to leave, we had gone barely five yards
when, from the crowd of onlookers, came a distinctly
Northern Ireland accent calling out our names and I
quickly became aware of a man in a black trenchcoat
approaching us. The speed with which he approached us
from the crowd combined with his accent caused alarm and
he was very quickly seized by two police constables. He was
taken to the mobile incident unit at the top of Bridge Street
where he was questioned. Paul led Wendy and me back to
the mobile and while he went inside to check on what was
happening we both acknowledged that the man's sudden
appearance from the crowd had startled us.

Paul asked us to step inside, and there the man apologised to us profusely for any concern he had caused. He
explained that he had come over to Warrington from
Ireland on behalf of the Peace 93 movement and that
he had travelled with all the flowers that the people of
Dublin had sent as a mark of respect for the victims of
the Warrington bombing. We sympathised with him about
the abrupt way he had been handled, but he was gracious
enough to understand why his actions, compounded by his
accent, had made us all so alarmed.

Quite soon after we returned home, Gordon Wilson
arrived. He was accompanied by a journalist, Tim Rayment
from the *Sunday Times*, and a photographer. I showed
them through to the conservatory and sat them down while
Wendy made them all a drink.

I had not realised how tall a man Gordon is – I would
say that he towered over me by a good six inches. He
told us how heartbroken he was by the deaths of Tim
and Johnathan and how much it had taken him back to
November 1987.

The conversation ebbed and flowed with ease, and I

found myself very aware of the power inside this man. He spoke with great conviction and compassion and, above all, with great emotion. He told us how, even after five and a half years, there was not a day went by when he did not remember his beloved Marie, and how he often still cried openly for his and his wife Joan's loss.

He also gave us some practical advice, telling us that Tim's death would place a great strain on our family relationships and that we should quickly come to realise that, just because we were married, we would not necessarily grieve in the same way or at the same time. He told us that resentment could quite easily occur at these times and that we must find ways of venting these feelings and differences, otherwise they could become destructive. Wendy and I listened intently to what Gordon had to say. It was patently obvious that he was speaking from experience and was giving us the benefit of that experience.

Gordon also told us of his plans to meet with members of the IRA in an attempt to persuade them to stop their campaign of violence. He said that he would go simply as Marie's dad, and not on behalf of any political party or organisation. He believed there was some chance of him making them see the futility of their actions. I recall Tim Rayment asking me whether I would be prepared to meet with members of the IRA as Gordon planned to do. I replied that I could not envisage such a situation and certainly not so soon after members of their organisation had murdered our son.

In all, Gordon and Tim Rayment stayed for perhaps an hour. We could all have easily talked for many more hours, but as Gordon explained, the main purpose of his trip was to attend Johnathan's funeral and he did not have much spare time. He then asked us when Tim's funeral was to take place. I told him that Thursday, 1 April was the most probable date, though it was still to be formally arranged. Gordon expressed his apologies for the fact that he would not be able to attend because of prior long-standing commitments.

As he left, we both shook hands warmly and said that we would meet again, as indeed we have on two further occasions.

Wendy and I were pleased to have had Gordon in our home. We knew that we had been in the company of a good man, and although I said to Wendy that if any individual could change the IRA it would be Gordon, I still had no confidence that he would succeed. Sadly, as it was to turn out, I was to be right in my pessimistic prediction.

Later that day, we were visited by two plain-clothes police officers who delivered to us papers headed 'Court of Her Majesty's Coroner'. We were required to acknowledge receipt of a statement called the 'Coroner's interim certificate of the fact of death'. This statement set out in very stark and simple terms the date and place of Tim's death, but it also stated that the 'precise medical cause of death has yet to be established'. The officers told us that this was normal procedure in the event of murder.

This was the very first time we had heard Tim's death referred to as murder, and use of the word left me feeling very cold. Both officers expressed their personal sympathies and then left. For several moments after they had gone, Wendy and I stared at the document that they had delivered, neither of us really knowing what to do with it. I decided that it had best not get mixed up with the enormous number of letters and cards which were strewn along the couch in the dining room, and so I placed it for safe keeping in the filing cabinet where I kept the kids' Day Books and all sorts of other household paperwork.

Over the course of the next five days we were very busy with all sorts of things, from the continuing media interest in our family to dealing with the Criminal Injuries Compensation Board. The bulk of our time, however, was taken up with funeral arrangements. Paul Matthews had arranged for a funeral director to come to see us at home, and of course we had the very distressing job of choosing a coffin and a headstone for Tim. Such tasks are upsetting enough when you are dealing with the death of a parent or grandparent, but when it is for your child, who only days before had been walking, talking and playing around the house where the funeral director was now sitting, your whole sense of what is real and what is unreal becomes blurred.

Brian Mulligan, the funeral director, was very quick to sense our mood and he skilfully guided us so that we did not have to spend any longer on these matters than was necessary.

The Reverend Gordon McKibben visited us several times to finalise funeral details, including the time, where family and close friends were to sit, which hymns we wanted, and who were to be the pallbearers.

Wendy and I agreed that Tim would be carried by Dominic, Phil, Terry and me, though on the day itself I was to rue not selecting two more to help us, for the coffin was extremely heavy and we had to walk a long way from the cemetery gates to the burial plot.

On one of Gordon's visits, I told him that I wanted to speak at Tim's funeral service and he agreed that this was a fine idea and was happy for me to speak in the middle of the service, between his opening address and the sermon to be delivered by the Bishop of Warrington, the Right Reverend Michael Henshall. The following day, however, Gordon visited us again and was a little embarrassed at having to tell me that I could not speak in the middle of the service as we had planned, but only at the beginning or the end. I chose to speak at the end because I preferred to conclude the service, as somehow it seemed more natural that way.

We also decided to have Michael Jackson's song 'Heal the World' played at the very end of the service as we were carrying Tim out of the church. This was a song that Tim had really loved to sing, and it meant a great deal to us to conclude the service with one of his favourites.

I have already described the fact that a feeling of great calm overcame me after Tim died, and this feeling stayed with me over the days following Thursday. I think it was due in part to the fact that I knew that Tim was at peace in a better place, and in part to the fact that I was still to have some time with him before his funeral. Indeed, what I am about to say next will, to some people, seem strange, but I actually found myself looking forward to having more time with Tim since the moment I had sat with him at the end of his life. I needed more time on my own to talk to him, to tell him how much I loved him, to hold his hand, and just to be with him. Wendy too was going to have her own time with Tim, though I had not asked her, nor she me, how these moments would be spent. We drove to the funeral director's where we had arranged that I would go in to see Tim first, so that Wendy would know what to expect. I entered the chapel of rest and closed the door behind me. Inside the room, there was just the coffin, Tim's body and me, and I walked slowly to the side of the coffin.

The sight that met my eyes hurt me even more than the first glimpse I'd had of Tim in the hospital on the Sunday after the bombing. Our son was totally unrecognisable, even from the boy I had left lying so still on the hospital bed the previous Thursday.

Describing how he looked and how he had changed is very painful, but the obvious difference I saw immediately was that his cheek had slumped so much that it distorted his face far more than when it had been swollen. His hair had been combed completely flat across his forehead from right to left, almost as if it had been stuck down with glue. His badly bruised left eye was still as deeply discoloured as before, but now in a grey, pallid face it made him look completely unreal. Above all else, however, real pain tore through me when I felt his hands. Because I had given it no thought beforehand, I was not expecting them to be so cold. It was an awful shock to touch them and to feel them so icy. As I held them, and then removed my own hands, I noticed how his skin's elasticity had disappeared.

The sights and sensations cut into me so deeply that my grief was abject and absolute. Then quite suddenly my mood changed to one of rage and anger, very like the feelings I had experienced the day before Tim died. I wept tears of sorrow and bitterness on seeing our beautiful son laid out before me like this. I muttered many things to him, but not the meaningful things I had planned to say. I simply could not come to terms with him being in a coffin, dead and cold. Where was the humour, the oh-so-near-the-knuckle cheekiness, the gorgeous heart-stopping smile that lifted his cheeks so high? Where had life's beauty gone?

I stepped out of the chapel of rest feeling I had been robbed not only of Tim's life but also of my final chance to say the private and loving things that I had so wanted to say to him. Wendy stood up as I closed the door behind me. She must have seen the look in my eyes because she asked me what the matter was. I told her that she should not go in to see Tim as it would upset her too much – it was better to remember him as he had been in life. I didn't say anything about how Tim looked and I never did until we began writing this book, when Wendy agreed that I'd judged it right.

I told Wendy that Tim was dressed in the Everton tracksuit and socks, and had the two Everton footballs, donated by the club, cradled in his arms. He was also

wearing the replica Neville Southall football shorts over
the tracksuit trousers. The shorts had been bought using
some of the £50 sent to us by a wonderful old lady of
ninety from North Wales. Marjorie Joy sent the money
before Tim died and told us 'to buy Tim something he
wants when he gets better'. After Tim died, we went
into Warrington and bought the shorts he had wanted
so much and which had cost him his life. We wrote to
Marjorie to thank her for her marvellous generosity, and
she wrote back to tell us how heartbroken she was at Tim's
death. Subsequently, we were to discover that Marjorie
has become almost blind and had moved into sheltered
accommodation, where she now has someone to read and
write for her. She is a wonderful, kind-hearted lady, whom
we will never forget.

My final act had been to remove from my little finger
the bloodstone ring that my father had bought me many
years earlier and which Tim had always wanted. I placed it
on his wedding-ring finger. I kissed the ring for a final time,
and then put the ring I was now wearing in its place to Tim's
lips. This ring was Tim's; he had bought it at Christmas with
some of the money he'd received in place of presents. I had
seen the ring in Tim's room on the evening of Saturday, 20
March, and I had placed in on the second finger of my right
hand that night. Apart from removing it once to place it
against Tim's lips, I have not removed it again and never
will until I die. Then I would want my son Dominic to wear
it until the time is right for him to pass it on to his son. As
you can tell, I have already planned for Tim's ring to pass
down through the future generations of males in the Parry
family.

During the afternoon Gordon McKibben called at the
house. He was accompanied by the Bishop of Warrington,
Michael Henshall. The Bishop told us of his feelings for
our family's loss, relating it to his relationship with his own

children, and how he would have felt had he lost one of them. Final details of the funeral service were arranged during this visit, and it was confirmed that I would give my address at the end of the service.

The next morning, we visited St Mary's parish church with Paul Matthews and Brian Mulligan, the funeral director. Details of seating arrangements were finalised and the sound system to convey the service to the many people expected to be outside was set up. Warrington Council were providing the sound system and Paul Matthews was to provide his personal Michael Jackson CD for the track Wendy and I had selected.

Brian Mulligan showed us where Tim's coffin would be placed inside the church and also instructed us how to raise and lower it from our shoulders. He suggested that it might prove to be a little heavy but I told him how light Tim was, and that I felt sure that the four of us would be fine.

In the afternoon, Wendy went into Warrington accompanied by Sandra Ambler, a close friend. She went to buy herself a new black jacket to wear at the funeral. While she was out, Father John Walsh called, and when I told him Wendy wasn't at home, he seemed a little ill at ease. This was hardly surprising considering that he had met me only once before, and that was at Warrington Hospital the night before Tim died. This was a perfectly understandable reaction, finding himself in the company of a person he barely knew at such a time. We settled down with our cups of coffee and John asked me the most helpful and natural question that he could possibly have asked. Very simply, he said, 'I never knew Tim, so will you please tell me about him.' Conservatively, I guess that I then spent two hours talking with John, and at no time did I detect his interest waning. The opportunity he presented me to talk about Tim was important, coming at that time, though I confess I did not realise just how important it was until later.

John proved himself to be not only a good listener but also a fine young man. He has an appealing blend of scholastic intelligence and everyday wit which makes him very engaging company. Subsequently, he has visited us several more times and has always been a welcome caller, though there is one small problem. If he calls after Wendy gets home from work, but before I arrive home, he tends to be given my evening meal! Most Roman Catholic priests, according to popular folklore at any rate, eat and drink you out of house and home, and John is no exception!

Wendy returned home just as John was about to leave, but he told us that he would be at Tim's funeral service the next day.

Not long after John had left, Tim's form tutor, Barbara Dutton, and Dom's form tutor, Kieran Burke, called at the house with several girls from the High School. The girls presented Wendy with flowers and one of them, Mel Vincent, handed me a huge Best Wishes card which had been signed with various messages by a great many children from the school.

Mel explained that she had bought the card when Tim was still fighting for his life and that she had not been sure whether or not to give it to us after Tim died. The advice from those she consulted was to give it to us, and we were pleased she did. Mel is another of that small band of very special people who have come to mean so much to me and my family for what they have done for us and for Tim's memory.

Until Mel told us I had not known that she and Tim had developed a fun relationship based on Tim's support for Everton and Mel's support for Manchester United. She told us that they ribbed one another continually, but that it had always been in good humour. Mel informed us that she and some of her friends had been talking to Tim only ten minutes before he was so badly injured. They had all been in a sports shop, where Tim had been trying on football shorts. The other kids had been taking the mickey out of Tim when he tried on quite a baggy pair. They had been amused by how thin Tim's legs had looked. In the same shop, someone had knocked over a display of footballs and she and Tim had helped to pick them all up. I could not help but muse on how it might have made all the difference had Tim not been so good-natured as to help pick up the balls that someone else had knocked over.

Mel has been very deeply affected by Tim's death and she has made visiting Tim's grave a regular event in her life. She takes flowers and always leaves cards with the message that she will never forget him. From time to time, she and her mother call to see us, and she always brings a card and flowers for Wendy. She deserves a very special mention because of her deep love for Tim. On one occasion, she brought her scrapbook of newspaper cuttings all about Tim, and told us how John Britton, the High School headmaster, had asked her to donate it to the school library. Politely, Mel had refused, but she did agree to photocopy it and to leave the copy there.

Here are two short poems written by Mel, the first of which is in her scrapbook:

IN MEMORY OF TIM

A funny, happy, handsome boy
So full of love and fun
You had so many friends
And I'm proud that I was one.
I dedicate this book to you
And so as time goes by
When people stop and look at it
They'll know the reason why.
You see, dear Tim, you really were

My very special friend,
I'll remember you forever
And hope my heart will mend.

Mel's second poem is entitled 'Memories':

As we walk along life's highway
Down the road called Memory Lane
We remember all the happy times
And wish them back again.
But life is not so simple
Oh how we wish it could be
For if it was, our darling son
You'd be walking here with me.
So we'll walk along without you
Our hearts so sad and sore
But the memories we have of you
Will stay for evermore.

Barbara Dutton handed Wendy and me Tim's first, and last, high-school report, and assured us that all the entries had been written before the day of the bombing. I have reproduced some of the entries below, preceded by a brief statement written by John Britton:

'We mourn the loss of this well-made young man. Let this report, written prior to his death, testify to his quality.'

ENGLISH

Tim shows great enthusiasm and excitement, especially in Drama. He completes his work on time but must check his spelling and punctuation . . .

MATHS

Tim is an able pupil, who usually works to the best of his ability. He can show a keen and lively interest but is too often ready to chat. Overall, Tim has made significant progress this year.

FRENCH

Tim shows keen interest, works hard and is always willing to participate in class activities. He can understand French very well and is able to use phrases with confidence . . . a very good start.

MUSIC

Tim is an able pupil who works soundly at all times. He shows considerable natural ability in practical activities, and responds exceptionally well to all aspects of listening skills. His creative work shows considerable originality, imagination and flair.

GEOGRAPHY

Tim has approached the work involved in this subject with enthusiasm. I am pleased with Tim's progress this year. Well done!

TECHNOLOGY

Tim has worked well on his graphic design project and has produced work of a good standard. Well done, Tim!

Finally, Tim's form tutor's summary:

> Tim is a lively, outgoing boy with a keen sense of
> humour. He is extremely popular within and beyond
> the tutor group and has established a wide circle of
> friendships in year seven and other years. Tim has
> shown real skill and ability in all sports activities and
> he is a valuable member of the school football team.
> Tim is usually most polite, courteous and helpful. His
> genuine enthusiasm and cheerful nature make him a
> real asset to the form.

> Signed: B Dutton

Wendy and I read through Tim's report with a great deal
of pride, especially at the kind and generous remarks from
Barbara Dutton, who clearly liked him. However, we both
became upset on reading of his general progress, as this
was another reminder of all Tim's potential gone to waste.
We noticed then that Barbara too was crying. It was very
evident that this had been a terrible blow to her, not just
because she was Tim's teacher but also because she had
considerable depths of compassion for our son.

Kieran Burke then handed a rather large package to
us. We opened it and to our great surprise and delight
discovered that it was a beautiful gilt-framed canvas
portrait photograph of Tim in his school uniform. This
was the picture that the press had somehow managed to
get hold of a day or two after the bombing. Ironically,
when Tim first brought this school picture home, Wendy
decided not to buy the prints because she did not like the
way he had combed his hair! Now, in our radically changed
circumstances, she loved the photograph as much as I did.
We decided to hang the portrait in our entrance hall so that
everyone would see it when they entered the house. It was

a moving moment indeed to hold the framed photograph and to stare into Tim's laughing eyes, which showed so clearly his love of life and the sense of fun he had always possessed.

Dominic and Abbi arrived home just before the party from school left the house, and Dom and Kieran Burke greeted one another with their usual mixture of smiles and grimaces – they enjoy what might best be described as an up and down relationship.

I remember particularly well how Dominic studied Tim's photograph. As Wendy wondered aloud how Tim would have looked as a man, his eyes filled with tears and he wept. Such displays of pain and sorrow in one's teenage children are all the more upsetting when one feels incapable of providing them with the comfort and reassurance they need. Dominic, I know, was feeling Tim's loss every bit as deeply as the rest of us, but being fourteen years old he sometimes found it hard to show his feelings.

Before going to bed, Wendy prepared the clothes that Dom, Abbi and she would wear to the funeral. She had telephoned her brother Phil and asked him to bring a dark suit for Dom to wear.

Before I retired for the night, I went into Tim's bedroom, as I had done many times over the days following the bombing. Closing the door quietly behind me so that I would not be heard by anyone else, I let my eyes survey my son's room. Nothing had been moved since the last night Tim had slept in his room, including the bedclothes and his pyjamas, which were folded and placed beneath the top cover.

There were many items on top of the bed which had been sent to us by sympathetic people from all over Britain and Ireland. There were crucifixes, Mass cards, rosary beads, scout badges, football club pennants, scarves and autographed footballs.

Turning back the top sheet of the bed and moving some of these items, I pressed my face into Tim's pillow and inhaled the smell of him deep into my nostrils. I picked up his pyjama-top and held that too. These were powerfully evocative sensations and stimuli, and soon I was shaking with emotion. My body shook as the tears fell from my eyes as heavy drops. I tried to bring Tim back to me through my senses, though the feeling of loss was enormously powerful as I lay alone with his pyjama-top clutched to my lips and nose.

I screamed silently at the butchery that had taken Tim from us. Again and again, I demanded to know from somebody, anybody, was there any justice in the world when a young boy of twelve could have his life snatched from him so brutally and unfairly?

I don't really know how long I spent consumed by agony and grief in Tim's silent room, but by the time I got to my feet the whole house was eerily silent.

Shortly afterwards, when Wendy and I lay in bed in the darkened room discussing the funeral, Wendy asked me whether I could smell anything, to which I replied, 'No, nothing, why?'

'Well, I can smell Tim,' she said. I asked her what she meant by this, and she explained that she could smell the bomb-blast odour that had been so pronounced on Tim's face.

We both reached the conclusion that Tim was in the room with us and had come to say goodbye. I know this must sound strange to some people, but Wendy sensed him so strongly that I too accepted his presence. I told him how much we loved him, and that we missed him very much. Believing he was with us in the room and speaking to him in this way made us both so calm and relaxed that we had the first peaceful and restful night's sleep since the bombing.

Thursday, 1 April

This was the day of Tim's funeral. Wendy and I awoke early and set about our preparations. We let Dom and Abbi stay in bed a little later than they normally would on a school day and called them down when breakfast was ready.

Wendy was busy making sure that the house was absolutely spotless and tidy. She hoovered and polished everywhere, and put everything away where it should be. I took care of the washing and drying of the breakfast dishes.

After putting the dishes away, I sat down again at the kitchen table, got out a small writing pad and pen, and began to sketch out in broad terms the things I wanted to say to the congregation in my address about Tim. Although I suffered one or two false starts, I was relieved that when I did get past the opening words, my thoughts on what to say came very clearly. Looking back to that morning, I guess that it took me fifteen to twenty minutes to feel that I had a clear idea of what I was going to say. I wanted to speak of Tim in life as well as of his death. I wanted to reach the hearts of as many people as I could with sentiments of love and longing to which they could relate. Above all, I wanted people to know that Tim was terribly and deeply missed.

Having decided what I was going to say, I folded the few sheets and went upstairs to place them safely in the breast pocket of my suit.

Meanwhile, a continual convoy of vans from local flower shops, as well as people on foot, arrived at the house to lay their flowers and wreaths on the driveway. This began as early as 7.00 a.m. and continued unabated until the driveway was a sea of colour. The combined perfume of the flowers was quite overpowering.

All our family gathered in the house, and in time-
honoured fashion everyone stayed in the kitchen making
endless cups of tea and coffee. Conversation was simple
and superficial.

Several times I went outside to read the messages on the
cards attached to the flowers and each time I stared at the
slate-grey sky, praying for it not to rain. I think we were
all dreading the prospect of it being wet as well as cold at
the cemetery.

Paul Matthews arrived and told us that a courtesy note
had been put through everyone's door in the street, asking
our neighbours to park their vehicles on their driveways to
allow ease of access for the funeral cars. He told us that
parking restrictions were being applied along the route that
Tim's cortège would take. It was obvious from what Paul
told us that Warrington Council and the Cheshire police
had planned every detail meticulously.

At 10.00 a.m., the funeral cars slowly reversed to the
bottom of the cul-de-sac where our house is situated. Brian
Mulligan, in charge of the cortège, walked down the drive
and shook all our hands. He explained that he would walk
in front of the hearse at the head of the cortège to the top
of the road. As he was talking, the hearse containing Tim's
coffin came into view. As soon as Wendy saw the hearse,
she ran back into the house, followed by her mother and
her sister Carol. Each of them was in tears and it was
several minutes before they regained their composure.

Back inside the house, our little niece Penny, who was
only four years old, asked Wendy what was in the coffin.
Unbeknown to me, Penny's mother Karen had mentioned
earlier that she might ask this question , and so Wendy was
able to tell Penny that the coffin contained Tim's toys which
were going to Heaven so that Tim would have his things to
play with. It's interesting to reflect on the questions that
young children ask at such times. Another close friend,

Kim, has a four-year-old daughter, Sam, and a few days earlier Sam had been upset on seeing her mum crying over Tim. Sam approached Kim and asked her whether Jesus would let her have Tim for a while. Puzzled at this unexpected question, Kim asked Sam why she had asked this, to which Sam replied, 'So I can make Abbi smile again.' We were all very touched by this lovely thought from such an innocent child, but Sam had always thought a great deal of Abbi, and she had obviously seen her great sadness since Tim's tragedy.

It was time for us all to take our places in the cortège of cars for the journey to the parish church of St Mary's. The cars followed the funeral director along the road from the house. He led the cortège at a very slow walking pace, and at the top of the road he got into the leading hearse which was carrying Tim's coffin.

The cars made their way towards Great Sankey High School and the cortège stopped outside the school gates to allow Wendy, Dominic and me to get out. Wendy was presented with a bouquet of flowers by a girl and boy representing the school. She kissed them both and I shook their hands as the whole school looked on. The school roll at Great Sankey is approximately 1300, and it looked to me as if every single one of them was assembled along the length of the school's front. I could see so many sad faces, and many of the girls crying freely with their handkerchiefs held to their mouths.

Originally, John Britton had suggested that Tim's class and a few other children should stand outside to represent the rest of the school. But he changed his plans and decided to assemble the whole school, knowing that no one would be able to concentrate on their work that day.

Several minutes later we pulled up outside St Mary's, followed by the many cars of friends and guests. As we stepped from the cars, the funeral director and his staff very quickly set about the job of easing Tim's coffin out of the car. Two of them supported the corners of the coffin while Terry and I took the weight, and Phil and Dominic then took the back of the coffin.

I was aware of there being hundreds of people lining Liverpool Road, where the church is situated. Just before we started into the church, I looked up and saw TV cameras high up on a gantry. Some days earlier Paul Matthews had told us that the BBC wished to film Tim's funeral, and that Sky news wanted to show the whole service live. It was some time later that we discovered that Terry's sister Jill, who lived in Sydney Australia, had seen news coverage of the bombing on Australian TV. She was outraged to hear of the events in Warrington, but she had a terrible shock when she saw her brother Terry carrying the coffin outside St. Mary's. It was only then that she knew the tragic events she'd heard about just a few days earlier, actually involved members of her own family.

As we walked along the path towards the church, I was pleased to see Tim's football team, Penketh United under-12s, on one side of the path with their team coach, Derek Finnigan, and Tim's Sea Scout troop on the other side with their leader, Ted Houghton. A day or so earlier I had called on Derek and Ted and asked them whether they would form a guard of honour along both sides of the path into the church, and both had readily agreed.

I knew Derek Finnigan quite well from going to watch Tim play for Penketh over the past three seasons, during which time Tim had become extremely fond of him. It was a standing joke that with regular monotony, every Sunday morning at nine o'clock, Tim would phone Derek to confirm match details for later that day. Many times, Derek told me that when the phone rang on a Sunday morning he immediately knew it would be Tim Parry. Quite why Tim could never remember the match details is not clear, unless his short-term memory was as bad as his dad's.

When Wendy and I called at Derek's house to talk to him about the guard of honour, Derek became very emotional. It was obvious that he had been equally fond of Tim. He had tears in his eyes for most of the time we were with him, and as was always the case when anyone else got upset, I did too. Here we were, two members of the supposedly 'stronger' sex, both in tears while our wives remained composed throughout.

We carried Tim's coffin to the front of the church and set it down on two wooden stands, then we took our places to await the start of the service, which began with the opening hymn 'The Lord Is My Shepherd'. Gordon McKibben began his opening address and with an immediate sense of foreboding I, along with everyone else, could hear that his voice was breaking up. He had obviously been nervous and tense for some days, and I felt sure that his voice was going to fail him. However, he carried on valiantly, and to my great relief the strength and composure in his voice began to return.

The local Catholic church was represented by Monsignor John Butchard of St Joseph's, who also addressed the congregation. Then we sang 'Make Me a Channel of Your Peace', which was Wendy's special choice.

Michael Henshall, the Bishop of Warrington, gave his main address, focusing his message on the utter waste of a young life by evil, cowardly men. He talked of Warrington being a watershed in the violence arising out of the troubles in Northern Ireland. I drew some comfort from the Bishop's outspoken and direct condemnation of the act of violence which had taken Tim from us. However, for much of the time he spoke, I stared at the portrait photograph of Tim which had been mounted on a tripod alongside his coffin, and tried to absorb the terrible reality that our son, whose smiling face looked back at me, was lying cold and still inside the coffin immediately next to his happy portrait, and that unbelievably this was his funeral.

My resolve to remain composed during the service almost deserted me when the Bishop finished his address and we all sang 'Abide with Me'. I have always found this to be a moving hymn, especially as I associate it with major sporting occasions such as the FA Cup Final. To listen to it being sung at my own son's funeral was far too much to bear, and I found it extremely difficult to keep my emotions in check.

Towards the end of the hymn I summoned every ounce of willpower I had to get myself under tight control again, as the time was approaching for me to stand before the congregation. The printed service sheet, 'In Memoriam – Timothy Andrew Parry, 1980–1993', announced my address as follows, and I cannot improve on it: 'Mr Colin Parry will speak in celebration of Tim's life.'

The words that I spoke were taken down verbatim by a number of national newspapers and reproduced the next morning, and so I am able to set them out in full.

I am here this morning immensely proud to speak as Tim's father, and I speak on my behalf and on behalf of my family. I have no political or religious message to give to you at all. It seems to me that I am not qualified to do that.

Before this tragedy, our immediate family probably amounted to no more than fifteen people. Following this tragedy, it seems to me that we now have an immediate family that runs into thousands, hundreds of thousands, millions probably. The kindness and the thoughts and the good wishes we have received from total strangers throughout England,

Wales, Scotland and, in particular, Ireland, have given us immense help in coping with the loss of Tim. So I think this morning I am qualified, uniquely well qualified, to speak on behalf of my family and my enlarged family, all those thousands of people, because they have said so many things to us that were absolutely spot-on.

They have said Tim hasn't died in vain. They have said good must come of this, and they have said that Tim will never be forgotten, and that's most certainly true. My most sincere hope now is that those hopes and wishes I have just expressed on behalf of everyone come true.

If my son becomes a symbol for peace and gives everyone a new sense of hope after so much tragedy, then that will be Tim's unique achievement.

Tim has touched so many hearts this past week and a half. I think that although he was extraordinary to us, in the lives of everybody else he was an ordinary boy, from an ordinary family, in an ordinary town, on a very ordinary Saturday when, along with Johnathan Ball, he suffered an extraordinary and terrible fate.

Tim clung on desperately for five more days and although in the end it was a fight he lost, he gave us a great deal of hope in that time, and he gave us more time with him. It may seem strange to say that you want time with your son when he has been desperately injured and is only breathing with the aid of a machine, but frankly, it's still your son.

The hardest part is never seeing him again. Our immediate family spent as much time as we could with him and, in particular, on the day Tim died, we had probably two to three hours with him. We kept telling ourselves that he knew we were there. I don't know whether he did or not, but as I said throughout this past week and a half, he was nothing if not a character. We kept waiting for him to wave a hand or do one or two other unmentionable things he used to do. He didn't do any of those, unfortunately; instead he slipped away with great dignity.

So many people have said Wendy and I and the family have been dignified and we are very grateful to have such an accolade given to us, but I think in truth the dignity that we have has been given to us by Tim.

Tim's fight for life and his tragic death have catapulted the family from almost total anonymity to constant attention. You may have noticed we chose to accept the media's right to bring Tim into everybody's lives. Partly, this was to save them coming to us, but mainly it helped us, and me in particular, to talk about Tim, and now it has become my obsession, to deal with what happened.

So many ordinary mums and dads wanted to be with us at this time and I think that, in a way, talking about Tim and making him real to so many people has probably helped them too, because everybody saw the pain we've felt.

I hope that everybody who has helped in some way personally, by card, letter or phone, will forgive me if I don't thank them all one by one. They know who they are, they have given us amazing support and we will never forget them.

I would just like to spend a few brief moments, if I may, talking about Tim when he was alive. I am biased, but I think Tim had grown into a fine-looking lad and, having been blessed with the good fortune of having a captivating smile, and knowing it, there were many times, with his flashing teeth and his twinkling eyes, when he managed to escape imminent parental correction. Like his older brother Dominic, he would periodically challenge our decisions and question our sanity. But for all that, like every parent in this situation, I would take him back tomorrow.

His death has torn an awfully big hole in our lives and the full effect won't be felt probably for some time to come. The immediate things, we are already struggling with . . . we stare into his room, we look into his eyes in that wonderful photograph. His eyes are still, they don't blink, they don't change, they don't move. We no longer hear his voice. His schoolbooks are closed, his football boots hang limp and his Sea Scout's hat hangs down.

We've experienced a terrible, deep, longing ache and emptiness since this tragedy, and I think we have yet to discover ways of dealing with this loss apart from talking about it, as we're doing now. We do ask our friends to make allowances for us in the future, because it will be more than likely that our one topic of conversation for quite some time will be Tim.

There is a terrible risk people will grow tired. I also suspect there is a risk that people's great support may be diminished by the amount of time and photographic material we have given to the press, and again we have done that, as the Bishop mentioned earlier, to keep Tim in the public eye. I think one of the many verses we were sent has meant a great deal to me and it's apparently a very brief Hebrew proverb which states: 'Say not in grief that he is no more but in thankfulness that he was.'

Tim had twelve all too short years, but they were superb, and for that, Tim, we thank you. It has not escaped my attention that Tim is being buried on All Fools' Day, either. Again, I think that's probably the last little twist from this character that we brought

into this world. So, goodnight, Tim, and sleep well.
We are with you for always.

I returned to my seat and sat down feeling a little unsteady.
I did not know whether my words had reached my friends
and family in the way I had intended. I wanted all those
who knew Tim, as well as the many more who had never
known him, to feel his presence and his personality. I
wanted them to feel him inside their hearts and minds.
I suppose what I am really saying is that I wanted
everyone to open their hearts and grieve freely, without
embarrassment or any of that British reserve which so
inhibits us from public displays of emotion.

Many times since Tim's death I have been on a kind
of emotional slow burn, by which I mean that while
my emotions are generally under control they are at the
same time simmering and directing me towards achieving
a specific goal. I have rarely been hostile or angry, even
though I am more than capable of such feelings, but I
have been aware that to influence people and events
requires strength, conviction and single-mindedness of
purpose rather than ranting or raving.

From the moment of giving my funeral address, I was
aware that I had a unique opportunity to keep my son's
name and memory alive for many, many people. Needless
to say, I did not consider my purpose to be either selfish
or egotistical, but simply a fierce desire not to have Tim's
death count for nothing. I wanted our son to be a symbol
for peace, and so I said it out loud and I meant it –
passionately.

I hoped that I could find the right blend of passion and
reason, strength and sense, understanding and urgency to
make a serious contribution, through our son, to finding
peace in Northern Ireland.

Of course, unravelling all of one's emotions to make

sense, even to yourself, is never straightforward, but from the time of Tim's funeral address, I think that clear objectives began to emerge.

The service ended with us carrying Tim's coffin out of the church to the music of Michael Jackson's 'Heal the World'. It was such an appropriate song, delivered with real feeling by the singer, and it simply felt right.

As I was about to get back into the funeral car, I saw Wilf Ball, and I shook his hand warmly. Although we had gone through so much together, this was the first time we had met. He looked beaten and bowed, but as time was to show, he bounced back like a man half his age.

The funeral cortège made its way from St Mary's to Fox Covert Cemetery in the Stockton Heath area of Warrington. This is a five-mile journey, and the whole route was lined with the people of Warrington, who turned out in their thousands to show their respect, love and sympathy for our family, and in doing so intensified the feeling growing inside me that we were actually involved in an event not unlike a state funeral.

At this point, I would like to use the recorded memories of Maureen Keaveney, a friend from my university undergraduate days. Maureen wrote these words for our mutual friend Peter Saxton, who was unable to attend the funeral because he was in Vancouver on business.

Sometimes a place becomes a collective single entity; at least, that's how it seemed that day.

As we drove into Warrington, the first sign of what was to come was the number of flags, on garages, office buildings, etc., all flying at half-mast. We stopped near the church of St Mary at about 9.30 a.m. A group of people had already gathered there, and were waiting quietly in the bitter cold, many of them with young children. An enormous bank of

pressmen had assembled to one side of the church,
and police were at work cordoning off sections of the
roads to allow the funeral procession free passage.

We drove on for about half a mile, and parked at
the place suggested by Colin, so that we could join
the cortège as it passed on its way to the church.
As we waited, small groups of people began to
gather along the roadside. Many were elderly, but
there were also young mothers with pushchairs, and
people of every age group. One very elderly man
with a walking stick took about ten minutes to walk
slowly and with difficulty to the street corner, where
he then stood silently waiting. At last, at about 10.50
a.m., the procession came into sight, moving like a
long, slow black train, with one police motorcyclist
at its head. It was impossible not to tremble as the
cortège slowly drew level, the first car entirely filled
with blue and white floral tributes, many of them
football-shaped, followed by the hearse, also a mass
of flowers, with the coffin topped by Tim's white Sea
Scout cap.

After Colin and his family had passed, we joined
the procession along the wide straight road leading
to the church. More and more people lined the
roadside, standing silently, many of them weeping.
Hundreds of people now stood in the area outside the
church, standing motionless and in complete silence.
As we left the car and passed between them, the
silence was powerful and overwhelming. Even the
cameras of the press seemed to have been muffled;
there was not a single flashbulb. Colin and his son
Dominic were two of the pallbearers, and we passed
behind them through a guard of honour made up
of Sea Scouts and members of Tim's football team,
all about his age and exercising rigid self-control,

with difficulty. One little lad had been crying, and stood with his fists clenched, in a small but supreme exercise of will. The utter silence and stillness was more tangible than any louder tribute could have been; Warrington's dignity was a powerful force, which transcended anger. That collective act of silent respect was its own recognition of the qualities of ordinary people.

During the service, the Bishop of Warrington spoke powerfully of his own anger, and of the need for peace, and at the very end Colin again showed his strength and dignity as he spoke of Tim's life and his wish that good would come from his tragic and untimely death.

Afterwards, we left the church where the silent crowd still stood vigil and then the funeral procession passed slowly through the streets of Warrington. This was the part that I found profoundly moving; thousands of people standing along the route to the cemetery, none of them just coming to stare, but standing, like the people at the church, in silent respect. All along the route, at every intersection, were police standing and saluting the procession. At the police station itself, about thirty or forty officers stood in line, one young policewoman standing, with her colleagues, to attention, with tears running down her face. At the fire station, the engines had been brought out, with the entire brigade in line, each man with one hand across his breast. Almost unbearable, an entire school of infant children, all in line and standing completely still and silent with their teachers. There were elderly men standing rigidly to attention, many of them saluting, whole factory workforces lined in rows, building sites where the entire workforce stood still, helmets off and heads

bowed. And everywhere, no one spoke or seemed
to move; it was as if the whole town stood frozen in
homage to Tim. I have never experienced anything
like the feeling of awe and grief seeing the people of
Warrington proving their courage and dignity as one
collective identity.

At last, to the cemetery, high on a windy hillside
overlooking the town. And down the slope, just a
few yards from the place reserved for Tim, a field of
flowers marking Johnathan Ball's tiny grave. A brief
but moving ceremony, with small gestures frozen like
snapshots; Abbi throwing into the open grave the
small toy she had hugged to herself all that long
morning; Colin and Wendy, with incredible calm and
dignity, reaching to throw small clods of earth into
that dark gash in the earth; the mourners, huddling
together against the biting wind.

And then it was over, the drive back, precision-
planned, with police motorcycles speeding alongside
or swooping ahead, clearing intersections, facilitating
the passage of the long cavalcade of cars. As young
Tim begins his long sleep, we begin the ritual of food,
drink, even laughter. We speak of him and drink
a toast, and go off at last through the still-sombre
town, as life begins to resume, though never ever
the same.

The brief graveside service ended with Gordon's words
being swept away by the wind. I heard little of what he
said, as family and friends huddled closely together to
shield themselves from the biting wind. Abbi bade her
last farewell to her brother as she stepped forward to let
a little teddy bear, dressed in Everton blue, fall into the
grave. She clung tightly to me as she straddled the soil
banked around the open grave.

Abbi and Dominic had conducted themselves perfectly throughout, and Wendy and I were immensely proud of them. I was particularly impressed with Dominic, who had become a fine young man on this day, burying his brother. He had not let anyone down, least of all himself, as he carried his brother with strength and dignity, keeping his head held high the whole time. He had matured five years in just five short hours, and I loved him so much.

Wendy had shielded and protected Abbi throughout the day, and she held her close as she reached forward to drop a single red rose on to the coffin of the beautiful son she had borne and lost. After saying our final farewell prayers to Tim, we turned and slowly made our way back up the hill to the cars. The police escort that had led us all the way across Warrington at 5 mph now led us back again, but this time we travelled at the normal speed of 30 mph. By this time the crowds, which had stood three or four deep in places a little earlier, had all dispersed.

We all returned to the Butcher's Arms, our local pub. Phil, the landlord, had agreed to close it to the public at 1.30 p.m. so that we and our family, friends and guests could have the place to ourselves. I circulated among the many people who had been through this incredibly difficult day with us: my lifelong friend Roger Kerrison and his friend Kath were there – Roger had been my best man and I had been his at our respective weddings all those years ago; several of my dearest and closest friends from my Swansea University days had travelled from the London area to be with us; Maureen Keaveney, who wrote the words above; Martin Cannon and Malcolm McLeod, my two flatmates from 1966, and Diana McLeod, Malcolm's delightful wife, also a friend from my university days. Malcolm had been on the telephone to me almost every evening from the Sunday after the bombing up to Tim's funeral. His concern was tangible, and it meant so much to me that this close

friend from all those years ago should check that I was all
right with such regularity. How ironic it was that just two
months earlier I had taken Wendy and the children for a
weekend break to Banbury in Oxfordshire to meet these
long-standing friends, along with Peter Saxton. They had
met Tim only once in mid-January and now, on 1 April,
they were at his funeral.

My secretary, Norma Warham, was there together with
my colleague David Hughes with his wife Margaret, and
Philip Croft, my boss. Their presence at my son's funeral
meant a lot to me. Norma, with whom I've enjoyed a
tempestuous relationship over the years, had shown herself
to be very protective and very supportive over these awful
two weeks. She had not flinched once from carrying out her
role with great authority but also with great compassion.
My other staff had not been able to attend the funeral,
but I knew that they too had been deeply affected by all
that had happened.

The time we spent in the Butcher's Arms was very
comforting to us all, as it allowed the considerable emotion
which had built up over the day to diminish gradually.
Everyone seemed at ease with each other, and I found the
atmosphere relaxing. I mentioned to many of the people
there that it was precisely the kind of gathering that Tim
would have thoroughly enjoyed.

It seems to me to be rather ironic that the gathering of
family and friends after a funeral can be a pleasant time,
though generally such thoughts are kept to oneself for fear
that they may be misconstrued. Collectively, it's as if an
audible sigh is emitted and the tension lifts sufficiently to
allow smiles and humour to reappear. So it was in the
Butcher's Arms, and perhaps it was exemplified best by
Father John Walsh, who sat at a table with Dominic, his
friend Ian Donnelly, and Rob Ellis, a friend Dom and Tim
had made on our French holiday in 1991. Dom told me later

that he and his friends had enjoyed the jokey relationship they had shared with John. It seems that they pressed him very hard on the question of celibacy, asking him how he coped with any needs that might arise. John told me later that he dealt with this very easily indeed, by telling the boys that he would take a cold shower whenever that problem confronted him.

Paul Matthews had by now become a firm favourite with everyone he met and had proved himself to be a considerable ambassador for the police service. Indeed, to his eternal embarrassment, a few days later I wrote a personal letter of thanks to his Chief Constable, thanking the force in general and Paul in particular. I know that he had been allocated the difficult and unenviable task of minding the Parry family, but he gave much more of himself than his official role called for. His help will never be forgotten.

I will return now to the words written by Tina Smith relating to how she heard of the Warrington bombing.

It is 20 March 1993. I saw a news bulletin which was mainly about the bombing in Warrington. My first thoughts were of Colin and his family, hoping and praying they were not hurt. I didn't see any television then until late Sunday night.

I was sitting at the table doing some course work I had to finish off. As I glanced at the television, I saw Colin and Wendy on the screen. It didn't click at first as I didn't realise they were talking about the bombing. I told my mum that I recognised their faces but she just stared back at me. I knew something was wrong. I looked back at the television. I could see that both Colin and Wendy were crying. Then it hit me. I knew that one young boy had died and another older boy was seriously injured. I asked my mum if

it was Tim or Dom. She didn't know the boy's name
but had seen a photograph. I ran upstairs to get my
holiday photos, but she still wasn't sure. My mum
suggested that I try Teletext. The numbers seemed
to take for ever to come around. When it did come
up, I couldn't believe what I was reading. I sat there
staring at Tim's name on the TV, tears streaming
down my face.

After watching more of the news, I decided to write
a letter to Colin and Wendy just to let them know
I hadn't forgotten Tim and I was praying for his
recovery. I stayed on the settee all Sunday night with
the television on, waiting to hear of any improvement
in Tim's condition. At work, I was a total wreck. I
couldn't concentrate properly and found it hard to
stop myself from crying.

I decided to buy Tim a teddy so it would be there
for him when he woke up. My mum chose a monkey
holding a football and wearing the Everton colours.

I didn't go into work on the Thursday as I wanted
to stay home and see as many news programmes as
I could. Each time the news was the same.

At about 12.30 p.m., my grandma let herself into
our house using the spare key. I was sitting, as usual,
in front of the television. As I looked at her and
smiled, she just said that she was so sorry and then
threw her arms around me. I had missed it on the
news. Tim's machine was switched off at 11.20 a.m. I
can remember shouting 'No, no' over and over again
and crying inconsolably. My grandma stayed with me
for a while until I calmed down a little. I stayed in my
bedroom then for the rest of the day.

At about 5.30 p.m. the telephone rang. My sister
answered it. She told my mum that it was someone
wanting to speak to me so she took the phone. Then

she shouted for me. I was annoyed because I had told her I didn't want to speak to anyone. She just said to me, 'It's Colin.' My stomach turned. He wanted to thank me for the letter and was making sure I had heard the news. I couldn't believe Colin had phoned me on the day his son had died. I felt as though I was the one who had lost a son because he was so supportive and was making sure that I was all right. After I put the receiver down, I looked at my mum and we both had tears welling up in our eyes.

I was off work again the next day. I had a visit from a sister from our church. She said that she would pray for both Tim and myself and have a special mass at the convent. She still asks my mum now how I am getting on.

I got in touch with Colin on the Sunday to ask about the funeral, which was the following Thursday, 1 April. I booked the day off work to go. The church was packed. The service ended with 'Heal the World', a record you can still hear coming from my bedroom most evenings.

As the coffin was being carried out of the church, I saw Abbi clutching the monkey I had sent for Tim. This brought a little smile to my face beneath my tears. It was later placed in Tim's grave.

I got to talk to Colin and Wendy at the cemetery, and after Tim's burial I gave Colin a big hug. I promised myself that I would not cry in front of them as I was their support. Wendy asked me if I minded Abbi putting the monkey in with Tim, but I was glad that she did, because after all it was for him.

We were invited back with the rest of the family to the Butcher's Arms for the buffet there. I was introduced as Tim's 'mature' girlfriend!

Even though I had only known Tim for two weeks,

he made such a big impact on me. The hardest part is knowing that I'll never see him again. I used to call him 'My little love' because that was what he was.

I've been to visit Colin and his family several times since the funeral and I visit his grave every four or five weeks. I made a special trip on what would have been Tim's thirteenth birthday – 1 September – except this time there were no red trainers to give him, just a single red rose.

And so this most traumatic of days drew to a close; our friends said their goodbyes while our family returned to the house where we watched much of the day's activities on the major TV channels.

I thought long and hard about our future, but the only thought that I could sustain for more than a brief moment was the heartache for our lost child, Tim. As I studied the faces of everyone around me that day, they all seemed, superficially at least, much as they had been two weeks earlier, but behind the bland masks and the day-to-day expressions there was no disguising the impact that Tim's sudden death had had upon us all.

5

The days that followed Tim's funeral seemed aimless and without shape or structure. There were things to be done but nothing had quite the same emotional weight as the preparations for the funeral, and so our moods tended to reflect this feeling of emptiness and lack of direction. This disorientation was compounded by various events, often when we least expected them. One example was on the Saturday after Tim's funeral when Wendy and I went into the Butcher's Arms at lunchtime to settle the food bill with Phil, the landlord; the atmosphere changed the moment we entered.

The pub was by no means full. As we walked through the inner double doors, we could hear the usual chatter of voices rising above the jukebox and the fruit machine. But then a bushfire seemed to take place; the first people to recognise our faces must have stared a little too long so that the people at the next table stopped their conversation too, and in just a few seconds a hush fell over the pub so all that could be heard was the sound of the machinery.

Never before have I felt so uncomfortable. I felt like a leper might have done. Obviously, we both knew that it was not hostility we were encountering, just outright shock and surprise that we should be there, I suppose, at such an incongruous time.

We walked the few feet to the bar, but with all eyes on us it felt like a few miles. Thankfully, the bar staff were their normal, friendly, smiling selves. One of them went to fetch Phil and as we sorted out the bill he suggested we should have a drink. I think it was Wendy who suggested we should have a pub lunch. We sat at a table in the middle of the lounge and waited to be served. Neither of us could maintain a normal conversation because we felt that all eyes were upon us, it certainly seemed so.

Losing Tim in such a public way had plunged us into the public eye without us having any idea of what it would mean in day-to-day terms. The impact we had on the clientèle of the Butcher's Arms that Saturday was to be repeated many times during the coming days, weeks and months. At first, we were unable to meet people's eyes, but then Wendy and I agreed that it was better for us to hold the other person's gaze, and to smile at them in order to break the awkwardness of the moment. Naturally, there were times when this approach was not reciprocated, but most of the time it produced the desired result of having the smile returned. I must say that the most pleasing public reaction was when complete strangers shook our hand, embraced and even kissed us. Many went further, graciously praising us for the way we had handled our grief.

This is what happened at the Butcher's Arms when, shortly after we sat down at our table, the man on the next table stood up as if to go to the bar but instead walked over to us. Very politely, he asked whether he could sit with us for a moment or two. We said, 'By all means,' and then he proceeded to tell us of his admiration for our fortitude and his great sadness for Tim. He only stayed for a few minutes, but those few minutes meant so much to us. They made us feel normal again. Meanwhile, his wife and two young daughters, who remained at their table, smiled at us each time we looked across to them.

This man's gesture was not unlike a referee's whistle following a minute's respectful silence at a football game, for at the precise moment he sat down with us the conversation in the pub resumed its normal level.

Wendy and I came to realise how ill at ease and awkward many people felt when they suddenly came face to face with us, and we consciously tried to be the ones to break the ice with a smile or a gesture. Actually, we knew only too well how we would feel meeting someone else who had suffered our fate. Only fifteen months earlier, a squash-playing friend of mine, Roy Greene, had lost his seventeen-year-old son, Philip. He was murdered in a knife attack in Liverpool and I vividly recall how nervous I was at the prospect of seeing Roy. When we met a few weeks after Philip's death, I asked Roy the very same questions I was to be asked, and I still am asked, over and over again: 'How are you?' and 'How are you coping?' They are simple questions and well intentioned, of course, but they are not, as I now know, simply answered. Most times, rather than give the truthful answer, which would take several minutes and would cause the questioner some embarrassment, I simply say, 'Oh, I'm fine', when I'm often anything but fine!

On the Sunday following Tim's death and again the following Sunday, Roy called at the house to comfort us. Having lost one of his own sons, he was able to speak to us from a position of real knowledge and genuine pain. His words were simple, but he bore his own pain openly with us, whereas, over the many months following Philip's death and before our own tragedy, I had only seen the mask he wore for the sake of the people who were not scarred in the tragic way he had been, and we now were. I had often thought how well he bore his grief, never stopping to think that it was all inside him and that he was unable to share it at all with others who could never really begin to understand the awful sense of loss, and the longing to have your child back.

Roy's wife Pat, whom we met only recently, has increasingly devoted her life to finding ways of educating young people about the terrible dangers of drug abuse. Pat is driven by a fierce determination that her son Philip's life shall not have been taken in vain. Her odyssey is one I can relate to well, for I now find myself driven in the same way in that I am not prepared for Tim to have died in vain.

At the beginning of the week in which the town held its memorial service for the victims, Wendy and I called into the High School to discuss various matters with John Britton. While we were there, Tim's form tutor, Barbara Dutton, called in to John's office to see us. She told us how quiet Tim's classmates were and how her attempts to re-establish some kind of routine were proving difficult. I asked her whether she felt it would be of any help to the children if I spoke to them. She thought this a good idea, and I agreed to return the next morning to see Tim's class.

Back at home, we were visited by two ladies from the Victim Support organisation. Ann Harvey is the organisation's only full-time salaried employee in the whole of Cheshire, and she was accompanied by an older, unpaid assistant named Jamie. They explained the function of the Criminal Injuries Compensation Board to us and the fact that we would be entitled to a lump-sum compensation payment in respect of Tim's death because it had been caused by a criminal act. Jamie offered to take care of completing the claim form on our behalf and we accepted her offer gratefully.

It struck me later that although Cheshire is not one of the largest or most heavily populated counties, for it to have only one person with full-time responsibility for helping people who are entitled to compensation from the government's scheme shows just how little attention or assistance is given in this country to the victims of crime. By contrast, there never seems to be any shortage of individuals or organisations geared to promoting the rights of the criminal. Ann and Jamie, despite being totally dedicated to their roles, were a limited resource for dealing with such a terrible problem.

That evening, we had a rare opportunity to unwind a little when Stephanie Harrison and Sydney May from the Walton Neurological Unit called to see us. Piers's mother Yvonne joined us and we all had a little too much to drink. Stephanie entertained us by revealing the off-duty side of her personality. She ended the evening riding on Dominic's back around the room, and by the time they left it was well after midnight. I think because Stephanie, Sydney and Yvonne had been so closely involved with Tim, letting our hair down in private with them did not seem such an awful thing to do. Indeed, they had made us laugh again and it felt good.

Thankfully, the next morning, Wendy's birthday, did not bring with it a hangover, and we kept our promise of the previous day to speak to Tim's classmates. Barbara Dutton introduced Wendy and me to the class and told them that I wanted to say a few words to them and it was important that they listened carefully.

I had already decided to try to avoid any sort of preaching or heavy sermons with these eleven- and twelve-year-old children. Looking at their faces, only a very few of which I recognised, it struck me how very young they all were. As far as I could tell, they were all looking at me, and every one of them sat silently as I told them that I wanted them to remember Tim as a good friend, even though there had probably been times when they might not have been on the friendliest of terms. I told them that my fondest memories of Tim were of him as a joker and a lover of sports of every description, and that above all else Tim had almost always been a very happy and cheerful boy,

and that was how he would want them to be. With a lump
in my throat I emphasised that the last thing he would want
would be for them to be sad and miserable. Throughout my
short address I could feel the tears welling up in my eyes.
The only means I had developed of preventing myself from
sobbing at times like this was to break my speech and to
breathe extremely deeply and very slowly. On this occasion
I feared that if I did not maintain my outward control my
mission would fail, and instead of the reassurance I was
trying to give them I'd have caused heartache for the class.
I concluded by telling them that where Tim had gone there
was no pain but only true and lasting peace.

I almost ran out of the classroom when I had finished
talking as the strain of keeping my feelings in check was an
enormous effort. All those innocent, trusting faces staring
back at me as I tried to lift their spirits had cut deep into
my emotions. I could not help thinking how young children
everywhere depend so much on their parents and other
adults to care for them and protect them. So the feeling
that I had not been there at the critical moment in my
young son's life when he needed me most became just
too unbearable as I turned my eyes on Tim's friends and
classmates.

In the corridor outside the classroom I felt weak and
drained and it was left to Wendy to exchange our goodbyes
with Barbara. Later, I kept recalling the face of Gareth
Bouldsworth, Tim's best friend in class. Tim and Gareth,
or Gaz as he is known, had quickly established a superb
friendship. They were physically quite unlike one another
– Gaz was short and dark with a crew cut, Tim was tall and
fair – but there was a real affection between the two. Gaz
has a loving and mature nature for one so young, and Tim's
death knocked him for six. We got to know his parents,
Brenda and Ricky, well over the weeks following Tim's
death, and I found it quite impossible not to break down

frequently with them. They would talk of Tim so often, and with so much love, that it totally overwhelmed me. After spending several deeply satisfying, almost cathartic evenings with Brenda and Ricky, I could see where Gaz inherited his depth of emotion from. I have never known two people speak so freely and so movingly of our son, especially surprising considering that they had known him for only a few months.

Some weeks after the visit, I wrote a personal letter to Gaz, thanking him not only for being Tim's great friend but for being ours too. I told him that Tim had thought the world of him, and I asked him to promise never to lose my letter, so that one day he could show it to his own children and explain to them all about Tim. I'm sure he will treasure this letter for the rest of his days.

Later that same day, another of the special people who has come into our lives in the wake of Tim's death appeared. His name is Albert Spiby, and a more inauspicious start to a friendship it would be difficult to imagine. The doorbell rang, and, when I went to answer it, I found standing on the doorstep a short, thick-set, dark-haired man in his early thirties who looked as if he had not shaved for several days. Dressed in torn trainers and badly fitting coat, he certainly looked down on his luck.

'I've come to bring you these,' he said, as he handed me some badges displaying Tim's face. He continued by explaining that the words I had spoken at Tim's funeral had affected him so deeply that he had decided to reproduce them on his computer. He gave me a printout which he had laminated in plastic. I could not help contrasting his down-at-heel appearance with the very professionally produced articles he had given me. Perhaps my bourgeois values caused me some inner turmoil at that moment, because for a second I was torn between judging the man on his appearance and judging him on his actions.

I'm relieved to say that the inclination to judge him on
his appearance was short-lived, and I stepped back from
the door to invite him in.

Looking ill at ease and uncomfortable, he initially
declined my invitation. I asked him where he had travelled
from and he told me – Walkden in Manchester, which I
estimated to be perhaps thirty miles away. Linda Donnelly,
a friend and neighbour, had brought Albert to the house
after meeting him at the top of the road. At first, I took
it for granted that he had left his car there, and so, when
I enquired about his journey, I was taken aback to be told
that, as he did not own a car, he'd travelled all the way by
public transport.

Realising that not only must it have taken him hours to
get to Warrington, but that he must have been pretty tired
too, I now insisted that he come in and have a drink and
something to eat. Again he declined, but I pressed him
and eventually, somewhat shyly, he entered the house,
where I introduced him to Wendy.

Albert would not sit down, and he politely refused tea
and coffee. In the end he asked for a glass of tap water,
but this was all that he would accept from us. Conversation
was still not easy as Albert was no more relaxed inside our
house than he had been on the front doorstep. He did,
however, tell us that he was unemployed, lived alone and
had been affected by the deaths of Tim and Johnathan Ball
as nothing else had ever affected him previously.

He asked what he could do to help, but I had no
answer. It was clear from his facial expressions that he was
absolutely sincere in his desire to do anything we asked of
him. I told him that if we thought of anything we would be
sure to let him know. After taking his name and telephone
number, I offered to drive him to Warrington bus station,
and again it was only after I insisted that he agreed.

While we were in the car, Albert informed me that he

intended being outside St Elfin's Church where the town's memorial service was to be held the following day. He planned to hand badges of Tim and Johnathan to VIPs as they entered the church. As I dropped him at the bus station, I thanked him again and told him that I expected we would meet again soon.

I returned home, deep in thought about the kindness of this man, a total stranger, obviously without much in the way of financial resources, who had decided to do something positive about the outrage in Warrington.

An hour or so after our first meeting with Albert, Wendy and I had to carry out a poignant task that caused us both great sadness. Knowing that we would be obliged to inform the Department of Social Security of Tim's death and that the child allowance Wendy received for Tim would be stopped, we called into the Warrington DSS office to hand in the child allowance book for alteration. The DSS staff member who dealt with the administration was most sympathetic throughout, but this did not diminish the feeling that in yet another way we had just taken Tim out of our daily lives and routines. No longer was the dinner table set for five, no longer did Wendy iron the family clothes and place them in five separate piles, and now no longer would we be entitled to child allowance for three children. Step by inexorable step, Tim was losing his presence and status as a real person. He was instead becoming a memory. This was an inevitable but nonetheless deeply depressing process which was terribly difficult to bear.

We returned to the house, and were cheered by the arrival of a long-standing friend, Mick Ambler, and his daughter Leanne. Like many of our closest friends, Mick was a regular caller, just making sure that we were coping with everything and showing that he was on hand to offer any help he could.

As we chatted over a cup of coffee, the telephone rang and Wendy answered it. I noticed a very broad grin spread across her face. Intrigued, I tried to pick up snippets of her conversation while maintaining my own conversation with Mick and Leanne, but this proved difficult. Eventually Wendy said, 'Colin, it's the Princess of Wales for you!' To say that I thought she was pulling my leg would be a monumental understatement.

As I took the telephone from Wendy I said to her, 'Come on, don't mess about, who is it?', to which she replied, 'It really is the Princess of Wales.' Something about the width of her smile and the pink colour of her cheeks made me believe that she wasn't pulling my leg after all.

'Hello,' I said, 'this is Colin Parry', and from the moment I heard the words 'Hello, Colin, this is Diana, the Princess of Wales' I too developed the same inane grin that I'd seen on Wendy's face a few moments earlier.

The Princess told me how shocked and saddened she had been by the deaths of Tim and Johnathan and that she had just told Wendy how disappointed she was that she was unable to attend the memorial service to be held the next day. However, she assured us she would be with us in spirit. I too expressed my regret that she would not be present, but thanked her for her kindness in telephoning us in this way. She told me that she hoped we would be able to meet on another occasion, and I said that she would always be welcome in our home.

In situations like this, you have to think on your feet and trust your instincts, and my instincts told me that informality and directness were the best approach with the Princess, who was so relaxed and easy to talk to. She acknowledged my standing invitation and replied that if she were ever in the area she would love to meet us.

Later, when Wendy and I discussed our conversation with Diana, I discovered that she had told Wendy that she would have liked to have given her a big hug. Sadly the Princess had not said this to me too! When I asked Wendy if she had really believed it was Diana when she first picked up the telephone, she said that at first she had suspected it was her friend Kim playing a birthday trick on her by putting on a posh voice. As it turned out the telephone call was a better birthday present than anything else Wendy received on this, her thirty sixth birthday.

We both formed a very good impression of Diana, whose relaxed informality had impressed us greatly. She was genuinely concerned for us, and this made us all the more angry when the daily newspapers picked up on our chance remarks about the phone call, given during a Sky News interview the following morning. The morning stories were of an apparent palace rift which had led to Diana being prevented from attending the memorial service.

Both Wendy and I felt we had betrayed the Princess by telling Sky News of her phone call, but the interview team and crew had arrived very soon afterwards and we were still coming to terms with the fact that the Princess of Wales had actually been talking to us. I'm afraid that we naively mentioned the conversation, and it was included in the interview, which was broadcast live via satellite from our home. Unfortunately the tabloids chose to cover the story from a 'palace politics' point of view rather than a humanitarian angle. We were deeply embarrassed and felt personally responsible for providing the newshounds with a juicy bone. This was the first, and I'm glad to say the only, time I have suffered the fate of politicians and many others in the public eye, in having the press distort information.

I was happy to have an opportunity to counter the stories when I was interviewed on BBC Radio 4's *Today* programme by Sue McGregor the following morning. Sue was seeking my opinion about the men of violence

rethinking their campaign following the deaths of Tim and
Johnathan. At the conclusion of the interview I asked for
a little more time so that I could explain the Princess of
Wales's message to us. While I could not undo the tabloid
newspapers' story, I felt a little better for having had the
chance to put the record straight.

On the morning of the memorial service, Paul Matthews
called quite early and informed us that John Smith, the
Labour Party leader, and his wife, had asked through
'channels' whether they could visit us at home, at 1.00 p.m.
Paul also told us which other VIPs would be present at the
service. The list included the Prime Minister, John Major,
on behalf of the government, Prince Philip, the Duke of
Edinburgh, on behalf of the Queen, and President Mary
Robinson and her husband, on behalf of the Republic of
Ireland.

We had kept our close family members advised of the
memorial service arrangements as they all wanted to be
there with us. It would be our first time together again
since Tim's funeral seven days earlier.

Paul informed us that the police had been maintaining
an especially close security check on St Elfin's for some
days and that trained sniffer dogs were being used to search
for any trace of explosives in or around the church. It
was clear that the visit of so many VIPs to Warrington
was being treated very seriously by the police and the
security forces.

The police recognised the vulnerability of Warrington,
well served as it is by the motorway network. The IRA
had demonstrated that the town of Warrington was an
easy place to get into and out of. The fact that three
IRA members had been arrested after the gasometer
bombing had been, from a police point of view, a very
good result. Police Constable Mark Toker, however, had
not been so lucky. He was shot three times after stopping

Above left: Shortly after we moved to our present house in Warrington, late 1987. Tim is playing with the neighbours' boxer, Zil.

Above right: Tim with Dom and Abbi at the house in Wigan, 1987.

Below: Family holiday in Minorca, 1988. As usual, Tim did not want to get out of bed.

Left: Tim with Dom in the conservatory, summer 1990.

Bottom left: Tim, the new recruit to the Sea Scouts, summer 1991.

Above: Tim with Piers (who was with him in Bridge Street on the day of the bombing), Abbi (*front right*) and Vicki, the daughter of family friends Kim and Dave Cook. The photograph was taken in the conservatory, spring 1988.

Left: Tim at the poolside at our camping site in Gascony, August 1992.

Below: Tim receiving his annual deep clean from Wendy, Christmas Eve 1991.

20:28
24.12.1991

Below: Family stop-over at a camping site in Blois, Central France, August 1992.

Left: The Three Musketeers. We like this one, it's a good photo of the three men of the family.

Above: Complete family photograph. Colin set the camera on the timer, ran round and sat down, trying not to look breathless.

Left: Tim with Abbi and Dom on his first day at Senior School, September 1992. Dom and Abbi were not as keen to be photographed as Tim.

the bombers' getaway van to carry out a routine vehicle inspection. Just a few weeks later the IRA struck again with devastating results for our family, the Ball family and the other victims.

At the appointed hour, several cars pulled up to the house and half a dozen plain-clothes police officers jumped out. In the middle of the convoy was a chauffeur-driven Rover from which John Smith and his wife Elizabeth emerged.

Paul Matthews opened the front door and showed our visitors into the lounge, where we all introduced ourselves. Paul disappeared to make everyone a cup of tea and we settled down for what I expected would be an informal and informative chat.

Our visitors expressed their very sincere regret over the death of Tim, and asked us how we were. We gave our usual reply: 'We're coping by keeping busy and taking one day at a time.' I presumed that this answer was sufficient, for it did not trigger any supplementary questions from our visitors.

I confess that for one who frequently talks a good deal with strangers, I found myself being very deferential towards John Smith and his wife. In part, perhaps, this may have been due to the plain fact that Mr Smith looked rather uncomfortable and ill at ease. Sensing that he was not relaxed did not make it any easier for me to act as the ice-breaker, even though it is normally a role I don't find any difficulty in filling.

Mr Smith talked about the gasometer bombing and how it could so easily have caused considerable devastation to that area of the town. He praised PC Mark Toker in particular and the police generally for apprehending the three IRA terrorists who had threatened the lives of so many of the people of Warrington.

Elizabeth Smith like me, seemed, happy to defer to

her husband, and spoke very little while she was with us, though she did smile at us warmly throughout. In the meantime, John Smith continued with his chosen subject, speaking freely and fluently, the confidence returning to his voice and his delivery. For my part I had been so deferential from the outset of this visit, it was difficult to break John's momentum in order to develop a dialogue between us. Consequently he continued to talk uninterrupted apart from an occasional word or two of acknowledgement from Wendy or me.

As the visit progressed, I became increasingly frustrated by my inability to speak openly in my own home to the potential future Prime Minister. I found myself hopelessly incapable of talking about the subject I most wanted to broach – the murder of our son Tim.

From time to time, I've considered what it is that holds me back in situations such as this, and I've concluded that it must stem from my upbringing where good manners were given great emphasis. Also, to some degree, I must have inherited my father's belief in the ascendancy of people who are either high-born or find themselves in high office. When I am in the company of such people, and I have not been asked to speak, I am inclined to sit patiently and wait for the opportunity to arise. I try to avoid talking over someone in situations such as these, I guess because it would offend the values I have assimilated in my formative years. Of course, normally there is nothing wrong with this brand of courtesy, except when I have something important I want to discuss, and then it causes me great frustration.

My disappointment with John Smith, and indeed with John Major, whom we were to meet after the service, stemmed from the fact that neither man asked me anything other than the orthodox and polite question 'How are you?' As I have said previously, this question is rarely, if ever, answered honestly. You know they don't expect a long and detailed reply and so you don't give one. This is the unspoken understanding between the questioner and the person being questioned and is part of the ritual that has developed in our polite society.

However, I was disappointed most of all with myself rather than our two party leaders. They have developed the skill of setting the agenda and sticking to it. In that way they are able to avoid the awkwardness of dealing with difficult and often unpredictable questions and subjects.

So it was throughout John and Elizabeth Smith's visit. The only time the subject changed was when Dominic came into the room. He was introduced to our guests, and John Smith, in a very friendly and almost avuncular way, asked Dom what he was hoping to do on leaving school. Dominic said that he wanted to join the police, to which John replied that if this was his earnest wish, then he should work as hard as possible to get good GCSE and A-level grades and then read law at university, for the police increasingly favoured graduates joining the force, especially law graduates.

Not long after this exchange, Philip and Karen arrived early for the memorial service and, after they too had been introduced to our guests, John and Elizabeth Smith bade their farewells and sped off towards Warrington.

I certainly do not intend to be critical of the late John Smith, Wendy and I appreciated his and his wife's kind motives in calling to see us, and particularly their thoughtfulness at Christmas when they sent us a card expressing their best wishes to us.

The family assembled at the house and we all set off in a convoy of cars to St Elfin's Parish Church. At the traffic lights near the church, policemen directed us into the local Sainsbury's car park, where a section had been reserved for those invited to the service.

As we walked along the road leading to the church,

there were large numbers of local people gathered behind
barriers erected by the police to allow controlled access
for those attending the service. Several of them clapped
as we passed, and others called out their best wishes. Many
policemen lining the road smiled.

As we were about to enter the church, Wendy and I
caught sight briefly of Bronwen and Paul Vickers. This
was the first time we had seen them. Bronwen lost her
left leg in the explosion. Thankfully, although they were
with her, her two young children were unharmed, despite
the fact that the youngest, Harriet, was only two weeks
old on the day of the bombing. Bronwen was to tell us
later that Harriet, amazingly, had not even been woken
by the bomb that had so seriously disabled Bronwen.

We entered the church and could see that every available
seat had been taken. We were handed a service programme
and shown to our seats, which had been reserved three
rows from the front. Moments later, Wilf Ball arrived and
sat next to me.

Wilf chatted away to me in a very relaxed manner and
seemed keen to establish a friendly rapport. He began
telling me about how Marie, Johnathan's mother, had left
him the day after the funeral, to return to her husband
and three sons. Rumours of this split had reached us over
the days following the bombing, but Wilf confirmed the
facts in the open way you would normally reserve for
an old and trusted friend or relative. It occurred to me
that neither he nor I was in a normal situation, and he
probably felt a bond existed between us as we had both
suffered the same terrible fate. From that moment on,
Wilf has always been ready to talk to me and has often
confided in me. I have always considered this to be a
compliment, and all the times he has been subjected to
press criticism I have sympathised with him, because those
who have not suffered the extraordinary and completely

unexpected tragedy our families have, cannot imagine the devastation caused, nor can they, or should they, sit in moral judgement upon us. Whatever mistakes we may make, we have suffered the greatest moral indignity of all – the murder of our children – and let no one forget or, worse still, underestimate that fact.

Canon Jock Colling, the rector of St Elfin's, gave the opening address to the congregation. The VIP guests sat in the front pews, listening attentively to his words. The Duke of Edinburgh sat alongside President Mary Robinson of Ireland and her husband; Prime Minister John Major, John and Elizabeth Smith, and David Alton, MP, sat together; on the opposite side of the aisle, Warrington's mayor and mayoress, the leader of the council, the town's chief executive, and the two local MPs, Doug Hoyle and Mike Hall, along with the local MEP, Brian Simpson, all sat together.

TV cameras were visible at floor level and overhead as the service was carried live on Sky News and edited for the main evening BBC and ITN news programmes.

The hymn-singing and the readings by members of the emergency services were very moving, but the most moving moment was when Archbishop Derek Warlock, the much-respected Catholic Archbishop of Liverpool, slowly and painfully mounted the steep steps leading to the pulpit. He had only very recently undergone serious surgery and looked very frail indeed as he took a minute or two to get his breath back before giving his address.

In his address, he warmly praised the town of Warrington and its inhabitants, likening their spirit to that shown by people in the Blitz. He was also extremely kind and sympathetic to the families of all those who had suffered, and particularly to our family and Wilf Ball's. I have often remarked that the Archbishop captured the mood perfectly and said all the right things.

I have also been asked what I thought of the message sent to Canon Colling from US President Bill Clinton. Everyone listened very attentively as Canon Colling read it to the congregation and we appreciated the President's personal and the American nation's abhorrence of such terrorist acts.

April 7, 1993

Dear Canon Colling

Let me join the people of Warrington in extending my deepest sympathy to the victims of the recent bombing and their families. My prayers are with them and all the other victims of the recent wave of terrorist violence.

The United States condemns in the strongest terms such violence and those who support and perpetuate it. That the most recent outrages have caused the deaths of young children and injuries to many more only emphasises the callous nature of such violence. The American people join the people of Ireland and the United Kingdom in expressing their sympathy to those touched by these outrages, in believing that violence from whatever quarter can never be justified, and in hoping that out of this tragedy will emerge a new determination to seek peace and reconciliation through dialogue.

In my recent discussions with the Prime Ministers of the United Kingdom and Ireland, I was struck by their dedication to the search for a peaceful solution to the troubles in Northern Ireland. In this, they have the full support of the United States.

With my condolences.
Sincerely

William J. Clinton

Only a few weeks later, Wendy and I were left wondering just how much the vast majority of ordinary Americans even knew of the Warrington bombings, let alone how they could feel the abhorrence mentioned in the President's personal message.

When the memorial service ended, Wendy, Dominic, Abbi and I, along with Wilf Ball, walked from the church to the rectory for a private meeting with the VIPs who had attended the service. I walked with Terry Waite and his wife Frances, and as we passed underneath the hanging branches of the trees along the way, I instinctively ducked my head as Terry did, to avoid the branches. It wasn't until I'd done this two or three times that I realised the branches were way above my head, and indeed above the heads of everybody else who was less than six feet four inches in height. It was only because Terry Waite must stand at least six feet six inches tall that he would have been in danger of decapitating himself had he not stooped.

Stepping into the brightly lit and welcoming rectory, we were shown into the room where Prince Philip was standing. As I entered, I could see plates with lots of snacks on a small coffee table in the centre of the room. I knew this would please Dominic who has a voracious appetite for snack-type foods. I kept my fingers crossed that he would not only be civil and polite with the people he was about to meet but also that he would not eat most of the food before everyone else could get some.

Prince Philip and I made eye contact when we entered the room and he smiled as I approached him. Holding out my hand, I said how pleased I was to meet him and thanked him for travelling to Warrington. He replied, 'The Queen sends her condolences and her very best wishes to you', and went on to tell us 'The Queen never attends memorial services.' I thought it best not to ask him why. I introduced Wendy and my children to him and he smiled at them all in turn. Other guests entered the room one by one and began mingling, and gradually the sound of chattering voices coming from a variety of discreet conversations drifted around the room. At this point I took it upon myself to introduce Wilf Ball to the Prince.

After a momentary pause, the Prince turned to Wilf and asked what he did for a living. Wilf explained that he had been an aluminium smelter for many years, but that he had retired through ill health in 1991 and that from then on he had concentrated on bringing up Johnathan. Without any warning, the Prince turned away from Wilf quite suddenly and looked at Dominic, saying, 'And what do you want to do when you've left school?' Dominic, by now accustomed to this stock question from visiting dignitaries, replied that he wanted to join the police, but only in London or Liverpool. In Dominic's mind, it is only big-city police forces which provide the kind of excitement you see in the *The Bill*, a TV series of which he is particularly fond.

After concluding his brief conversations, the Duke advised Dominic and me that he could stay no longer as he had a train to catch. He said his goodbyes and was gone.

Meanwhile, just a few feet away from Dominic and me, I could see Wendy in conversation with the Prime Minister. Abbi stood alongside Wendy and, judging by the expression on her face, she did not understand very much of what the Prime Minister was saying to her mother. I could see that John Major was holding one of Wendy's hands in both of his, and that Wendy looked as though she was listening very closely to what he was saying.

As Wendy continued her conversation, I turned to meet the Liberal Democrat MP, David Alton. He was very quick to tell me how much he admired the way Wendy and I had dealt with our great loss, and we soon got into a very wide-ranging exchange of views about Northern Ireland

and the possible reasons why Warrington had been selected twice for attack by the IRA. Throughout the conversation I had with David, I felt sure that he was as keen to hear my views and opinions as I was his. It was a worthwhile conversation and one that I enjoyed.

I decided that in addition to being impolite it would be a wasted opportunity if I devoted too much time to any single dignitary, and so I courteously took my leave of David for the time being and looked around the room. I noticed that the President of Ireland, Mary Robinson, and her husband were very close by, and so I walked across to them and introduced myself. She told me that she had listened to a radio interview I had given earlier that day to the Irish radio and television service, RTE. She also said that she had heard me refer to her as 'an ordinary woman', and as she said this to me I was quite convinced she was annoyed by my description. However, to my eternal relief, she suddenly smiled broadly and told me that she regarded my description as a compliment. The tension in me quickly evaporated as we talked very amicably together. Wendy joined me and we found the President and her husband delightfully easy to talk to. I could see why she enjoyed such remarkable popularity in her own country as she was instantly at ease with us and displayed great compassion and warmth. She told us that Warrington and the deaths of Tim and Johnathan had had a dramatic impact in the Irish Republic, where a huge amount of sympathy had been expressed over our loss. Wendy and I both acknowledged this and the President was clearly amazed when we told her that we had received several thousand letters and cards from all over Ireland. She asked if we had any plans to visit the Republic and we told her that we had no immediate plans. She then made us promise that if we did travel to Ireland we would accept her standing invitation to visit her in the presidential residence. A few moments later,

her PA handed me her business card and emphasised that
the President's invitation had been made very seriously and
that we must take it up if we went to Ireland.

Our meeting with the President and her husband had
been tremendously gratifying. Little did we know that we
would be able to take up her kind offer some three months
later, during the making of a *Panorama* documentary for
BBC Television.

As the round of meetings continued, I found myself
face to face with the Prime Minister. My first and clearest
recollection of this encounter was the warmth and sincerity
of John Major's smile and greeting. Just as he had done
with Wendy earlier, he held on to my hand after our
handshake. I must confess that I found this more than
a little disconcerting, but I made no attempt to remove
my hand from his, even after several minutes, because I
did not want to appear to be rude or discourteous.

His style was certainly most disarming, for as well
as maintaining very steady eye contact throughout our
meeting, he also exuded genuine sympathy with his facial
expressions. It was all the more unsettling and frustrating
for me not to be able to get a word in, because here was
a man whose body language said 'I'm a nice guy; you can
trust me and confide in me', and yet who never once, that
I can recall, asked me a question or gave me the chance to
make our one-sided meeting into a two-sided conversation.
Just as John Smith had effectively done earlier in the
afternoon, John Major closed all the avenues along which
I might have developed some conversational strategies,
though I confess that he did so with considerable charm.

He told me that he had been in Northern Ireland prior
to coming to Warrington, and that he was determined to
do all in his power to bring about a peaceful resolution of
the 'troubles', but that he was under no illusions about the
difficult path that lay ahead. For all the personal difficulty

I had in speaking to Mr Major, I still came away impressed by the force of his determination to do all in his power to find a solution.

Subsequently, events were to show how prophetic his words were, for eight months later the joint British/Irish initiative known as the Downing Street Declaration offered real hope that all sides might at last sit together at the negotiating table.

I feel a certain obligation at this point to explain that I am not party-political, but I was inclined to believe then, and I still am now, that John Major and the Irish Prime Minister, Albert Reynolds, put their personal reputations at stake in declaring jointly a way to peace in the island of Ireland.

During the evening, and especially during the time I spent in his company, John Major did not neatly fit the image so many people seem to have of him – of being weak and unclear in his policies. He spoke to me with great confidence and conviction throughout. One remark that he made I vividly remember because it made me understand that he too experienced considerable frustration, though in his case it was with what he saw as the entrenched attitudes of those seasoned Northern Ireland politicians we've all seen on our television screens so many times. I was forced to admit to myself that my frustrations were probably nothing compared to his.

Later that evening, as we were driving home, I asked Wendy whether she could recall her conversation with John Major. He had told her that Tim reminded him and his wife of their own son at twelve years of age, and that this similarity had upset his wife, Norma, even more than she already was. Wendy told me that the Prime Minister had also been very friendly to Abbi, asking her age and enquiring how she was. But overall, just like me, Wendy had found the business of uttering little more than an occasional 'yes' or 'no' less than satisfying, although she too had found Mr Major to be very pleasant on a personal level.

Eventually, I thanked John Major for taking the trouble to explain to me his views on what needed to be done to help Northern Ireland, and I made my way over to Archbishop Warlock. As I took the Archbishop's right hand, it struck me how thin and frail it was and, studying his face, I could see that he was probably still struggling to regain his health. I was also struck by the sadness and, if I might use a word that would not usually come to me, the mercy in his eyes. Here I knew was a good man, a man with the kind of faith that I often wish I had. We did not speak together for more than a few moments, because the gathering was coming to a natural conclusion, and I had no wish to tire him after what had probably been an extremely long day, but I particularly wanted to thank him for his very moving address, and tell him that I greatly valued his presence at the service.

Indeed, I was to say on a number of occasions when talking months later to Unionist and Nationalist families in Belfast that Archbishop Warlock and Bishop David Shepherd had shown the great lead that the two Churches united in their social and spiritual purpose can achieve. Certainly in Liverpool, which when I was a youngster was in many ways a city divided along Protestant and Catholic lines, great progress has been made in eradicating any lingering sectarian divisions. Many people attribute this achievement to the two Church leaders, and perhaps the closeness of the Churches was personified when Pope John came to Liverpool during his British tour and visited the two great cathedrals at either end of Liverpool's Hope Street.

The next day, 8 April, we left the house to spend a few days away, thanks to the personal kindness of Peter

Greenall, whose company Greenall Breweries, based in Warrington, owns De Vere Hotels. A day or two earlier, Paul Matthews had been asked to let us know that if we wished to get away for a short break we could select a De Vere Hotel and stay at the company's expense. After looking through the brochure, we selected the De Vere in Swindon because it was near the Cotswolds, an area we hardly knew but understood to be beautiful.

Upon our arrival, the hotel manager greeted us and took us personally to a magnificent suite comprising two very large bedrooms with a huge connecting lounge. We unpacked, had a drink from the bar, took a shower, and then made our way down to dinner in the restaurant. Wendy and I enjoyed a really lovely meal while Dominic and Abbi ate theirs with relish. During the meal, the manager asked us what plans we had for the evening, and when we told him that we had not made any he asked whether the cinema or the bowling alley interested us. Both attractions were in the same retail park as the hotel.

After a quick family conference, we settled for the cinema and decided to see *Forever Young* starring Mel Gibson. The manager told us that he would arrange for tickets to be waiting for us at the door.

We all enjoyed the film, despite its sad ending, though I'm sure that throughout we were all thinking constantly of Tim and how he should have been there with us. We had taken several photographs of him with us to Swindon, to make it seem like he had travelled with us.

Returning to the hotel, we had a couple more drinks at the bar and then went to our suite. Though I had not yet said anything to Wendy, I already felt wrong being so far from home and so far from Tim.

The next morning, after breakfast, we travelled to Bath and walked around the historic city, looking at shops and at the magnificent architecture but for all the beauty of the

place, the visit was utterly without meaning or purpose. I
had come to realise that we had expected too much from
this trip; we had thought that it would help by relieving
the awful burden of sadness and emptiness left in our lives
without our dear Tim, but we had misjudged the situation
and were all very homesick. At dinner that evening, in the
nearby Pizza Hut, I sounded everyone out, and it was no
surprise to discover that we all felt the same and it was
our unanimous decision to return home on Sunday, one
day earlier than originally planned.

That evening we visited the bowling alley. This too was
very kindly arranged by the hotel manager at no cost
to ourselves and once again, we tried to generate some
bonhomie, but try as we might it just did not work.

The following morning before returning north I managed to prove to myself something I had already known
for many years – that I am a rotten navigator. Having
decided we would go to a Cotswold village, I set off and
drove many miles in the opposite direction, ending up in
Devizes in Wiltshire. I didn't know whether to laugh or
cry when I studied my road map and realised that I had
driven for two hours the wrong way!

The one positive thing to come out of our rather forlorn
mini-break was that Abbi agreed to our suggestion that
she should move out of her tiny bedroom and into Tim's
much larger room when we returned home. I was very
pleased with Abbi's positive reaction, because I did not
want Tim's room, full of his memories though it was, to
become a kind of shrine. We all agreed that Abbi's room
would become an office where memorabilia relating to Tim
would be displayed. I began to see in my mind's eye how
I would have it set out, and for the first time since Tim's
fatal injuries were sustained I experienced the feeling that
there was something positive for me to do and my spirits
rose a little. It was then that the inspiration to write about

Tim and what we had gone through came to me. I knew that I would do it, but what I could not be sure of was whether or not a publisher would be bold enough to take my work.

After returning to the hotel we packed our belongings, thanked the hotel staff, in particular the manager, who had been so kind to us, and began the return journey to our home . . . Tim's home.

A Personal Prayer To God

(Written some weeks after Tim's funeral)

Dear God

How is our son Tim? Are you taking care of him?

Is he still the beautiful, happy, loving boy he always was?

Have you restored him to the way we made him – fair of face, smiling eyes, happy disposition and kind to others?

Wendy, Dominic, Abbi and I miss Tim so much because we love him so much.

What does he do all day, how does he spend his time, can he see us and does he know how much he means to us?

Can he hear us, and can you fix it so that he can communicate with us? How is this done? Can it be done? Have we enough of the right kind of faith to be able to receive any messages he may be sending to us?

What is it really like in Heaven? Is there a sense of time and place and does everyone have a human form? I hope so, then when the day comes for me too, I can hold my son again and kiss him and look into his eyes again to tell him how much I love him and have missed him.

Dear God, give it all some meaning that we can understand; make it have a purpose. For someone

so young and so loved to be taken from us in such
a random act of violence is so hard to understand.

Tim did no wrong, he did not deserve this brutal
fate. His sins were the sins of a young, innocent
boy. He was cheeky, a little rude now and again,
he didn't help about the house very much, he was
untidy, usually because he was in such a rush to be
out enjoying his life to the full.

He was such a friendly young lad with everyone,
young and old. He had so many friends in life and
now he has millions since his death.

For all these reasons, make sure he is safe and
cared for, but above all keep him with you till our
time comes to be re-united with him and then, if it's
all right with you, we'd like to take over again.

Tim's dad

6

In the days before we went to Swindon, the telephone never stopped ringing for more than a few minutes at a time. Most of the calls had been from journalists and I had become used to answering their questions and giving my comments, so this was not a particular problem, other than there being little respite.

However, we were beginning to receive unsettling telephone calls. The calls were not threatening, but the fact that they were from complete strangers asking personal questions about the family made me very uneasy. The callers were usually women who asked very direct and personal questions immediately I picked up the telephone. There were no polite introductions or common courtesies beforehand.

One of the harder things to deal with when you are suddenly in the public eye, and one which I had not anticipated beforehand, is the over-personal approach that some people adopt. These phone calls fell into this category. In a way it was ironic, because I knew I could deal with all manner of face-to-face questions from strangers without difficulty, but something inside me made me feel that a complete stranger phoning to ask the same questions was intrusive. I dare say it has something to do with the fact that you cannot see the person you are talking to and you have only a voice on which to base your feelings, so that the very slightest of misgivings are magnified considerably. The overall effect of these phone calls was to cause me considerable discomfort, and when

I discussed it with Wendy we decided that the simplest
solution was to change our number and go ex-directory.

The Monday after our return from Swindon was memorable for its silence and the acute sense of loneliness.
The telephone didn't ring because no one knew our new
number, and no one called round because no one knew
we were home.

Dom and Abbi went off to school at the usual time, and
Wendy and I moped around the house, not sure what to do
with ourselves. We had grown so accustomed to a continual
stream of callers, either to the house or on the phone, that
this new silence was utterly unnatural and unnerving.

We considered what we should do, and agreed that we
wanted to visit Tim's grave. We simply wanted to stand
there and commune with our son, but sadly our plans were
frustrated by there being so many people whom we did
not know standing nearby. Several were looking at the
flowers on Tim's grave, and as we drew nearer they saw
us and moved, but not far enough to enable Wendy and I
to be alone with Tim in the way we wished. For my part, I
was unable to shed the tears I needed to, and I willed the
people nearby to withdraw further to allow us the private
space we yearned for so that we could grieve in a personal
way. As so often happens, they did not recognise our silent
signals and the moment was gone.

By the time we got back to the house, sorrow, emptiness
and frustration all welled up inside me, and when I
looked at Tim's beautiful smiling portrait photograph
I broke down. The tears that had been building up
inside me for so many days came flooding out in hea-
ving sobs. Wendy reached out to console me by putting her arms around me, and she broke down too.
We cried together for several minutes, until I managed to say, 'Call your mum and dad and see if they'll
come over and spend the evening with us.' Wendy did

so, and to our great relief they agreed to come over straight away.

The evening was a real tonic after such a harrowing day. John and Betty told us that they were glad of the opportunity to be with us on their own for the first time since before the day of the bombing. Conversation alternated with tears until very late into the night, but thankfully the day drew to a close on a better note than it had begun.

One of the more unusual contacts we made at this time was with a chap called Ken Harris from Norfolk. Ken wrote and told us that Tim's death had affected him so deeply that he had felt compelled to travel from his home to Warrington, to bring flowers to Tim's grave. The journey took him nine hours by public transport.

Since that first time, Ken has made the journey on at least three other occasions, and after each visit he sends us a detailed account of his day, the time he left home, his journey, where he went in Warrington, whom he met and so on. On one of his visits, he actually met Wilf Ball at the cemetery, and he told us how pleasant that had been for him. Ken's only connection with Warrington is completely coincidental. His home town bears the same name as our road. He now seems to have formed a bond with the town and most certainly with Tim.

For quite some time, Wendy and I had intended to visit the other seriously injured victims of the bombing, and the next morning Wendy rang Warrington General to speak to Gordon Edwards and Liz Antrobus, both of whom were still receiving treatment for serious leg injuries, and to Bronwen Vickers, the lady who had had her leg amputated. After establishing that it was convenient to visit, we met Gordon and Liz in the room in which they were to spend much time together. They were a very friendly couple who were engaged to be married on

26 March 1994, exactly one year and one day after Tim's
death. They had both sustained very similar injuries and
had metal clamps on their legs. They described where they
had been when the second bomb had detonated, and then
told us of their determination to be able to walk down the
aisle together on their wedding day. Gordon and Liz were
gritty characters who epitomised the hidden reserves that
people often find in adversity.

After we had left Gordon and Liz, the nurse took us
along the corridor to see Bronwen. Bronwen's husband
Paul was waiting to tell us that Bronwen would not be
able to see us for a little while because she was receiving
treatment, but she asked if we wouldn't mind waiting as she
was looking forward to meeting us. Finally, when we did
see her, it was a very special meeting. Bronwen burst into
tears the moment we entered the room, and she reached
out her hands to us. We each took hold of her hands and
held her close in a warm embrace. When Wendy sat down
next to Bronwen, they continued to hold one another's
hands until the time we left. After her tears she smiled
at us so cheerfully that we had to remind ourselves of
the horrific injuries she had suffered. Conversation came
easily between the four of us and it felt as though we
had been friends for many years. Wendy gave Bronwen
a photograph of Tim which she kept by her bedside with
the photographs of her own two young daughters, Harriet
and Hannah.

Bronwen told us of her recollections of the bomb in
Bridge Street, and of two-week-old Harriet's amazing
escape. Mercifully, both of their children were uninjured,
although Paul had sustained ankle injuries from the shrapnel. Bronwen sat up in bed smoking a cigarette which she
had rolled herself using liquorice paper. She was exceptionally free of bitterness about what she had suffered, and was
absolutely determined to be walking before baby Harriet

did. As she talked of her determination, something about her voice made me realise that she would achieve her goal – and she did!

Paul Vickers is a very tall, bearded, gentle chap who was obliged to take long-term leave from his job with the Forestry Commission to look after their two daughters while Bronwen underwent extensive treatment to prepare her for going home. Considering the seriousness of her injuries, Bronwen's recovery was quite remarkable, and it said a lot about her single-mindedness. What we like so much about Bronwen is her irreverence towards people and life in general. She is the type of person who judges people on their merits, and she does not touch her forelock to anyone on account of status or position. It is clear that one has to earn her respect.

To avoid tiring her too much, we decided to leave after an hour. As we got up, there was a knock on the door and a man walked in who was obviously familiar to Paul and Bronwen, although not to Wendy and me. He was introduced as Mike Argumont, an ex-fireman who had been among the first on the scene in Bridge Street after the bombing. He then told us that he had saved Bronwen's life. He spoke rapidly and in a way that gave us little chance of replying, and I was surprised at his directness, especially when he told us that he had seen that Johnathan was dead and that there was nothing that could be done for Tim.

Listening to his remarks about Tim and Johnathan made me feel hurt and angry. I resented what he said; the way in which he talked about our son lacked sensitivity for our feelings. In the end I talked over him and warned him not even to think about describing Tim's injuries to us, as that was what I thought he was leading up to. I think at that point he realised he had upset me, and he moved on to a completely different subject.

'Do you know a chap called Bob Strange?' he asked.

'No, I don't,' I replied. 'Why, who is he?'

'He works for Kilroy Television and I met him when I appeared recently on one of their morning programmes,' he explained. He then said that Bob Strange was keen to speak to us, and if we gave him our home telephone number he would pass it on to Bob. I told him that I'd prefer it if he gave me Bob's number and I would speak to him myself. He wrote the number down, passed it to me and then Wendy and I left after telling Bronwen and Paul that we would call in again soon.

A few days later, Bronwen told us that Mike Argumont had apologised to her for his ill-chosen remarks about Tim and Johnathan. I accepted that he had been a great help to Bronwen on the day of the bombing and I had no wish to fall out with anyone who had been on the scene on that awful day but Tim's life was not something I could accept anyone talking about as though it had been a cigarette packet that had been picked up, found to be empty and cast aside.

Events such as this, where people were insensitive to our feelings were very rare indeed, and throughout these early days we continued to receive the most wonderful letters from all over the world, though the great majority were from Britain and Ireland. As well as letters from ordinary people like ourselves, we also received letters from members of the Royal Family, the British and Irish governments, and from the Church.

One particularly moving letter was sent by Sarah, Duchess of York, along with a lovely photograph of her two young daughters, Beatrice and Eugenie. In a handwritten letter, she offered her love, support and strength, saying that Tim had gone to a far better place, but adding that she knew our suffering was unimaginable.

Prince Charles sent a letter in which he extended his heartfelt sympathy and told us how well he remembered the loss of his much-loved great-uncle, Lord Mountbatten, killed by a terrorist bomb in 1979. Fortunately we were able to thank him in person later in the year.

The Prime Minister, John Major, had sent us a handwritten letter on the day Tim died, in which he had said how he could scarcely imagine the agony and misery we were suffering.

The Archbishop of Canterbury wrote us a kind letter telling us that Tim lived on in the love of God and that we would see him again one day.

The Irish Foreign Minister, Dick Spring, sent his condolences and deepest sympathy in a letter written on the day of Tim's death. He talked of Irish people being sickened by the inhuman violence perpetrated by terrorists and of his own sadness at the pain of our loss, for he too had a young family.

After receiving many thousands of letters from people in the Irish Republic, the opportunity to make our first trip there came after Wilf Ball, his neighbour Alan Johnson, Wendy, the children and I accepted an invitation to attend a Peace Concert which was to take place at The Point in Dublin on Saturday, 24 April.

Initially, we were a little apprehensive about our trip because the police told us that they had taken advice from Special Branch on the question of our security. But then they came back to say that they could not foresee any risks in travelling to Ireland.

Paul Matthews drove us to Liverpool Airport and Howard Davies, the policeman allocated to look after Wilf Ball, drove Wilf and Alan. Wendy and I had grown so used to having Paul in constant attendance that it never occurred to us to ask him how long his task of keeping a watchful eye over us was to last. He became so much a part of us that it actually seemed odd that he was not travelling to Ireland with us. We flew by Ryanair to Dublin and on

arrival we were shown into a private airport lounge where
we were met by Susan and Arthur McHugh, their children
and close friends. Susan and Arthur had led a massive
demonstration for peace in O'Connell Street in Dublin
on the Sunday after Tim's death. An estimated 20,000
people had gathered to voice their utter contempt for
what the IRA had done in Warrington. It was after seeing
news coverage of the demonstration that Angus Thorburn,
secretary of the Warrington Male Voice Choir, organised a
peace concert to take place in Warrington's Parr Hall, and
invited Susan and Arthur to attend the concert as guests of
the choir. During their weekend stay in the town, Angus
brought Susan and Arthur to our home to meet us.

Frank Buckley, a former road manager of the Irish
rock group U2, and Barbara Dowling, a Dublin solicitor,
had organised the Peace Concert, entitled 'Expressions of
Sympathy', to give Irish artists an opportunity to express
their opposition to violence through words and music.

I found that many of the expressions and much of the
language used in the explanation of the thinking behind
the concert struck a chord with me, and I cite just a few
examples here:

> The concert is being organised to allow musicians
> and performers to mark a moment in our history, a
> moment when we have the courage, the interest and
> the will to see beyond the indifference to violence
> that so easily creeps into our lives . . . if it can help
> create one tiny fracture in the crust of hopelessness
> and ambivalence that encases the subject of violence
> within our culture, then something worthwhile will
> have been achieved. Another small step in the direc-
> tion of a lasting peace will have been created by us
> all. Little cracks have a habit of growing, as is proven
> by the current surge of feelings and concern.

These thoughts confirmed so clearly the sentiments that the many thousands of Irish people had expressed in their letters and cards to us. A collective national awakening, born partly of a sense of guilt, took place in the Republic of Ireland following the Warrington bombing. This awakening was also given shape so effectively by Susan McHugh at her peace rally in Dublin.

On countless occasions over the months since Tim was killed by the IRA bomb, we've been asked why Warrington was so different from other atrocities committed by the IRA. My answer has always been that the people of the Republic woke from their passive acceptance of violence for the first time since the Troubles began in 1969. If I judge the mood of the people in the South from their words to us, then I know that they were appalled beyond anything they had known before at the deaths of our son and of Johnathan Ball.

This is not to suggest that we did not also receive many moving letters of sympathy from Northern Ireland. We did, but the Irish people in the South always conveyed the same message to us. They were adamant that the IRA did not bomb Warrington in their name, nor in the name of Ireland; that support for the IRA's campaign of violence is infinitesimal and that the people in Ireland yearned for peace.

Once we had finally decided we would go to Dublin for the Saturday concert, it occurred to me that the Irish state television company, RTE, might give us the opportunity to express our thanks to the Irish people while we were over there. I rang the station and I was very pleased we were invited to appear on the *Late Late Show*, hosted by Gay Byrne, who is something of an Irish institution, having fronted the show for more than thirty years. I was told that the programme was watched, on average, by more than a third of the population of the Republic, so it was a

great honour to be invited on to the most popular Irish
TV programme at such short notice.

After our meeting with the McHughs at the airport,
we were driven in a Mercedes stretch limousine to Jurys
Hotel in the heart of Dublin. We were shown to our suite,
which consisted of rooms for the children and ourselves.
As we looked around the huge rooms, we noted that this
was a level of luxury to which we were not normally
accustomed. All our previous journeys abroad had been
limited to annual holidays, and this usually meant staying
in tents, caravans or in very basic and usually very cramped
hotel rooms. In complete contrast, the size, furnishings
and facilities of our present suite of rooms surprised
Wendy and me, and led to Dominic and Abbi showing
their approval very obviously. They soon discovered the
wonderful novelty of having a refrigerator in their room,
stocked with a good supply of chilled soft drinks. Needless
to say, the fridge in their room, and the one in ours, was
depleted very quickly.

At a pre-arranged time, we all met in the hotel bar. The
McHughs very kindly offered to take Dom and Abbi with
their young children to the nearby McDonald's so that
Wilf, Alan, Wendy and I could become better acquainted
with Barbara Dowling and her colleagues. Everything
worked out rather well, and at a little past 9.00 p.m. we
were all transported from the hotel to the RTE studios.
Eileen Heron, the researcher from the *Late Late Show*,
took us to the hospitality room, and shortly before the
show went on-air at 10.00 p.m., Gay Byrne came in to
meet us all. I was surprised by how much make-up he
was wearing, and found it a strange sight. As the months
passed, and we spent more and more time in television
studios, I became used to this aspect of being in front of
the cameras.

Thirty minutes before we were due to appear, Wendy

and I were taken up to make-up, and my face, neck and the
back of my hands were lightly dusted with powder. It took
maybe three minutes for the young lady to do this, but I
then waited another twenty minutes for Wendy. I could not
understand why so much make-up was being put on her,
only to discover later that the make-up girl had thought
that Wendy was one of Cliff Richard's backing group! I
did not get to meet Cliff, who was appearing in the show,
because I'd left the photographs of Tim in the hotel room,
so Arthur drove me back to get them. While I was away,
Wendy and Abbi were introduced to Cliff before he sang
a couple of songs and chatted to Gay Byrne on the show.
Wendy told me that Cliff expressed his admiration for what
we were doing and had regretted not meeting me.

When our time came to appear on the programme, we
stood behind the screens that formed the back of the studio
set while Gay reminded the audience and the viewers of
the IRA bombing of Warrington. Wilf, Alan, Dominic
and Abbi were sitting in the front row of the audience
as we were introduced. I sat nearest to Gay Byrne, and
Wendy sat alongside Ben Elton who was sitting next to
James Galway. Whether the stars of the show knew we
were appearing I do not know, and they may have felt
just as odd sharing the stage with people who had lived
through such a recent tragedy as we did sharing the stage
with them. Having said that, the guests all faced the
audience and not each other, so that once you had taken
your seat you were no longer aware of the other guests.
I dare say that in normal circumstances sharing the stage
with internationally famous names would have unsettled
us, but in our particular circumstances normal reactions
no longer applied.

What followed next was a great surprise to me, for I was
given almost fifteen minutes in which to talk uninterrupted
about what had happened from 20 March through to the

day Tim died, five days later. This was so unexpected that
several times I checked with Gay Byrne whether it was all
right for me to continue, and even though he encouraged
me to go on, I was worried that I might have been using
time allocated for some other part of the programme.
Live television programmes place the presenter under
enormous stress, and I felt it was right for me to offer
Gay the opportunity to bring the interview to a close and
thereby save him the problem of doing it himself.

Towards the end of the interview I was asked whether
there was anything I wanted to say by way of a final
comment. There was, and it took the form of an appeal
to anyone watching or listening who had family or friends
in the United States, to tell them about the real activities
of terrorists in Northern Ireland, in the hope that they
could persuade them not to support, even inadvertently,
the likes of Noraid and other propaganda groups that raise
money for the IRA.

Before the programme finished, Gay walked across the
studio to the front row of the audience and spoke to
Dominic and Abbi. He asked both of them if they were
all right and then he said to Abbi, 'I know you're not
coping too well, are you?' I wasn't sure why Gay had
asked Abbi this question, and she seemed to shrink back
into her padded coat as she replied shyly, 'I'm all right.'

Up until that moment, I suppose we had felt that the
children would tell us if things were troubling them, but I
began to understand that this was a misplaced assumption.
Behind their outward assurance and their appearance of
normality, moments such as this brought it home to me
just how lost our poor children were. They looked and
sounded the same as they had on Friday, 19 March, but
they were not the same, any more than Wendy and I were
the same, or ever will be the same again.

I'm sure the question was not intended to suggest

that Abbi was not coping in the normal sense of the word. We had told Gay during our brief chat in the hospitality room before the programme began that Abbi had been dealing with all that had happened by being quiet and withdrawn. As I looked at Abbi's expression and listened to her simple reply to the question, I felt the most immense sympathy for her, and for Dom too, because their lives had been shattered by Tim's death in the same way as mine and Wendy's had, but where we, as adults, had the opportunity to talk about it to family, friends and the media, our children had nowhere obvious from which to seek comfort other than their parents, and at that precise moment I couldn't help feeling that we were failing them.

The way Abbi responded to Gay Byrne made me realise that the question was perceptive after all. The look on her face and the tone of her voice told me that there was a great deal of pain and confusion in her young heart and mind. Wendy and I had not been attuned to their needs as we should have been because in time-honoured fashion we had assumed, as they were not showing any apparent signs of distress, that Dominic and Abbi were, in spite of everything, coping.

Parents are not given an instruction manual that they can read beforehand to tell them how to handle every situation which may arise during their children's lives, and even if they were, who would ever expect to suffer the fate we had suffered? Tim's death had been so sudden, so completely unexpected and so dramatic that with each new day we faced different circumstances and new challenges, and of course it was easier to deal with problems and questions you could see rather than ponder on what was happening inside the hearts and minds of others, even your closest family. This, and the sheer volume of visits, callers and interviews, had led to us failing Dom and Abbi. Being busy can be a blessing and a curse, depending on one's perspective. For me, and increasingly for Wendy, finding and pursuing new and worthwhile goals has preserved our sanity, but there was an awfully easy trap to fall into, that of underestimating the needs of our children. Because they seemed well adjusted and they did not call out for help and support, we tended to believe only what we saw and heard. In these early days, we did not look deeper and take the necessary time to be sure that we were really attuned to their needs and their moods.

However, from that moment on we consciously involved our children in family decisions, by encouraging them to express their feelings openly and to tell us their needs. We tried to make sure that just because they were outwardly composed we did not make the mistake of automatically assuming that they were dealing with the loss of their brother, and the turmoil that followed, in the same way as us.

At the end of the show, as the guests all filed off stage, I noticed that Ben Elton was carrying what looked like a glass of whiskey. With all the aplomb of the aspiring amateur comedian, heightened by the Scouser's innate belief in his own talent for being funny, I asked him if it was whiskey or a 'sample' in his glass. Choosing to ignore my rather weak joke he replied, 'It's whiskey, would you like some?' I thanked him for his generous offer and took a sip to moisten my dry throat. We chatted briefly and he came across as a self-effacing and friendly chap. He went up even further in my estimation when he told me that many of his friends were from Liverpool and most were Everton supporters. As we parted, he was generous again, only this time it was with his praise and admiration for our family. The quick-witted, wise-cracking TV image Ben Elton exudes with such supreme confidence disguises what, in private, seemed to me to be a very caring, kind-hearted man capable of real warmth.

Our party left the RTE studios to be taken to a pre-arranged visit to the Mansion House, the official residence of the Mayor of Dublin. The Mayor, Gay Mitchell, had issued his invitation to us all after we had arrived at the RTE studios earlier that evening. He showed us around the main rooms of the house which were adorned with huge canvas paintings of former lords and High Court judges from the days when Dublin was a British city. My other very clear recollection of the pleasant, relaxed hour we spent in the Mansion House was the exceedingly well-stocked bar in the reception room. It was here that I had my first real taste of Irish whiskey, and it was with some hesitation that I informed my host of my preference for Scotch. Thankfully, the Mayor was not in the least bit offended when I proffered my opinion on this most sensitive issue.

Back at the hotel, Wilf and Alan decided to have a nightcap at the bar, but Wendy and I chose instead to turn in for the night as it was already after midnight and we were anticipating another busy day to follow.

Saturday morning was free of any 'official engagements' and Wendy and I agreed that we should take a walk with Dom and Abbi, from the hotel into the main shopping area of the city. Wilf and Alan declined the invitation to join us, saying they would meet us in the early afternoon in time for our visit to the McHughs' house.

The morning was dry and mild, the perfect weather for a casual stroll around the shops, or so we thought! We reached the top of Grafton Street and as it looked such an attractive shopping area we decided to explore it further. From then on, every couple of yards, we were stopped by well-wishers of all ages and both sexes. It was a bewildering but gratifying experience. For every person who stopped to shake our hand, there were ten more who smiled, called out a greeting or waved a hand. Flower-sellers recognised Wendy and thrust bunches of flowers into her arms, and one even embraced her as he did so. People expressed their gratitude to us for being in Ireland, and thanked us for attempting to understand what could have caused people to plant the bomb that killed Tim and Johnathan. Many reiterated the remarks of their countrymen who had written to us by saying that the IRA did not commit such atrocities in the name of Ireland and had no support among decent, ordinary Irish people.

The experience of that morning served to confirm our belief in the goodness and kindness of the vast majority of Irish people. At no time did we encounter anyone or anything even remotely unsympathetic. It was warmth, kindness and smiles wherever we turned.

Dominic and Abbi were truly amazed by the whole experience that morning, and I was particularly pleased that they had witnessed such friendship first-hand because it helped them to understand that it was not 'the Irish' who were to blame for Tim's death, but the men and women who were spawned out of ancient animosity with such cold-hearted evil in their hearts that they could justify any brutal act on the grounds of political expediency.

Dom, in his usual way, had already developed a free and easy relationship with Mick, our stretch limo driver, and with one or two of the hotel staff, and had seen that our Irish hosts were very caring people who were glad to have us in their country.

Needless to say, any intention on our part to do some serious shopping was abandoned as we proceeded with our stop-start journey down Grafton Street. After an hour or so, and having walked only some two hundred yards, we went into Bewleys for a coffee and a break from all this astonishing attention.

When the time came to return to the hotel, we stood at the top of Grafton Street to call a taxi, but after several minutes none had appeared, so we set off back to the hotel on foot. As we walked along, a driver rummaging in the boot of his car recognised us and asked where we were going. When we told him, he insisted on taking us back to our hotel personally – just one more friendly act at the conclusion of what had been a most moving experience for us all.

After a quick change of clothes, we were taken to the McHughs' house. As the car drove into their street, we saw that every house was bedecked with white flags fluttering from their upstairs windows emblazoned with the single word 'Peace'. We were greeted as the car pulled up outside the house, the adults giving their attention to us and the children from the surrounding houses giving their attention to the stretched Mercedes.

Susan and Arthur introduced us to their friends and fellow peace campaigners. There was a plentiful supply of refreshments and a very appetising buffet spread across the dining-room table. The afternoon was spent very pleasantly in a classic conversational gathering, all of us mingling and moving on until eventually everyone had had a conversation with just about everyone else.

Two of the McHughs' guests there to meet us were Paul Smyth, a youth worker, and his girlfriend, Kim. Paul and Kim come from Belfast and were the first people we'd met who had had a long association with peace movements in the North. I was interested to discover that Paul was a Protestant and Kim a Catholic, although neither was practising. We talked about the difficulty of keeping the momentum of peace movements going after the initial groundswell of grief, anger and emotion has produced a cocktail powerful enough to bring divided people together. Paul was well aware of the pitfalls, and he told me about his

very good friend and mentor, Ciaran McKeown, and of his
work in peace movements, including the most famous of
them all – the peace movement led by Betty Williams and
Mairead Corrigan in 1976 following the deaths of children
run over by a fleeing IRA terrorist shot dead by British
soldiers.

It was reassuring to hear from Paul and Kim that despite
setbacks people committed to peace were still plentiful in
Northern Ireland. The new dimension this time, however,
was that the Peace 93 campaign had sprung to life in the
Republic.

By the time of our visit to Dublin, there had already
been problems for the fledgling movement when a group
from Northern Ireland who were opposed to the use
of plastic bullets by the British Army had joined the
mass demonstration in O'Connell Street carrying black
placards. Some people in the crowd mistakenly thought
that these people were IRA supporters and abused them
by spitting and stamping on their placards. Tussles broke
out and the people from Northern Ireland returned home
with considerable resentment about the treatment given
to them by a section of the Dublin crowd.

Susan McHugh went to Belfast in order to apologise
to these people for the treatment they had received,
but by all accounts she got a fairly hostile reception.
It was at this point that she began to realise what a
difficult and rocky road she, her husband Arthur and
their friends were walking. Where peace movements are
concerned, the immediate emotional outpouring can only
carry things along for a comparatively short time, and
then calmer heads must prevail if a coherent structure,
free from political interference, and with simple, clear
and achievable goals, is to emerge with any chance of
long-term success. Although I have given my view in a
single sentence, it is obvious to anyone who supports the

existence, and hopefully the sustained growth, of a lasting peace campaign in Ireland, that the objective of peace is both elusive and complex. This is self-evident, otherwise why would all previous campaigns, led by good people with the best of intentions, have failed to deliver the ultimate prize of peace?

One of the most significant things I learned from the cross-section of Irish people we met in the Republic, there did not seem to be many who placed a united Ireland at the top of their political agenda. Indeed, I would put it more forcefully than that: there seemed to be only one political priority which occupied everyone's mind – how to end the violence so that the process of exploring all possibilities of finding peace in an atmosphere free from coercion and intimidation could begin. Half jokingly, I put it to one of Susan and Arthur's close friends that a united Ireland and Northern Ireland's continuation as part of the United Kingdom would no longer be irreconcilable if the Republic rejoined the UK! For several seconds, he thought about this rarely considered option, and said, 'Perhaps that's not such a bad idea after all!' We smiled but chose not to pursue this line of thought. The main priority of the afternoon continued to be the theme of getting to know each other.

During the course of the afternoon, a BBC production team arrived, headed by the producer Nikki Stockley. Nikki explained that she was making a programme on the McHughs for an episode of *Everyman*. She asked whether we would agree to be filmed for the programme, and we said we would be happy to make any contribution she thought appropriate. As well as filming inside the McHughs' house, Nikki wanted some outside shots, and someone suggested Dublin Bay as a location. In convoy, we drove to the bay and were filmed striding along the beach. Wendy and Abbi flew a kite in the blustery wind blowing off the bay, and later Abbi, unaided by Wendy, managed to get the kite to a considerable height.

Paul Smyth and I had a further conversation as we stood on the beach, and I was increasingly impressed by his detailed knowledge of Northern Irish issues. He asked me whether I would have the time to meet Ciaran McKeown while we were in Dublin, and I said that it was unlikely, given our tight schedule during this trip. However, when we were back in our hotel room in the early evening, I spoke with Ciaran on the telephone for several minutes. He conveyed his heartfelt sympathy to me for the loss of Tim and said that Warrington had tapped deep into the consciousness of the Irish people, particularly those living in the Republic. We both agreed it would be good to meet some day.

As we were transported from our hotel to the Point for the concert, we were told by Barbara Dowling of a huge explosion in the City of London, causing massive damage to commercial buildings over a considerable distance. A *News of the World* photographer, Ed Henty, was killed in the explosion.

This news cast a dark shadow over us all and brought back to Wendy and me the horrors of the Bridge Street bombing and the awful afternoon we spent at the hospital. I was deep in thought when Barbara said that various television companies wanted to interview us at the Point for our reaction to the City bombing. Wendy and I agreed to give our comments, but declined to give a full interview as we were unaware of all the details at that stage.

When we arrived at the Point, one or two 'handy lads' took up position on either side of our family to make sure that we weren't jostled as we went in. Once inside, we met Frank Buckley, one of the concert organisers, for the first time, and were introduced also to our 'protectors'. I noticed that there was an air of tension about the place, but I think this had more to do with the smaller than expected audience and the needs of the various artists than with the deeply disheartening news from London.

We were taken to a large room and provided with drinks while the organising went on apace. Perhaps an hour after our arrival, we were directed to our seats on the balcony to the right of the stage. We had a good view, and could see that the audience was reasonably substantial.

Before I became too settled, I had an official duty to perform on stage. The Mayor of Warrington had asked me to deliver a gift from the people of Warrington to the people of Dublin by handing it to the Mayor of Dublin before the concert began.

The Mayor of Dublin gave a touching speech about the horror of what had happened in Warrington and of how pleased he was that we were in Dublin so soon after our tragic loss. He presented me with a gift to take back to Warrington's mayor, and then I replied with a few words of my own to the audience. Again, I returned to the theme I had used on the *Late Late Show*, that misinformed people in America and a small number of misguided people in Ireland who give succour to the terrorists must come to realise the total futility and cruelty of the actions of the men of violence. I was given a long round of applause by the audience, but the point was not lost on me that the people gathered for this concert were, by their very nature, people who supported the cause of peace.

The evening was extremely entertaining, with bands, interspersed with poets, giving their own brand of peace messages. Of all those I heard, however, I was most impressed by the moving and imploring words uttered by a local notable named Pat Ingoldsby.

DO NOT KILL ANYBODY FOR ME

You do not have a mandate from me.
No matter what your reasons are for killing people,
you do not do it for me.
I do not wish my name to be on
your guns or knives or bombs or bullets.
I have remained silent for too long.
I am guilty of the awful ambivalence.
'The ould enemy.'
'Who broke the Treaty of Limerick before the ink was
    dry?'
'Perfidious Albion.'
'Burn everything British but their coal.'
That is what we learned down here and some of it sticks.
I have not had my brothers or sisters tortured until they
    begged to die.
I have not seen my father shot dead in the bath.
I don't know what it is like to live in the middle
of raw hatred and gut-churning fear.
I don't know what the solution is.
I probably don't know enough.
I do know what fear feels like.
It feels like when I said no to the hard-faced man with the
    collection box in the Dublin pub.
It feels like right now as I write these words
and break my long silence and say
'You do not have a mandate from me.
No matter what your reasons are for killing people,
you do not do it for me.'
I have got the right to say this.
I always had.
You do not represent me
even though for a long time
my passive silence seemed
to tell you that you did.
Do not do it in my name.

Do not do it at all.
No more.
No more.
No more.

All too soon, our stay in Ireland came to an end, but our family visit to Dublin confirmed that the sympathy and love of the ordinary Irish people expressed in the many thousands of letters we had received were absolutely genuine.

Our departure from Dublin Airport was a sad occasion, for it meant saying goodbye to many friends we had made in such a short time. Susan and Arthur McHugh and their friends were there to see us off. I thought about the weekend and of all we had seen and heard, and I asked myself had we really only been there for two days? So much had been crammed in, that it seemed we had been there for a week rather than just a weekend.

On the Monday morning, I began my second week back at work. Looking back, those early days and weeks at work passed by in something of a haze. I was not capable of focusing on anything for more than a very short time, and my presence was little more than a token. My staff, friends and colleagues were extremely patient with me and tolerant of my dream-like state. My boss, Philip Croft, and I had a long talk about what was expected of me and he stressed that I could take whatever time off I needed. In fact, I recall him saying, 'Take the whole year off if you need to; your family comes first, so make sure that you look after them.' It was a relief to hear Philip's reassuring words because I had been worrying, not only about the time I was losing from work, but also about how soon I would begin to make a real contribution again.

At the same time as I returned to work, Wendy returned

to her job as cook at Tim's old junior school, but she found it too difficult to deal with the memories it brought back and she was unable to return on the second day. By agreement with her employer, she transferred back to another school where she had worked previously for four happy years. Wendy remained there until later in the year when she moved to a sixth-form college across town.

When I initially returned to work, I decided to see as many people as I could, to tell them that they could talk to me as they had done previously and that they need not avoid me. However, I was straightforward and told them all that I was not yet in control of my emotions and was inclined to get upset without warning. By saying this, I was not trying to frighten people away, though I could have understood perfectly well if my remarks had had that effect. As the days passed, it was rare for anyone at work to mention Tim or the bombing at all, and though this came as no surprise to me, it meant that I had to find other outlets for talking about Tim. Slowly I came to realise that the media, with its constant high level of interest, was providing me with that outlet. It was to become my safety valve.

I was standing in the kitchen of our house one Saturday lunchtime just a few weeks after Tim died when Barry Haverty appeared at the front door. Barry is the father of Neil Haverty, the other boy who went into town with Tim and Piers on 20 March.

I had only met Barry once before, and so I was a little surprised to see him. He asked me whether I could spare him a few minutes and I told him to step inside.

'I've wanted to call and see you a few times,' he told me, 'but each time I got upset and went back home'.

I encouraged him to tell me what he wanted to say. He then began to share with me his memories of those final moments before the bomb went off. He told me that he had met the boys in town and had gone into many of the sports shops with them. Just minutes before the bomb, he suggested that they had been in town long enough and he would drive them all home, but the boys would have none of it. As they all stood outside McDonald's, Tim told Barry, 'We want to look around a bit more before we go home.' Barry then noticed Tim drop a sports brochure into a bin on the opposite side of the road from the one which, we now know, contained the bomb. Barry had wanted to look through the brochure himself, so he reached his hand inside the bin's side opening to try to retrieve it, but to no avail.

What he told me next upset him very much. He said to me, 'I really had a go at Tim, because he just tossed the brochure away after I'd told him that I wanted it.' I asked him how Tim had reacted to being told off in this way and Barry's answer did not surprise me in the least. 'He just smiled at me,' he said. By this time, tears were welling up in Barry's eyes as he recalled those final moments with complete clarity. He left the boys to complete their shopping and walked to the top of Bridge Street. In the time it took him to walk those few yards, the bomb exploded and there was mayhem. Barry sprinted back towards the scene to search for the boys but was prevented from getting too close by an off-duty policeman. The next thing he told me was that he could see a body lying in the street near the shattered bin. 'I thought it was a man,' he said to me, 'because he looked so big, but now I know that it was Tim.' I looked at him as he cried. I believe he told me his account because he had to face me with it. He looked drained and was silent for a long time. I then reassured him he had done the right thing to come and talk it through in this way.

In circumstances of personal tragedy, some people will

choose silence, solitude and introspection, but I needed
to talk in order to vent my feelings, for it was only
by doing so that I prevented an enormous build-up of
frustration. I realised that our small circle of close family
and friends could not be expected to be Good Samaritans
indefinitely, as they too had to be given time and space
to come to terms with their own feelings. I felt it would be
wrong and selfish to expect my needs to take precedence
constantly over theirs. However, by not always turning to
them every time a friendly ear was needed, individuals
in the media instead became close to us for a time, and
very important to me in sharing private moments of great
sadness and anguish during some particularly frank and
open conversations that were sometimes on, but mostly
off, the record.

Nikki Stockley from BBC's *Everyman* programme and
Sarah Oliver of the *Daily Express* were two early examples of people who spent several evenings in our home
discussing aspects of Tim's death with us. On a number of
occasions, I drank rather more than was good for me and
this usually led to uncontrolled outpourings of grief. Nikki
and Sarah were very understanding and compassionate and
perhaps without knowing it gave me the vital opportunities
I needed to pour out my deepest feelings, thereby helping
me to hang on to my sanity.

As Wendy and I gradually came to understand our own
feelings, and our different needs in terms of expressing our
grief, we tried to accommodate the differences between
us. This was not easy, and from time to time tension
mounted between us. However, at the critical moment
someone usually called at the house or on the telephone, and this would generally oblige us to be courteous again.

Recognising the danger signals, I took evasive action
and found that venting the full range of my emotions on

new acquaintances who were dealing with us in their professional capacity as journalists or television programme-makers was both safe and very effective. At times of high emotion, one person's outspokenness may be another person's pain, and it can be a self-indulgent luxury to unload your own feelings regardless of the effect it has on those closest to you.

Wendy came to realise very early on that my need was being fulfilled in the way I have described, and it is to her eternal credit that she never tried to stop the succession of appointments with journalists. There were times when I know she was tired and wanted a quiet evening without anyone visiting, but even then she did not grumble about our visitors, be they friends, family or journalists.

At these crucial moments in our relationship, Wendy's intuitive recognition of the growing benefit I was deriving from the media was vitally important. We could so easily have disagreed over this and, had we done so, I believe that we would have been sorely tested. That our ship did not run aground was entirely due to Wendy's skilful navigation. I may have been the mouthpiece, the spokesman and the incessant talker, but Wendy quietly got on with the vitally important role of keeping the home and family together.

Wendy would never have chosen to have the press and television people camped in our lives, but she knew that the platform they provided for telling so many people about Tim was desperately important to me. She did not try to dissuade me from continuing with the round of interviews, although she often said, 'You do it, you don't need me there, I don't know what to say anyway.' Needless to say, although I was aware of her nervousness and knew she often found it an ordeal to take part, she knew that I would not do these things without her.

I was convinced that our strength, in the eyes of the public, was in being together. People saw our joint strength, and understood that we complemented one another. We were never competitive when being interviewed, and always tried to be supportive, not for show, but simply because it was the way we were. However, I would not have continued without Wendy's agreement, and it is a mark of her selflessness that she put my needs first.

The most exciting media proposal we had had so far had come from Bob Strange of Kilroy Television. When he contacted us to talk about a documentary aimed at discovering how Tim could have become a victim of the troubles in Northern Ireland, Wendy and I were firmly agreed on the kind of programme we wanted to make. The meeting took place in our home on Wednesday, 28 April, and was the start of four months of planning and filming to produce, in time for what would have been Tim's thirteenth birthday on 1 September, what we hoped would be a thought-provoking *Panorama* programme presenting an honest analysis of the dire and deadly results of a quarter of a century of failing to find a peaceful solution to the problems of Northern Ireland.

7

Bob Strange, Wendy and I had several meetings to flesh out the content and form of the documentary programme we were to make for Kilroy Television.

Bob told us that the idea of making the programme first occurred to him when he watched the news conferences from Walton Hospital during the days following Tim's transfer from Warrington. The idea had little form until he saw Tim's funeral service televised. He became so upset at the injustice of Tim's death that what had been no more than a vague idea until this time became a very clear vision.

Initially, he had been extremely hesitant about contacting us to discuss his idea, not knowing how we might react, but when I made contact with him, he drove north from London to see us at very short notice, arriving early in the evening of 28 April.

For the first few moments after we met, Bob was affected by the same state of nervous unease that so many people suffered when first making our acquaintance. He accepted Wendy's offer of tea and sandwiches only after several polite refusals, but then he settled down, looking more relaxed as the conversation began to flow easily.

It soon became very obvious that Bob was an extremely emotional man who found it very difficult not to break down when reliving his feelings at the time when Tim was fighting for his life and then when he died. He told us that no other event in his life had affected him so much, and that he had been compelled to follow the events day by

day. Through this experience he came to realise what a
powerful programme could be made about Tim's death
and his parents' need to discover why it had happened.

We talked for several hours before he left to set about
the job of committing his company to make the programme
for the BBC. Bob returned to Warrington a number of
times, and on each visit he was nearer to putting all the
pieces of the contractual jigsaw together. He had amazing
stamina and always preferred coming to see us rather than
conducting business by telephone. He would drive north,
meet with us for a couple of hours, and then as often as
not drive straight back again.

Wendy and I were both alarmed when we saw the kind of
vehicle Bob travelled in. He favoured either a very elderly
Ford Granada or an equally decrepit Ford Fiesta, neither
of which I would have trusted to get me into Warrington,
let alone a round trip of some four hundred miles.

A couple of weeks had passed since our first meeting
when Bob rang one evening to tell us that the BBC had
decided to put the programme out under its flagship documentary series *Panorama*. To say that he was excited would
be a huge understatement – he was thrilled to bits!

The next stage was for a senior member of the *Panorama*
editorial management team to meet us, and this was
arranged for a few nights later, again at our house.

For the umpteenth time, Bob drove from London to
Warrington, only on this occasion he was accompanied
by Nick Robinson, deputy editor of *Panorama*. Nick, like
Bob before him, made a really good impression not only
on Wendy and me, but also on Dominic and Abbi with
his easy style and his genuine concern for our feelings in
making the programme.

I assured Nick and Bob that although we would inevitably encounter some emotionally difficult moments during the making of the programme, we were nevertheless

All three, clean and tidy. Taken in the lounge, October 1992.

Friday 26th March 1993. Bridge Street, Warrington, the day after Tim died.

Thursday 1st April 1993. Tim's funeral. Colin, Dom and Wendy's brother-in-law, Terry, carry Tim from St Mary's Parish Church, Great Sankey.

Girls from Great Sankey High School representing the school at Tim's funeral. Mel Vincent is third from left, holding a service card.

(*From left to right*) Wendy's brother Phil, Colin, Wendy's father John (obscured), Phil's wife Karen, Abbi, Wendy, Wendy's mother Betty, Paul Matthews, Dom (obscured), Colin's father Eric (obscured), Terry and Wendy's sister Carol. The family are walking towards St Elfin's Parish Church, Warrington, on the day of the Memorial Service, Wednesday 7th April 1993.

Left: Wendy and Colin off the Falls Road, West Belfast, July 1993.

Below: On the peace line.

Below: With Julie Singleton at a Tiger's Bay bonfire in the early hours of 12th July 1993, the morning of the annual Orange Day parades.

one hundred per cent committed to doing it so that Tim's death, and his family's determination to make it count for something, would be appreciated by as many people as possible.

Nick and Bob had to put the production team together and organise research staff who would go on ahead, a bit like Red Indian scouts in a western film. Their job was to arrange meetings with people appropriate to the programme. We expressed very clearly our wish to avoid, as much as possible, elected politicians who we feared would utter the rhetoric that we, and millions like us, had heard so many times before. Instead, we agreed that the programme should bring us into contact with as many ordinary people as possible, to represent all sections of opinion in Northern Ireland, the Republic and the USA. The one absolute restriction we imposed was that we would not meet known terrorists, or people likely to sympathise with terrorist activity. We made it absolutely clear that the thought of being in the company of anyone who would try to justify Tim's death with a political rationale was anathema to us. Fortunately, we were pushing at an open door, and there was no resistance whatsoever to accepting our limited preconditions.

Once all the preliminary pieces were in place, Nick very generously invited the family to London to look around the BBC Television Centre. Dominic and Abbi were particularly thrilled with this, because they had never been to London before, despite many requests to do so when all the children were growing up. Wendy and I had always promised we would take them, but as is often the case the promise had never been translated into firm action, until now. Sadly it was a trip that Tim had never made either, although he had come closest in 1989 when Everton and Liverpool contested the FA Cup Final at Wembley. I had managed to get two tickets but not the

three I needed to take both Tim and Dom with me. Dom
had very generously told me to take Tim because he knew
how much it meant to him for Everton to be at Wembley.
But rather than take one and not the other, I had decided
to go alone. To cap it all, not only did Liverpool win,
but Tim's much-prized Everton scarf blew out of the car
window on the way south!

To try to make up for this, I bought Tim a replacement
scarf outside Wembley Stadium. I was sure he would
forgive me for losing his original scarf when he saw
the new one I'd bought him, but this didn't go to plan
either. Travelling home after the Final, I had the new
scarf blowing out of the window, only to find, on arriving
home, that it had unravelled completely into hundreds of
individual fibres!

Our first family weekend in London was very interesting,
especially when we were taken into the editing room for the
early-evening news programme at 6.00 p.m. Before that we
were shown around the newsroom where we met several
household names from the BBC news-reading team.

First we were introduced to Moira Stewart and Peter
Sissons, who were preparing for the six o'clock news.
Moira Stewart was remarkably informal and full of fun. She
remarked that although she is tall and has very long legs,
she is quite short from the waist upwards. Consequently,
she needs to sit on a cushion to raise her up to the height
the cameras need, but this causes her to slip to one side on
her chair, which leads to her being shouted at all the time
for slouching in her seat! A little later, when we watched
the news from the producer's editing room, when Moira
was off-camera, we heard someone cry, 'Sit up, Moira!'

As we talked to Moira, I became aware of the contrast
between the very serious image all newsreaders must
project and the light-hearted lady she really is.

Compared to Moira, Peter Sissons seemed an altogether

more serious person, but then he too revealed his alter ego when I told him that we had seen him recently on one of those long school photographs so popular in the days of grammar schools. Not surprisingly, he was very curious about this, and so I explained that a friend and neighbour, Brian Donnelly, had attended the Liverpool Institute School at the same time as him along with another famous old boy, Paul McCartney. On hearing this, Peter told us that he and Paul McCartney had been good friends for many years.

We kept our initial meeting with Moira and Peter quite brief because we knew that they were required to go into the news studios for final preparations before the news was transmitted, but they both told us to come into the studio once the broadcast was over.

Our host in the newsroom then took us to meet Michael Buerk, whom Dominic had already spotted. Dominic is a great fan of the programme *999*, which Michael Buerk hosts, and was keen to meet him. After courteous introductions all round, Michael told Dom to sit alongside him and talked at some length about the making of the programme. I could see from Dominic's eyes that he was totally absorbed by what Michael was telling him.

The time came for us to be ushered into the editing room, just a couple of minutes before 6 p.m. I commented to Wendy how friendly the people in the newsroom were, whether we had spoken to them or not.

In contrast to the newsroom, which had been orderly and quiet, the editing room seemed chaotic and frenzied. The four of us were shown where to sit, opposite a bank of TV monitor screens which filled an entire wall. The pictures on the screens constantly changed from one news story to another as the producer tried to decide in which order the items would go out to the nation.

We were given a timetable for the news stories, and then

we watched in total fascination as every one of them was rescheduled. None of the production team took any notice of us. It was as if we were not even in the room. Tension and stress were certainly running high as the clock ticked ever closer to six.

The nervous energy you could feel in the room did not diminish once transmission had started. I remember that one particular BBC reporter was in Paris to cover a news story about schoolchildren taken hostage in their school. The editing room had pictures but no sound. The reporter was fiddling with the microphone in his ear, and could hear London, but London could not hear him. As the minutes ticked by, making the decision whether or not to take the story critical, the poor reporter began dabbing his forehead to remove the beads of perspiration that were starting to appear.

Voice contact was made by telephone after the reporter borrowed a few francs from someone nearby, and then just as a discussion began about how to cover the interview, the picture disappeared! In the end, the story was relegated to a lower position and was covered by voice only with a still caption showing a road map of Paris, with a cross marking the place where the siege was taking place.

My lasting memory of this thirty minutes is one of high drama and, I'm sure, high blood pressure for all those involved. I felt certain that anyone over the age of thirty-five working on the production side of television, and particularly live TV, would be at constant risk of a heart attack. By the time the news was over, the room had become oppressively stuffy and I was quite relieved to step back into the larger, airier rooms outside.

We were taken to the studio where Peter and Moira were sorting their papers, putting their pens away and removing their microphones. I noticed that unlike other television studios we had seen, such as Granada's Albert

Dock Studio in Liverpool and the RTE studios in Dublin, the BBC News Studio had fully automated cameras – there was not a cameraman in sight.

Peter Sissons was now noticeably more relaxed than earlier, though Moira seemed just the same. She called Dom over to sit in her chair and read from the autocue. At first he was not too sure about this, but then decided to try it. He asked when he should begin, and was told that the autocue would move in response to his voice. He read several sentences and then abruptly stopped. When asked why he had stopped, he answered that he had seen a spelling mistake!

Peter Sissons then called Abbi over to try the hot seat, but she was far more reluctant than her brother. In the end, though, she gave in to the overwhelmingly superior numbers urging her to try it. However, unlike Dominic, who read for a couple of minutes, Abbi confined herself to just a few seconds.

When Peter told them that their efforts had been taped and we would be sent a copy, I wasn't sure whether they were pleased or terrified. Perhaps the best indication of their true feelings is that whenever the tape is played at home to show visitors, they will not stay in the room, and on one or two occasions have even resorted to dire threats to dissuade me from showing the tape.

Before being taken back to our hotel, we went to a private office where we all enjoyed a drink and some lovely sticky cream cakes. Dominic, thinking he was out of sight, stood at the window and ate three of the cakes, and only when his hand slowly reached for a fourth did I intervene to tell him others might want one!

Later that evening we had dinner in the hotel with Bob Strange and his wife Pam, and then adjourned to the lounge for coffee. As we talked about our respective families, I distinctly overheard American accents coming from the table next to ours, and, on impulse, I got up to go and speak to them. Excusing my interruption of their conversation as politely as I knew how, I asked whether I could join them for a few moments. They looked a little bemused but invited me to sit down. Before I began to ask them questions, I told them that my reasons for wishing to speak to them were serious and would be explained to them very shortly.

I asked where they were from. 'Albany, in New York State,' they told me.

'Is that near New York City?' I asked.

'Upstate,' was the reply, which I took to mean that it was quite some distance from New York City. Nevertheless, I took it for granted that living in this part of the USA meant that they would be more international in their outlook than their countrymen from a small Midwest town might be.

They told me that they had arrived in the UK only two days previously, and so I asked whether they had heard about the recent terrorist bombings in Britain. The City of London bomb had been widely reported in the media back home, they said. I continued, 'Did you hear or read of the IRA bombing in Warrington?' All three of them looked blankly at me, and one asked me, 'Where's Warrington?'

This confirmed my suspicions were well founded; that the deaths of Tim and Johnathan had not been reported on any significant scale in America. I set about explaining where Warrington was, who I was and what had happened on 20 March. I tried, as diplomatically as possible, to suggest that the US media, perhaps under pressure from the powerful Irish-American lobby, had decided that the deaths of two innocent young boys in Warrington at the hands of the IRA would not do the Republican cause any good at all and that this was why they had not reported the case in as much depth as the City of London bombing.

I watched their faces closely to see how interested they were in what this stranger was telling them, but I reached no firm conclusion. My conspiracy theory did not elicit any reaction, and I realised that apart from having had my suspicions confirmed, it would serve no further purpose for me to take up any more of their time. So I thanked them for listening and apologised for any inconvenience or embarrassment I may have caused them. As I departed, they very graciously offered me their condolences.

A little dejected, but unsurprised, I walked back to our table to face the quizzical looks of Wendy, Pam and Bob. I told them about my impromptu research and the results. Nobody was shocked by what I had learned although they too were disappointed.

Some weeks later, when we spent time in Boston making the *Panorama* programme, we were again to encounter this peculiar American insularity.

Saturday morning was spent in detailed discussion with Bob, Nick, Clive Syddall, Kilroy TV's managing director, and John Bridcut, the producer appointed to make the programme. While we drank endless cups of coffee and kicked issues around, Pam very kindly volunteered to take Dom and Abbi first to Harrods and then to Madame Tussauds, with her own two boys. An hour or so after they set off they were back, because Dom had decided he was far too grown-up to visit Madame Tussauds. Instead, he went back to his room where, unbeknown to us, he rang room service not once but several times, to order sandwiches and soft drinks. It was only on the Sunday when we came to check out and saw room service charges on our bill that we learned of his clandestine activities. He defended his actions by saying he did not know room service was chargeable!

Clive Syddall and John Bridcut were both informed about the structure of the programme which we had already mapped out with Bob and Nick, and they seemed happy with it. John had to set about the job of putting his production team together and then visit Wendy and me in Warrington to agree the final timetable. One very important matter agreed during the morning discussion was the target transmission date for the programme. This was to be the Monday following what would have been Tim's thirteenth birthday. His birthday would have been on 1 September, and the programme would be shown on 6 September.

The weekend was enjoyed by us all for a variety of different reasons. The children had been to London. They'd seen their first West End show, *Crazy for You*, and thanks to the theatre manager they had gone back stage to meet the performers. They'd been to Harrods – apparently an ambition of Dominic's for quite some time, although I never knew of it. Best of all, they had seen television in its raw and most exciting state – live! For our part, Wendy and I had met key people we were to work with, and had made positive progress on the nature and direction of the *Panorama* programme, and we had also enjoyed the social side of the weekend.

After the excitement and varied events of the weekend, everyday life returned to its previous mix of work, domestic chores and continuing press and TV interviews. Of the many interviews we undertook, some were especially memorable. The first of these, which I recall with great clarity, was an interview with *Hello* magazine. The reporter who conducted the interview was a very sympathetic lady by the name of Madeleine Kingsley. I have to admit that I don't subscribe to magazines and frankly I had never heard of *Hello*, but when I received a card asking me to phone Madeleine, I decided to do so more out of curiosity than anything else because they were the first magazine to request an interview. Madeleine came very close to tears during the interview, so moved was she by Tim's death and its impact on our family. It may have been the fact that she was not afraid to show her own feelings when interviewing us, as much as anything that Wendy or I said, that persuaded Dominic and Abbi to be photographed with us. By this time, both our children had developed a strong aversion through shyness to being photographed or filmed. They generally stayed out of sight when any interview was taking place, and even though I always asked them to be with us it was quite rare for them to agree to do so.

When *Hello* was published, it was a peculiar feeling to see the article and our photographs sandwiched between interviews with Liz Taylor and Malcolm McDowell! In this particular edition, the magazine also featured a series of black and white photographs and a short article about the marriage of the former Beirut hostage, Brian Keenan, a man I greatly admire. I must say that I felt I had more in common with Brian than I did with the aforementioned Hollywood movie stars.

Another interview at this time, which I recall very clearly but for quite different reasons, was with two researchers from a Channel 4 series designed to feature people of courage. When I was contacted, I was both flattered and interested in the programme's concept as it was explained to me over the telephone, and so I agreed to a preliminary interview taking place at home. The interview proceeded smoothly enough until, as sometimes happens quite without warning, I became upset while talking about Tim. I was in some difficulty for several minutes before I eventually regained my composure and we concluded our discussion. Later that evening, after the researchers had left, I commented to Wendy that I would be surprised if any more was heard from them. Wendy asked why I felt this and I said that my getting upset would have worried them that I would break down under questioning on the

programme. I was to be proved right when, after many
weeks, one of the researchers involved, rang me to explain
that they felt it was too early yet for me to cope with the
type of programme they had planned. Although I did not
agree with her, I saw no point in disputing her opinion,
and that was the end of that.

Another interview, which I found very worthwhile,
took place with the writer Brian Masters. He had been
commissioned by *The Times* newspaper to write an article
on the theme of people who have been bereaved and how
they cope with their grief. Brian's article was based on a
series of separate interviews with people who had suffered
well-publicised bereavements. The list of his contributors
included Ann West, the mother of Lesley Ann Downey,
the young girl murdered by Ian Brady and Myra Hindley
in the Moors murders; Gordon Wilson, whose daughter
Marie was killed by the IRA bombing in Enniskillen in
November 1987; Diana Lamplugh, whose daughter Suzy
disappeared in 1986; and Pat Cottril, the mother of Fiona
Jones, the recently married young woman murdered while
cycling in northern France.

Brian's questions throughout were intelligent and thought-
provoking. It must have seemed to him that he was
almost taking a sabbatical by writing this article, as it
was in complete contrast to the niche he had cornered
in the biography market. In recent years he has written
celebrated books on serial killers such as Denis Nilson
and Jeffrey Dahmer, the American who ate parts of his
victims.

As Brian said to us, you risk forgetting the victims of
callous crime when you write about serial killers like these.
Their deeds are so hideous and vile that they become
almost mesmerising in their ability to provoke endless
analysis. I'm sure that Brian found value in meeting these
interviewees, and I have him to thank for encouraging

me in my desire to write this account of the year since Tim's death.

Hunter Davies interviewed me for his weekly page in the *Independent*, though his interview was carried out from a different perspective to most of the others. He drew on our family's past and included in his final published text how Wendy and I met and how long we courted before marrying. I also liked the inclusion of my long-standing, if slightly tasteless, remark that I was a 'precision grinder'. This was my in-family joke, referring to the fact that Abbi was born on Dom's third birthday!

Hunter's interview was well balanced, touching on the good things that Tim's life had brought to our family as well as recounting details of the day of the bombing and his death. I found his style of writing pleasing and straightforward, and he struck me as the kind of man I'd enjoy having a pint with in the pub. His description of me was accurate and without over-elaboration: 'his seventies moustache is growing grey, Liverpool accent intact. Direct gaze, a feeling of strength, but not evangelical. He could be a PE teacher, one of the lads; tough when needed.'

The final interview I will mention from this period was particularly memorable for me. Nikki Stockley, the *Everyman* producer, who was still putting together her programme on Susan McHugh, the Peace 93 campaigner from Dublin, asked me where Tim liked to go most of all. I replied instantly, 'Goodison Park, Everton Football Club's ground.' Nikki asked me whether I would agree to be filmed there and without any hesitation I agreed. We arranged to meet one Friday afternoon in late May after I had finished work, and it turned out to be a beautiful sunny day. I was filmed sitting in the stands looking down on the pitch, and then walking from the corner spot to the centre circle. As I did so, I became completely oblivious of the camera, and simply went back in time to all those occasions when I'd taken Tim and Dominic to see Everton play. My father had first taken me in 1951 when I was just four years old, and in forty years of watching Everton I had never set foot on the pitch where so many of my heroes of old, and Tim's heroes of today, had played. Although it was the close season and the goals had been taken down, it still felt good to stand in the centre circle and slowly turn through 360 degrees, staring up into the sunlit stands as I did so. My memories of Tim were intense and strongly focused as I stood perfectly still in the eerie silence of this imposing football stadium where I'd seen so many great games played over the years. At that moment, I was sure Tim was looking down on me and saying, 'Go on, Dad, score one for me!'

When filming was finished, Nikki and her crew followed me back to Warrington where the interview continued with Wendy and me at home. When this edition of *Everyman* was eventually shown we were on holiday, but Nikki sent us a copy of the tape and, after watching it, I was a little disappointed that all the scenes inside Goodison were cut, even though quite a lengthy part of the interview with Wendy and me was used. However, Nikki, to her eternal credit, sent me a tape many months later with the rushes of me at Goodison. This tape is now among the many I have collected in my library about Tim. It comprises videotapes of everything we ever saw about Tim on television, along with the thousands of letters and cards we received, and all the other articles we have been sent, such as photographs, poems and sketches.

Not many days after my walk on the hallowed Goodison Park turf, another football event took place which was to prove to be really tough on my emotions. Tim's football club, Penketh United, had decided to dedicate a player of the year award in Tim's name, and Derek Finnigan, Tim's team coach, asked me to choose the winner from

Tim's own under-12 team and present the award at the annual prize-giving day. Choosing the player to receive the award was easy; nor did I find it difficult to make a brief speech congratulating him and thanking the club for naming the award after Tim. But then Derek called me back to the front of the crowded room to give me Tim's own trophy for representing the club in the season just finished. By the time I'd shaken Derek's hand, collected the trophy and returned to the side of the room, the tears were already in my eyes. I left quickly and went back to my car where I could express my feelings alone. As I did so, I had to fight back the resentment and anger burning inside me that Tim was not there to collect the trophy himself, just as he had done at the end of the three previous seasons.

This was one of those private moments, and there have been several, when my sadness and loss were mixed with bitter resentment that Tim would never do again all the things he had enjoyed doing so much with his friends, and that he would never encounter all the things he had the right to look forward to as he grew into manhood. At this moment these things, these simple, straightforward pleasures that Tim would never know, came flooding into my mind, just as they had done before and as they will do for the rest of my days. He would never marry, he would never make love to a woman he loved, and he would never bless this world with the beautiful children I know he would have produced. Each of these thoughts caused me intense pain and plunged me into the depths of despair.

I sat in the car with my head on the headrest and waited for these feelings to subside before driving home. Wendy could see that I had been upset and knew it was best not to make too much fuss. A means of dealing with these highly charged moments was beginning to emerge in our relationship, and this involved recognising the importance of each other's right to solitude as a way of dealing with the

awful reality that Tim was never coming back. We avoided
long, troubled silences or angry outbursts which would
have been dangerous and deeply unsettling. So there was
a joint, if unspoken acceptance of the benefits of periods
of solitude and inner reflection. Gordon Wilson's words
of advice, given to us when he came to our house after
attending Johnathan's funeral, came flooding back. He
told us then that we would not necessarily grieve together
or in the same way simply because we were married, and
of course he was right. For my part I'm still inclined to
bouts of anger and bitterness that block out everything
and everyone else. Wendy, by contrast, is much more
controlled, partly I think because she is such a practical
person. She busies herself with the many activities that she,
like so many other wives and mothers, tends to take care of.
She is less inclined than I am to show her innermost feelings
openly. This is because her intense grief is for personal and
private consumption only.

Over the course of the following weeks there were
many events to keep us busy and to keep the walls of
sanity soundly in place. In late May, our children's school
organised a Fun Run to raise money to pay for a memorial
garden within the school grounds in Tim's name. The Fun
Run was an annual event that usually attracted no more
than a hundred entrants, but when word got out that this
year's was for Tim, 650 men, women and children of all
ages turned out on what was to be the filthiest, wettest
night imaginable, but they all ran, walked or crawled the
four-mile course. Everyone who finished was given a medal
and Dominic's and Abbi's now hang proudly in the office
at home which is full of Tim memorabilia. Abbi came in
359th and Dominic 615th! I have to admit that they were
never built for athletics. Nevertheless, Wendy and I were
proud of them as we stood in the rain-drenched school
field watching everyone complete the run.

The Fun Run's sponsorship money, and a further £1500 raised by Albert Spiby on a sponsored twenty-three-mile walk from Adlington, near Chorley, to Warrington, was put together to finance Tim's memorial. This was subsequently unveiled on the first anniversary of his death on 25 March 1994.

Two days after the Fun Run, during the school half-term, the four of us went to Spain for a week's holiday. We stayed in an apartment in Malaga and spent the week discovering just how tough holidays were going to be from then on, as a family of four instead of five.

There were several reasons why we had a holiday at this time. There was the very basic desire to escape from our goldfish-bowl existence, at least for a while. Wendy and I also needed to work on re-establishing ourselves as a family unit. We had to find out whether we could handle a week away from home and away from the constant support of family, friends and the media, and, at the root of it all, could we possibly enjoy a holiday without Tim given that so much of the fun on past family holidays came directly from Tim's sunny personality and his ability to mix and make friends so quickly and easily with everyone he met?

Complicating these questions even further was the fact that Dominic and Abbi were approaching fifteen and twelve respectively and, as many parents know, children do not make friends at these ages as easily as they do when they are younger. As they grow older, their personalities become more complex and, like adults, they worry about rejection; they also have shyness to contend with, and no matter how much we might wish them to be more outgoing in a holiday environment, it just doesn't happen simply because we want it to. Add to all these perfectly normal teenage problems the murder of your brother, and you begin to understand that this was no ordinary package holiday.

Dominic and Abbi spent more time talking to one another and walking about together than we had ever known. For one week, it seemed that normal hostilities were suspended. Both of them were resigned to the fact that it was unlikely that they would make friends in such a short time and so they stayed close to each other and to Wendy and me.

One thing was clear, however. Dom had made up his mind that he would go home with a good suntan, and he worked hard at getting it. Copious amounts of oil and cream were absorbed into his skin as he slowly cooked under the Spanish sun. Abbi too looked much healthier as the week wore on. Their pasty winter-white complexions gradually turned golden brown, and as always happened on our continental holidays their hair turned blonder or, in Abbi's case, whiter than it already was.

We walked around the resort of Benalmadena and got to know our way around quite well. Much to Dominic's delight, we even found a McDonald's, but generally we ate at a small restaurant run by a British couple who cooked the kind of food Dom and Abbi would usually eat, while Wendy and I tried the local dishes washed down with affordable Spanish red wine.

On our second day at the resort, we encountered a very loquacious Ulsterman called Dan. He worked in the timeshare resort we were staying in, and had been advised by the timeshare company of our arrival. After going through the obligatory invitation to extend our timeshare ownership, he then confined himself simply to being our guide, friend and mentor for the remainder of the week.

He took us around the town in his black open-top jeep, which had an anti-roll bar and huge wide wheels. It will come as no surprise to you to read that Dominic was most impressed with this macho machine with its gleaming paintwork and black leather seats.

Apart from Dan, we did not meet anyone and so we got used to spending time in each other's company. Each evening before we began our meal, I called upon us to remember our departed son and brother by raising our glasses to Tim. Without fail, every time I did this, a lump came into my throat. We talked fondly about Tim as we ate together, remembering happy times, especially previous holidays. As I knew I would, I often became upset and tearful at these times, but Dom and Abbi, to their credit, never looked embarrassed or awkward about their dad being upset in public. Certainly I always felt better, almost as if I was cleansed, after these family occasions. Nothing could bridge the yawning gap left by Tim's death, certainly not a holiday, but there was a sense of relief that in a very quiet and low-key way we had benefited from the time together on our own, doing simple things and enjoying simple pleasures.

By the time we returned home, we looked much healthier than we had when we set off, but our inner well-being was still extremely fragile as we were no nearer to knowing or understanding what life was going to be like henceforth. An important week had passed without mishap, and frankly that was all we could reasonably expect as we put a brave face on things for each other's sake. The bonus was that we had talked about Tim without too much faltering – apart from me, that is. But even now, when I talk about Tim, my breathing becomes shallow and irregular and my heart starts pounding so much that I half expect that others can hear it.

8

Late in November, a particularly powerful letter arrived from someone we'd never met, a woman called Linda Byron. Although it was just one of many thousands of letters we received after 20 March, it stated so many things with which I agreed and in a way in which I would have expressed them myself that it seemed to sum up the rationale Wendy and I had for making the *Panorama* programme.

Linda said in her letter:

I wrote to you in March following the Warrington bomb outrage. I expressed the view that perhaps there was something pre-ordained in this awful tragedy of two very appealing young boys being killed and a father with obvious communication skills having the ability 'to tell it like it is'. I certainly had a flash of insight, a psychic experience, call it what you will, at your press conference, that something very special was happening here. Listening to your television appearances since that time, I have come to believe that you share this view of some deeper reason or purpose to the tragedy . . . I really do believe that you have, and will, make a big contribution to the peace process in Northern Ireland.

As you come to the turn of the year, like all bereaved people, I am sure you will think, *This was the year we lost our son, but just remember, it was also the year the nation found him, the terrorists*

*were shamed by him and the seeds of peace were
sown by him*. Perhaps, paradoxically his and your
biggest contribution was changing hearts and minds
in England . . . Obviously the road to peace will be
tortuous but I hope you gain great comfort from the
role that you and Tim have played in it.

Many times since this tragedy took Tim from us, I have
considered the statistical odds against such a random act
of terrorism taking our son's life. I keep coming back to
these unanswerable questions:

Why Warrington?
Why Bridge Street?
Why that litter bin?
Why the day before Mothers' Day?
Why that precise moment?
Why did Tim not get well away from the area after
  the first bomb?
Why did Tim run towards, and not away from, the
  second bomb?
Why did the shrapnel hit Tim, and
Why did it hit his head and not another part of
  his body?

When I reflect on all these questions, I come to the same
conclusion every time, that the odds, even if they could
be calculated, would be astronomically long on Tim being
killed the way he was.

This process inevitably leads to further questions, such
as the one implicit in Linda's letter: 'perhaps there was
something pre-ordained in this awful tragedy'. I dare say
there are those who would laugh at any notion of destiny
playing a part in Tim's death, arguing that it was a totally
random act, no more and no less.

Increasingly, I have come to believe that this explanation is too simple and is a denial of the fact that every life has a unique purpose, great or small. Tim had a short but happy life in an ordinary family. Had he lived a full life, I guess he would probably have enjoyed a normal life with normal pleasures and the kind of highs and lows that we all experience along the way.

Being robbed of his life has turned me into something of a crusader. I was possessed with the single-minded determination to make people look at Tim, to know about him and, most important of all, to know that his death would not be allowed to be forgotten. Whenever I reconsider whether this is the right thing to do, I always draw great strength and fresh commitment from the many letters Wendy and I have received, urging us to go on.

So it was with *Panorama*. Here the BBC was saying, You have a story to tell, so tell it. By my nature, I have always been outspoken, sometimes foolishly so, but that's the way I am. I could no more deny myself this unique opportunity from the BBC than I could forget Tim. I am driven to keep his memory alive so that it may serve as a constant reminder to those involved in terrorism, as well as to those who are simply indifferent or even tired of the whole bloody business, that murder and intimidation are not the way to bring about a settlement in Ireland; they achieve only one thing, the crippling of the lives of innocent families.

A key aspect of making the *Panorama* programme, and one that we considered very seriously, was that it meant we would be away from our children for almost a month at such a critical time. We experienced conflicting emotions: should we further the cause of peace with Tim or sacrifice it for Dom and Abbi? We had to be sure. Wendy asked her parents to move into our house for the whole period. We talked to Dominic and Abbi about their

feelings, and they reassured us that they would be fine with
their grandparents. Dominic was particularly insistent that
we should make the programme about his 'kid brother',
although he was a little less understanding when we told
him that he and Abbi could not accompany us on the final
part of the programme – our trip to Boston.

Filming began with Wendy and I discussing over the
kitchen table what we hoped to achieve by making the
programme. We were told to ignore the camera and just
chat together as we would normally. Needless to say, this
is easier said than done, but the producer, John Bridcut,
was satisfied with our initial efforts.

The next day, the new brain scanner at Walton Hospital
was dedicated to Tim, and the camera crew endeavoured
to film the proceedings, which took place in an extremely
small area crowded with guests and press photographers.
The dedication of the scanner was the result of a request
made by Mr Miles to Wendy and me when we were at
Walton. We both felt that it was a fitting tribute to Tim,
who had been the first patient to go through the scanner.
After the dedication ceremony, the camera crew came
home with us for a buffet meal, which gave us all an
opportunity to get to know each other a little better.

The crew were selected by John Bridcut and Clive
Syddall. Jonathan Partridge, the cameraman, was from
South Africa. Simon Farmer, the sound engineer, came
from London, and Julie Singleton, the production assistant, was a Geordie in exile. Julie's job was to take care
of accommodation, travel plans, food and, most importantly, to carry the ready cash around in her bumbag for
contingencies. Indeed, Julie looked after all our collective
needs and did it with good heart and good humour.

Perhaps because we were all so very different, the group
dynamics worked well. Certainly a camaraderie built on
good chemistry developed over the days and weeks we

spent together, and this helped to strengthen our vision of the programme; only very occasionally can I recall there being any discord between Wendy and I on the one hand and John Bridcut and the crew on the other.

The only other person to spend time with us during the making of the programme was Mike Day, the Press Officer appointed by the BBC. It was Mike's job to deal with any local or national newspapers who approached us during the making of the programme. Understandably, the BBC, which was investing a large sum, was determined not to have the programme's impact diminished by unplanned publicity.

As time went on, Wendy and I began to feel rather sorry for Mike Day, because the crew appeared to believe that part of his job was to be a spy in the camp. As a result, the welcome mat was not always out when Mike arrived. Although we were aware of this difficulty in the relationship, there seemed little that Wendy and I could do about it apart from be friendly with Mike on a personal level.

Mike's role extended beyond the completion of filming. It was his responsibility to organise pre-transmission press conferences and news coverage via newspapers, magazines, and so on, but throughout the time we were filming Mike was generally in the background.

It was Friday, 2 July when Wendy and I flew from Manchester into Belfast's Aldergrove airport for our first-ever visit to Northern Ireland. We were surprised that the visible security at the airport was so low-key. We had expected to see a lot of armed policemen and British Army vehicles inside and outside the perimeter, but there were none to be seen.

The film crew arrived from Heathrow a little later than us, and Julie immediately busied herself hiring the two Austin Montego estate cars and a transit van which were to carry the people and equipment over the weeks to come.

John and the others loaded the van while Wendy and I drank coffee. I had offered to help with the loading, but was politely told that they were used to it and so it was better to let them get on with it, but then John asked me to drive one of the two cars so that he could make calls on his mobile phone to the programme's key researcher in Northern Ireland, Gwynneth Jones.

Gwynneth was employed by Ulster Television, the independent regional television station in Northern Ireland. With her local knowledge, she was to prove an extremely valuable addition to our team. Born and bred in Northern Ireland, her obviously Welsh name intrigued me, but the explanation was simple enough – her father was Welsh!

The first stop after leaving the airport was our hotel, the Forte Crest in Dunmurry. Cases and personal baggage were hurriedly deposited in our respective rooms before we sped off to Dungannon for our first meeting, which was with Gordon and Joan Wilson from Enniskillen.

We met at a place called the Inn on the Park, a convenient meeting point for all concerned. The Wilsons were due to fly to America later that same day for a holiday, so we were delighted that they could spare the time to meet us.

Gordon had made a very positive and lasting impression on Wendy and me and we were pleased and more than a little relieved that he and Joan were to be the first people we would meet in Northern Ireland. The meeting also gave us our first real insight into the work that goes into documentary film-making as well as some of the frustrations involved.

Wendy and I were told to wait outside, and on John's signal walk inside but not to look directly at the camera. We followed our instructions to the letter, and on stepping inside the doorway were greeted by Joan and Gordon. We all exchanged warm handshakes and, after Gordon had introduced Joan, the four of us walked across to the bar where we ordered drinks. Drinks in hand, we set off to a corner seat to begin our conversation. However, just as we began, John stopped us and asked us to do it all again. We all trooped back to our original positions to repeat the exercise. Thankfully, this time John did not call us back. I have to say that I could detect no obvious differences between the first and second shoot, except that we now had two rounds of drinks on the table.

The choice of a corner table enabled us to pair off, with Wendy chatting to Joan and me chatting to Gordon. My discussion with Gordon was proceeding very smoothly and fluently when Jonathan called a halt, saying that the camera's battery needed to be replaced. This only took a minute or two, but it was a frustrating interruption to our free-flowing dialogue, especially as when the filming stopped John asked us not to carry on talking.

We resumed our conversation and it was a relief to find that we were able to pick up where we had left off without too much difficulty, but then a couple of minutes after that Jonathan again called a halt. This time it was because the videotape needed to be replaced. Again we all awaited the 'go' signal and when the discussion did restart, I couldn't help feeling that it had lost some of its spontaneity. I was very conscious of the fact that I was putting my questions to Gordon in a slightly different way from the first time and they did not seem as effective third time round.

The interview ended with the reassuring realisation that the camera and boom microphone had been quite unobtrusive. I remembered all the times I had filmed family and friends with my cine camera and, more recently, my video camera, and how often people became unnatural once they were aware of the lens pointing at them. Based on these experiences, I had some misgivings that we would stumble over our words or simply dry up as we were being filmed – thankfully neither fear materialised.

Another slight worry I'd had before the filming began was whether I should plan my questions in advance, or whether I should stick to my normal interviewing practice of asking questions as they came into my mind during the course of the interview. Perhaps I should explain that, having been in personnel management for twenty-five years, I have conducted many hundreds of job interviews, and although interviewing a job candidate is different from the kind of journalistic interviewing I was now carrying out, the process is essentially the same. An interview is merely a process of discovery. Asking questions, followed sometimes by supplementary questions triggered by the course of the interview was not an alien business for me. Perhaps because of this experience it fell to me, rather than Wendy, to ask the questions. At least, she seemed more comfortable for it to be so.

Subsequently people have asked me whether the questions were my own or whether I merely acted as spokesman using somebody else's prepared questions. I can state quite categorically that the questions were always my own and, had it been otherwise, I would not have been interested in making the programme.

After an enjoyable lunch, Joan and Gordon set off for Dublin to catch their flight to America, while we returned to Belfast to get our first glimpse of the city we had only ever previously seen on television. Our guide was Brian Feeney, an ex-SDLP city councillor. We were to meet Brian twice during the course of making the programme, and between these two meetings his son was to discover a bomb beneath the family's car. Fortunately, it was a fairly crude device which was easily spotted. Nevertheless, the matter-of-fact way in which Brian talked about it was a chilling reminder to us of how commonplace such things are in Belfast, and that although he was no longer active in local politics, Brian was still a target for the terrorists.

On the first occasion we met Brian, it was decided that he would drive the Montego and give a commentary as he went along. Jonathan squeezed himself and his camera into the passenger seat to film Brian talking and driving through the areas we were being shown. We felt sorry for Jonathan enduring such cramped conditions, but he assured us that he had put up with a lot worse situations during his career.

Simon and John shared the boot space behind the back seat where Wendy and I sat in comfort. Simon had given Brian and me radio microphones so that our conversation could be recorded as he drove us around the areas that showed most starkly the divisions between Catholic and Protestant, Loyalist and Republican. Only two days before our arrival, the most serious Loyalist street rioting for twenty years had broken out, but this time the RUC were the target for their anger. A Loyalist march, planned to go through a predominantly Catholic area, was cancelled by the RUC, causing considerable annoyance to the organisers, and as a result a demonstration against the RUC was organised in the Shankill Road area. One of those in the demonstration carried a hand grenade, presumably intended for the RUC, but it had exploded before he could throw it, killing him and causing a number of injuries. This led to civil disorder in Loyalist areas, on a scale unseen for years.

As we were to discover, the build-up in tension was largely based on the increasing feeling of isolation among some hardline Loyalists. They felt that Catholics had gained a good deal in terms of political, social and housing benefits by employing civil disorder as a tactic, and perhaps it was time for Loyalists to do the same in order to redress the balance. This was a desperate philosophy, but without doubt it had captured the mood of many disillusioned Protestants in the Shankill and other Loyalist areas.

As Brian drove us into some of these areas, including Tigers Bay, the Shankill and Glencairn estate, we saw kerbstones painted alternately red, white and blue and houses festooned with Union flags, standing amid great landscapes of wasteland and dereliction. Many of the buildings were unoccupied with their roof timbers exposed, windows smashed or bricked up with breeze-blocks. I remember particularly well one street on a hillside, where every house on both sides of the street was unoccupied, with every doorway and window bricked up. Yet one house in the middle of the terrace was still being lived in. Not only that, but the lady of the house was painting the inside of her window frames and still clearly taking pride in her home despite being surrounded by nothing but empty and wrecked houses. Her house also displayed the customary Union flag.

Wherever we went in Loyalist areas, men and young boys were erecting huge bonfires to be lit at midnight on the eve of the Orange Day parades. Wendy and I contrasted the size of these bonfires with those built in our own community for Guy Fawkes' Night on 5 November. The fires in Belfast made the ones back home look no bigger than the fire you would light in your front room.

Brian's commentary was excellent, very informative and so comprehensive that there were very few questions I needed to ask him. However, I did ask him about his own background. He had studied at Reading and Cambridge universities and had a doctorate in medieval politics. As he told me this, I smiled wryly at the thought that medieval politics was probably the perfect qualification for understanding Ulster politics as deeply as Brian so obviously did.

On our tour of the Loyalist areas, he pointed out the so-called 'peace lines' separating Protestant and Catholic communities from one another. Typically, the barriers stood anything from fifteen to twenty feet in height. They represented the terrible division of a society along sectarian lines. The past twenty-five years have led more and more to this separation of ordinary people. The Protestants feel very strongly that they have been deliberately squeezed out of their traditional areas by the policy of successive British governments to relocate Catholic families. Over the years, this has led to the minority Protestant population moving to districts where Protestant families are concentrated. We heard this process referred to as 'ethnic cleansing' by a number of Protestants living in the Shankill Road area, which is itself surrounded by predominantly Catholic communities.

We were experiencing little hope or optimism by the time our circumnavigation of the ghetto heartland had ended, but we were grateful to Brian for his skilled explanation of life 'the way it is' in those parts of Belfast that he had shown us. I was interested to note, as we toured around the Catholic Falls Road area, that so much of the housing was new. This was often in stark contrast to some of the housing in the Protestant areas, and especially the bleakly depressing Glencairn estate. The rows of old terraced houses at least looked tidy, but the Glencairn estate was a classic example of 1960s planning mistakes. Concrete tenement buildings were devoid of any sense of community. Shops and other amenities, which most of us take for granted, were in short supply. Of course, there are inner-city areas in mainland towns and cities which are no better than Glencairn, but we first saw it on a wet, grey day with burned-out cars still smouldering from riots just two days previously, and the impression we came away with was one of profound depression and a real absence of hope. It would be very hard indeed for the human spirit to blossom in a place like the Glencairn estate. I say these things without any intention of being gratuitously offensive to the people who live there, but out of sympathy with them for having to live in such a soulless place.

Whether by accident or design I do not know, but the next morning we travelled north out of Belfast to a youth peace camp near Coleraine. This experience served to lift our spirits considerably after the low point reached the previous afternoon. In fact, it was to be the general pattern throughout our time in Northern Ireland, that one visit would depress our spirits only to be followed by another which would raise our hopes again.

So it was with the peace camp. It was here that we met Paul Smyth again. You will recall that Paul and his girlfriend Kim had been at the McHughs' house in Dublin when we first travelled to the Republic. Paul is youth leader of a camp that comprises an old farmhouse, some outhouses and an acre or two of land for growing crops and rearing a few animals. It also proudly boasts a brand-new accommodation building, financed to some extent by EC grants. On the Saturday that Wendy and I arrived with the TV crew, a group of sixteen- to twenty-year-olds was staying for the weekend. There were rather more girls than boys, but an even mix of Protestants and Catholics. They lived in various towns across Northern Ireland, but the one thing in which they were all united was a belief in the need for peace. Their religion, politics, sex and home town all came a distant second to the common desire to work for peace and reconciliation.

Most encouraging of all was the fact that there were three among them who had directly suffered tragedies due to the troubles, but who were still completely committed to non-violent ways of bringing about peace. One girl, now in her early twenties, had seen her father shot dead in front of her when she was just thirteen, and two of the boys had lost their sisters in a brutally atrocious way when a so-called Loyalist paramilitary attack had been carried out against a local businessman who owned a mobile roadside café. In their desire to teach the businessman a lesson – not to trade with Catholics – the caravan had been sprayed with bullets, killing the two young and innocent girls, sisters of Sean and John.

Although they had suffered grievously, both had chosen to resist the urging from their own sides to take revenge. Sean freely admitted to us that he had been wavering at one point and had contemplated taking up arms himself. But he had been associated with peace movements before his sisters' death and in the end turned his face away from violence and revenge and back towards peace and reconciliation. Wendy and I both found great strength in these young people and were heartened by their attitudes. Sean was a lively, outspoken young man as they all were, and not in the least how those sceptical about peace campaigners might characterise them. John, the other young man who had lost his sister, was disabled with a crippled leg but nonetheless was a real character with a tremendous zest for life, a great sense of humour, and an unquenchable desire to do all he could for peace.

For well over an hour we all sat around having an honest, no-holds-barred debate about the prospects for peace. There were strong differences of opinion on key issues. For example, most of the Catholic youngsters believed that Sinn Fein should be allowed to sit at the negotiating table. Their opinion was not based on support for Sinn Fein politics, but on the view that it was unrealistic for them to be kept away. A view they also expressed strongly was that extreme Unionists were hypocritical in their position vis-à-vis the Loyalist paramilitary groups, the UVF, UFF, and so on. They implied that whereas Sinn Fein was quite openly the political arm of the IRA, extreme Unionists were not really distinct from the UVF and UFF at all. I challenged them to give me proof to back up this view, but I got none, or at least none that I could say convinced me.

The peace camp was not a community without its share of prejudice, half-truths and bias, and I don't suppose there was ever any possibility that it could be otherwise within the overall context of Northern Ireland.

Notwithstanding this, however, the common denominator among all those staying there was a thirst for peace and a readiness to accept and accommodate each other's differences without the need for violence.

It was also interesting to note, as we did many times during the weeks that followed, that the view of most Catholics we spoke to was that they favoured Northern Ireland remaining within the UK rather than becoming united with the Republic. This opinion usually had more to do with the harsh economic and pragmatic realities of life than it did with being pro-Union and anti-Republic, but nevertheless it shattered one of the pieces of political baggage I'd brought to Ireland with me, namely that all Catholics are Republicans. It just isn't so.

One of the tougher problems that some of the kids in the camp told us they had to deal with was the pressure from their parents to stay away from peace movements and support their own community. Many of them told us that they were diametrically opposed to their parents' political position. This obviously made life very difficult for them at home.

By the time we left the camp, we felt we had witnessed a good and heartening side of Northern Ireland, and we hoped that we'd met some of its future political leaders and opinion-makers.

On the drive back into Belfast, we could see the huge cranes known locally as 'David and Goliath' in the Harland and Wolff shipyard, beyond which lay Belfast Lough. Although we saw many impressive sights in Northern Ireland, this symbol of a shrinking British industry was still very striking.

We spent the afternoon with a Protestant family living just off the Shankill Road. Alfie and Gina McCrory and their five sons were our hosts for three hours. They live in a small but modern house in a square behind the Shankill. Alfie is a community worker and Gina a housewife. The crew rearranged the McCrorys' lounge furniture to ensure we could all get in, and the camera and boom microphone were put in place before the interview began.

Alfie is a man with clear and definite views, who answered all my questions with the conviction of a man who has to live in his community long after the cameras have left. I found him easy to talk to as he did not hold back, although we knew that Gwynneth, our researcher, had experienced some difficulty in getting Alfie to agree to the interview following the rioting that had taken place over the preceding couple of days. A BBC TV news crew had been attacked two nights before, and since then there had been a perfectly understandable unease on Alfie and Gina's part to be seen with another television crew. Alfie stressed to Wendy and me that until the rioting he and Gina had planned to take us along the Shankill where everyone on the street would have shaken us by the hand and expressed their genuine sympathy to us over Tim's death. The atmosphere was no longer conducive to do this in Alfie's opinion, and I was certainly not going to argue with his local knowledge.

After the interview inside their home, Alfie and Gina took us on to the Shankill, but before any filming began Alfie walked ahead on his own up the road for two blocks to engage in private discussion with three men. When he returned, he explained that he had told the men who we were and why we were filming. Apparently this satisfied them sufficiently for approval to be given for us to film inside a couple of shops, but then the crew had to remain in one place as Wendy, Alfie, Gina and I walked along the road for some outdoor shots.

When the original filming was completed, I asked Alfie about the men he had conferred with, and although he laughed off my suggestion that they were local para-militaries, I remained unconvinced; after all, why else would he have been obliged to explain what was happening and then seek their approval? Still, we came to realise that things are often not as they seem in Northern Ireland.

The first shop we were taken into was a confectioner's. The lady owner, her assistants and the customers all expressed their sympathy to us and said how pleased they were that we had come over to see things for ourselves first-hand. This was to be said to us many times, though it was usually accompanied by the pointed remark that it was very rare indeed for English people to be seen in the troubled areas. We always accepted that the welcome given to us was genuine wherever we went, but when we stepped into the second shop with Alfie and Gina the atmosphere was anything but welcoming. Without ever discovering from Alfie why, we encountered no warmth and little enough sympathy. The interview with the shop-owner, who was clearly in no mood for conversation, was mercifully brief and saved us all from too much embarrassment.

We were to spend more time with the McCrorys, but our first encounter had been valuable, enabling us to learn directly of the hopes and fears of an ordinary Protestant family caught up in an area that they themselves described as a ghetto. It was Alfie who talked to us about the belief gaining ground in Loyalist minds of a hidden agenda

between the British and Irish governments aimed at finding
a way of getting the British out of Northern Ireland. He
warned us of a terrible backlash were this ever to happen.
In answer to my questions, he repeatedly told us that
the Loyalist paramilitaries were just a reactionary force
to counter the IRA. If the IRA ended its campaign of
violence, Alfie told us, the Loyalist paramilitaries would
have no further reason for carrying on with their campaign.
He also spoke about the growing perception in the minds
of Protestants that because of the Anglo-Irish Agreement
of 1985 the RUC was less and less their police force as it
had always been seen to be, and was more and more under
the control, even if indirectly, of Dublin.

As everyone has seen on television, political graffiti is
commonplace in Northern Ireland. The Loyalists depict
King William astride his horse at the defeat of the Catholics
at the Battle of the Boyne in 1690, while Republicans
favour the forearm padlocked across a green map of
Ireland. These, and variations on the same theme, are
seen throughout the province, but we noticed in several
places new references to the RUC being paid in punts,
a clear reference to the Loyalist belief that the Irish
government has an increasing say in the governing of
Northern Ireland.

Before we departed from the McCrory household, Gina
very kindly provided sandwiches and cake for everyone.
Considering that their home had been significantly dis-
rupted during our invasion, we thought they had been
remarkably hospitable throughout.

Looking back on that afternoon, the one thing we found
distasteful was when Wendy went to the spot where Brian
McCallum had died. This was the man who had accidently
blown himself up with the grenade. Graffiti in the Falls
Road referred to him, with bitter irony, as the 'handyman'.
When we asked why, we were told that this epithet was

given to him because, quite apart from killing himself, he
had blown his own hand off. Wendy stood at the spot where
he had died; it was marked with flowers and cards. Some
of the cards referred to him as a 'brave soldier'. We found
it morally repugnant that these words should be used in
relation to a man intent on hurling a grenade at policemen,
just as we were to find it similarly repugnant one week later
when we were shown a headstone engraved with the names
of IRA 'volunteers' who had died since 1969.

We returned to the hotel in the early evening very tired
after our first two days of filming. It was proving to be
mentally far more exacting than we had anticipated. We
realised just how hard the production team, under John's
direction, worked. Breaks were virtually non-existent,
with snacks and refreshments generally grabbed while
travelling from one film location to another. Furthermore,
filming went on till very late in the day as a rule; we would
all be up, breakfasted and out by 8.30 a.m. and then not
return sometimes till 8.30 p.m. or even later. Perhaps
naively, Wendy and I had not realized how punishing this
schedule would be.

The next day, Sunday, 4 July, we were to experience
the most emotionally draining experience of the whole
four weeks. We travelled to a very small town in the
north called Rasharkin. There we met the family of Gerry
Dalrymple. He was one of four men murdered by Loyalist
terrorists in the neighbouring coastal town of Castlerock
on 25 March, the day Tim died. At the time it was seen
as a tit-for-tat killing for the IRA bombing in Warrington.
Unbeknown to the other three, one of the four men killed
was a member of the IRA.

As we pulled up outside the home of the murdered man's
eldest son, we saw Joe Dalrymple, his wife and his two
young daughters and son all lined up in their Sunday-best
clothes. We walked up the path as Joe walked down to

greet us. I could see that he was beginning to cry even before we met, and his tears brought tears to my eyes and to Wendy's. We exchanged words of welcome before Joe took us to meet his family inside the house. Finally, he introduced us to his mother, Patricia, who, just like Joe, was upset before we even exchanged greetings.

We were taken through into the kitchen where a lovely buffet had been prepared for us. The crew set up the equipment and filmed what was to be a tearful conversation. Everyone expressed mutual sympathy and questioned what kind of people could perpetrate such acts of barbarity. Patricia and Joe said they lived in a town where Catholic and Protestant lived side by side together in peace, and they told us that they had received as many expressions of sympathy and support from their Protestant friends and neighbours as they had from their fellow Catholics.

Joe was at pains to tell us that the violence that takes place in Belfast was rare in smaller communities, and that his family bore no ill will towards Protestants; they simply wished that peace would come to this troubled part of the world and come soon.

We received great hospitality at the home of the Dalrymples and wished that the men who had killed Gerry could have seen the effects of their barbarous behaviour on this delightful, peace-loving family.

By the time we left Rasharkin, we were all in a very quiet, reflective frame of mind. The afternoon was spent at the Giant's Causeway, a place of remarkable beauty on the northern coast of Antrim. During our time there, Wendy bought a small black ceramic dog to take back with us to place on Tim's grave. For years, Tim had wanted us to buy a dog, but because we already had a cat, we decided it would not be a good idea. Wendy bought the dog so that Tim would be able to see it sitting beneath his headstone;

it would keep silent watch over him in the stillness of the place where he now lay.

After a few hours spent taking in the spectacular scenery, Gwynneth drove Wendy and me back to Belfast. To my great shame, I fell asleep on the back seat. I think the fresh air at the Giant's Causeway must have had a soporific effect, on top of which the busy schedule of the past couple of days was beginning to take its toll.

Once we were back in Belfast, Gwynneth drove us around the Lower Falls Road area, where we saw a number of house gable-ends with murals depicting support for Sinn Fein and the '75 years' struggle, 1916–1991'. Army patrols were very evident in this Catholic area, in contrast to the Loyalist areas where we had seen none.

Watching British soldiers on the streets of a British city was a very strange feeling. Typically, they would be in groups of ten, generally on the move with one or two walking backwards to watch out for attack from the rear. There were usually one or two at a time kneeling or crouching in the doorways of houses or against a wall. It was even more bizarre to see soldiers down on one knee in residential areas with their weapons raised, looking down the sights, while there were very young children playing games no more than a couple of feet away. These early images of Belfast street life served as an awful reminder of how dire the situation in Northern Ireland is. As well as the foot patrols, the number of armoured Land Rovers and other, larger, personnel carriers was far greater than we had imagined it would be.

Joint Army/RUC checkpoints on the major roads in and out of the city, especially on the edge of the commercial centre, were manned by armed soldiers and policemen. For us, one of the more surprising aspects of the checkpoints was the courtesy and good humour of the RUC policemen. I cannot recall one occasion when the greeting and the help offered by the police was anything less than first-class, and I was intrigued by the fact that it was always the RUC officer who would speak and never the soldiers on duty.

The one time we had a slight brush with anyone in uniform was when we wanted to drive beyond a manually operated barrier across a city-centre road. At first glance, I thought the man on duty was a policeman, but then I realised he was a private security guard. His manner was quite different and rather brusque when I asked if we could have access to the blocked-off street. He cut me short as I explained our purpose, and told me to do a U-turn in the road and go back. When he told me a second time even more impatiently, I decided to give up and do as he said. Having followed his instructions and turned our vehicle around, we noticed that Julie was chatting to him. Her smile charmed him into allowing our vehicles access after all. We never did establish what it was that Julie said to him to bring a little human warmth to the situation.

An essential part of the process of maintaining the programme's shape and balance was the organisation of as many face-to-face meetings as was practicable in the time available. Perhaps the most appropriate analogy to reflect this philosophy would be to describe the whole process as like putting together a jigsaw, with the added complication of not knowing what the final picture would look like.

The next piece in the jigsaw, then, was a journey to Portadown, where we spent several hours with a local businessman, John Bolas. I would describe John, an Irish Protestant in his early to mid fifties, as being a typically ebullient and gregarious Ulsterman. He was a joy to spend time with, because despite having suffered the same fate as many small businessmen in Northern Ireland in having his business premises completely or partly destroyed by bomb damage, he remained optimistic and determined to carry on regardless.

After telling us that his dry-cleaning business in Lurgan had been destroyed by an IRA bomb in March 1992, he showed us around his Portadown shop, which had sustained extensive blast damage from a more recent thousand-pound IRA bomb which had exploded a short distance away in the main town centre shopping area. Like John's shop, many other shops nearby had their windows boarded up, and many displayed the sign 'Sale – bomb-damaged stock'.

John told us how much he loved his home town and how its residents, many of whom he knew personally, got along together well. He stressed to Wendy and me that he had no prejudices and simply yearned for peace. Rather like me, his challenge to all the conflicting parties was to set aside the preconditions they placed in the way of progress towards a negotiated settlement. John's position seemed to me to be that both the moderates and the extremists have the right to state their positions and join in the debate, but the men of violence must renounce violence before they can be included.

On a lighter note, John proved to be a great help with a practical problem I'd encountered. I'd travelled to Ireland, appropriately enough, in an old pair of bright-green shoes, but had forgotten to bring any other casual shoes to change into. My old green shoes were just about acceptable with my old green cord trousers, but hardly looked the part when dressed in anything else. When the filming with John was finished, he took me across town to a shoe shop whose owner he knew well, and after he had explained who I was and my predicament, the shop's owner very kindly gave me a generous discount off a pair of brown shoes. John also presented Wendy with a beautiful crystal vase just as we were ready to leave Portadown.

It was 6.00 p.m. as we waved goodbye to John and set off on our long journey to Listowel in County Kerry in the Irish Republic. This was one of the features in the programme which Wendy and I had suggested when the various elements to be included were being discussed.

Quite soon after Tim died, we received a book of condolences from the town of Listowel. A lady called Del O'Sullivan, with a group of close friends, had organised this book, which contained just over two thousand signatures – I know because I sat and counted them one evening! At the time, neither Wendy nor I knew what size Listowel was, but we imagined it was medium-sized and that the number of signatories represented a fair proportion of the town. Subsequently, we were told by Del that the town's population was only around three thousand people, and that it had not been thought right for children under the age of eleven to sign the book. This meant that the vast majority of the town's people, and not just a fair proportion, had signed their condolences. As far as the programme was concerned, it struck Wendy and me that beyond visiting Dublin, we should also travel to a rural community to meet ordinary Irish people. Where better than Listowel? we concluded.

We agreed with John Bridcut that the researcher should go on ahead to ask Del and her friends whether they would agree to be interviewed about the Warrington bombing, but without informing them that Wendy and I would be coming too. The idea was that the camera would capture the look of surprise and, we hoped, pleasure on their faces when we met for the first time.

The journey from Portadown to Listowel took eight hours, although we did stop for petrol, and also for dinner at a delightful pub-restaurant in the centre of a town called Tullamore. This was at the approximate halfway point in our journey.

Over dinner, I decided to get to know more about the crew and John. Jonathan, the cameraman, was married

with a young child and planned to return to his native South
Africa one day. He had filmed in some of the world's hot
spots, such as Afghanistan, Somalia and Yugoslavia. He
is totally dedicated to his work and had just acquired a
new and much lighter camera which was his pride and
joy. Simon, the sound engineer, was an ex-heavy-metal
band member who had somehow drifted into his current
occupation. He is single and had developed the knack of
frequently reducing Julie to an hysterical wreck with his
jokes and funny one-liners. He, Jonathan and John had
worked together on several programmes previously and
knitted together well as a team. Like Jonathan, Simon
had worked in some of the notorious hot spots around the
world. Julie, dear Julie, is a lady with boundless energy
and a good heart, and she possessed the art of getting her
way, generally to the advantage of us all, a prime example
of which was getting our seats upgraded on the Virgin flight
to Boston.

John Bridcut, the boss, is ex-public school and had
learned his trade with the BBC over a number of years.
Now, like so many people in television, he was freelance
and running his own company. After one particular
programme in India which he, Jonathan and Simon had
worked on together, John had been christened by the other
two 'Bridders of the Punjab'.

John's management of the crew was good. He led by
example and his obvious dedication to his profession.
However, beneath his placid exterior there was a very
clear and determined mind which sometimes brought
him into conflict with Wendy and me. We felt that
the programme's original concept was to bring us into
contact with ordinary Irish people, in order to get their
perspective on the Northern Ireland troubles. John, on the
other hand, obviously felt that the programme needed a
few interviews with politicians and one particular situation

involved an elected councillor and one of his constituents. These developments made Wendy and me increasingly uneasy, until finally we objected strongly to the councillor/constituent scenario. It did not in fact appear in the final programme.

Naturally enough, we appreciated that John was under considerable pressure to bring the programme in on time and on budget. He was often preoccupied to such an extent that he did not always remember to explain his plans fully, and so, from our point of view, it sometimes seemed that we were moving away from first principles. I must stress that the working relationships were very good for most of the time, but just occasionally Wendy and I felt we had not been properly consulted and that decisions were taken without our involvement.

In trying to explain why these occasional differences between us arose, I can only say that the conflict may have had its roots in the gap between John's professional programme-making instincts and the obvious amateurism which Wendy and I brought to the programme. There were times when Wendy and I felt as if we were the junior partners in the enterprise, and our misgivings were not always allayed by John's quintessentially English politeness and good manners.

Meanwhile, during our journey south, where one crosses the border at Newry from Northern Ireland into the Irish Republic, it was fascinating to see at first hand the security measures established to prevent quick passage from one side to the other. Under the direct view of a large bunker on the hillside, cars pass through a series of meandering bends in the road and over steep road ramps. Reduced to crawling speed, we zig-zagged our way across this border zone and then pressed on with our high-speed journey through the Republic. We noticed one or two obvious differences in the landscape either side of the border. In

general, the road surfaces were much better in the North
and there were fewer built-up areas in the South, but the
size and quality of some of the houses we saw as we sped
along in the Republic were superb.

After a break for dinner, there was overall agreement
to abandon any idea of having an overnight stay en route.
Instead, we decided to proceed with our journey. I must
say that it had been many, many years since I had enjoyed
a long drive so much. The open roads, even those with less
than perfect surfaces, were a joy to drive on. Traffic was
light and generally slow-moving, allowing us to pass safely
and easily. Wendy fell soundly asleep in the car after dinner
and only woke on the bumpy road approaching Listowel.
We pulled up outside the Listowel Arms at 2.00 a.m.,
hurriedly unloaded all the baggage and equipment, and
after a couple of nightcaps, turned in for the night.

Wendy and I were allowed the luxury of a lie-in the next
morning while John and the crew set up their equipment in
the lounge bar, in readiness for our surprise meeting with
Del and her friends. After breakfast, we strolled around
the town looking in shops before Julie took us to the
coast for some sea air. We stayed for an hour or so in a
small hotel which served hot coffee and scones with jam
and cream, before making our way back to Listowel. The
car was parked at the far side car park so that we would
not be seen and Julie went inside to establish with John
about when we should make our entrance. After some
deliberation, we were told to walk towards the hotel's
entrance, but to turn our faces away from the window as we
passed, just in case anyone should be looking outside.

Julie had told us where Del was sitting and on entering
the room we walked slowly towards the corner table.
As luck would have it, Del was the first to look up
as we stood immediately alongside the table. Her look
of momentary confusion was quickly followed by total

surprise and then by the widest smile I'd seen for a long time.

Del stood up and shook our hands, saying, 'They said only the BBC were coming, they never said you were coming too. What a lovely surprise!' Her smile stayed in place as she introduced each of her friends in turn. We took our seats and drinks for Wendy and me appeared from somewhere, along with a large bouquet of flowers for Wendy from the hotel manager.

The conversation flowed easily in an atmosphere that was instantly relaxed and informal. Del and her friends told us how powerfully the Warrington bombing had affected them and the town in general, and how much they had wanted to convey their sense of outrage to us. We explained that we had wanted to visit Listowel not only to thank Del and as many others as we could, but also to find out how a small rural community in the Republic felt about Northern Ireland.

Some of our basic assumptions about the people living in the Republic were soon proved wrong. For example, we discovered that very few people from this part of the Republic had ever been to Northern Ireland, or, it seemed, wanted to. Some admitted to us that they would be afraid to go to the North. In contrast whereas nearly everyone we met had either lived in or visited Britain. Indeed, many had relatives who had settled on the mainland. Everyone we met spoke in very complimentary terms about their fondness for Britain and the British people. When, in fact, we had expected to find much less warmth for Britain and the British people than this, and we had taken it for granted that the vast majority of people living in the Republic would have spent some time in the North.

Time and again it was emphasised with great force that the IRA and Sinn Fein had little support in the Republic, though I remember one of Del's friends saying to me that to abandon the goal of a united Ireland would send a message of hopelessness to Nationalists in the North, which could lead to further violence born out of frustration. I suggested to her that the most reliable and recently available information pointed to the fact that only a quarter of the citizens of Northern Ireland were in favour of Ireland being unified. She seemed unaware of this.

Among the people we met in Listowel, there was a growing fear of Loyalist attacks on the Republic. There also seemed to be a general acceptance of the fact that a united Ireland that took no account of the wishes of the Unionist community would merely change the terrorist attacks from IRA outrages in the North and in Britain to UVF/UFF outrages in the Republic. During our time in Listowel, no one we met openly expressed support for the nationalist cause.

Early in the evening of our first day in Listowel, Del invited Wendy and me for tea at her house where we met her husband and their children. We spent an enjoyable hour or two getting to know them, before Del took us back to the Listowel Arms. After freshening up, we were entertained in the town's Heritage Arts Centre with a very lively, traditional evening of Irish acting, singing and dancing.

When everyone was talking freely in the lounge bar of the Listowel Arms, the nearest thing I heard to anti-British sentiment was when an elderly chap drew a distinction between the present-day Provisional IRA and their predecessors in the original IRA. He took a lot of time and trouble to tell me that the IRA in the 1916–21 period was a revolutionary force of freedom fighters trying to throw off the burden of British rule, whereas he condemned unreservedly the Provisional IRA as nothing more than thugs and gangsters who represented no one other than themselves. He too stressed that their support in the Republic was virtually non-existent.

Our time in Listowel was really heart-warming, thanks to everyone's wonderful hospitality throughout. When the time came for us to leave, we expressed our gratitude to and affection for Del, her family, her friends and the townspeople we'd met, all of whom had made us so welcome.

One day we would like to visit this region of Ireland again and see some of the natural beauty of the area. Certainly, the warmth of the people and the lovely countryside make it a delightful corner of the island of Ireland.

During our journey to Dublin, Wendy and I reflected on our visit to this quiet corner of Ireland. We shared the view that the Republic is now a mature democracy whose people recognise the hopeless futility and considerable danger of one side trying to force its view on another. Everyone we had spoken to agreed that an end to violence was absolutely vital if the seeds of peace were to take root and grow. In an atmosphere free of violence, real co-operation could begin and in the fullness of time, this may or may not lead to a united Ireland. However, what struck Wendy and me more than anything else was the myth that the IRA in the North represents the common view of Irish men and women. In thousands of letters, many books of condolences and face-to-face meetings, they told us very forcefully that it does not. Needless to say, we found this constant assurance very encouraging. To cap it all, when I asked the direct question 'Should the Irish government freely give up its constitutional claim to the North?' I never once heard the answer 'No'.

But it was not all positive news, and one of the most disappointing things we heard came from the leader of a Listowel youth group. The group had just returned from a visit to Listowel's twin town of Downpatrick in Northern

Ireland. During their time in the North, they travelled in
their own bus into Belfast to see the city. At one point
during the tour, a group of youngsters attacked their
bus with hammers, smashing the bus's rear lights. The
youth-group leader told us how unnerving this experience
had been for them all, but he still felt that such visits were
worthwhile as they had been received very well apart from
this one ugly incident. To his credit, he continued to see the
benefits of exchange visits and was very keen on taking his
group to England in the future.

As we headed towards Dublin, John Bridcut decided
that he wanted outdoor shots of us driving down a country
road. We stopped outside a small town called Newport, to
choose the exact location where Jonathan would film us.
However, as we got out of the cars to check things over,
a large number of big and very unpleasant flies began
buzzing around our heads. They showed such considerable
interest in our hair and our ears that we all ran back to the
cars and drove off as quickly as we could.

This proved to be the only time we were treated
unpleasantly in the Republic.

On the outskirts of Dublin, we pulled off the road to have
lunch in a large modern restaurant, where the manager
recognised Wendy and me. He very kindly bought us all a
round of drinks. Just before leaving, Wendy and I changed
into our formal clothes, ready for our meeting with the Irish
President, Mary Robinson.

The President's official residence is a beautiful white
house known as Aras an Uachtarain, set in the wonderful
grounds of Phoenix Park. We drove up to the front of the
house where we were greeted by an Irish Army officer in
dress uniform. He took us through to a reception room
where the President's personal adviser, Bride Rosney, welcomed us. Bride, whom we'd met at the memorial service,
chatted to us for a few minutes before President Robinson

came into the room. Appropriately, the President wore a green suit and, most encouragingly, a very friendly smile. She said to us, 'It's good to see you again, and I commend the considerable symbolic importance of what you are doing in the aftermath of your terrible loss.' Several photographs were taken, before the President suggested she show us around the gardens so that she could tell us the history of the house. Radio microphones were fitted to the President and to me so that our conversation could be recorded as we walked along. Wendy had stated, as she often did, that I could do the questioning and she would walk along with us.

We set off along a wide gravel footpath between two very large lawns, but after we had walked twenty or thirty yards Simon signalled to John that the noise of our footsteps on the gravel was drowning out our voices. Very politely, John asked President Robinson whether it would be possible for us to walk on the grass instead, to overcome the sound problem. This was agreed and we moved on to the lawn.

This unplanned interruption was very fortuitous because our time with the President was limited and an explanation of the history of the house seemed like it was going to take up all the time. Thus I was able to bring the conversation on to the questions I had prepared for her. As we stepped on to the grass, I quickly asked her how she had felt about the news coverage given some weeks earlier to her much-publicised handshake with the Sinn Fein President, Gerry Adams.

In what I thought was a typically honest way, she told Wendy and me that wherever she travelled and whomsoever, she met, it was always her policy to shake everyone's hand and to show no favour in any way to any person. Her handshake had been misrepresented in some sections of the British press, as bestowing a kind of official approval on the politics of Sinn Fein. Quite

naturally, the President was very clear in her insistence
that her handshake had carried no message whatsoever,
but was simply a matter of common courtesy.

I reminded her of the reaction to the handshake among
some of the more prominent Unionist politicians in Northern Ireland. Some had suggested that the President would
no longer be welcome in Loyalist areas. She responded by
saying she was confident that she would be able to reassure
those Unionists, who now doubted her impartiality, the
next time she met them.

The exchange of views on the Adams handshake took
rather longer than I had intended and, almost before we
knew it, we found ourselves back at the house. However,
in order to get off the lawn and into the house we had
to negotiate quite a steep grass embankment. This was
handled with supreme ease and athleticism by President
Robinson and Wendy, but to my acute embarrassment I
slid back down on my first two attempts. The shoes I was
wearing had leather soles and heels and gave me no traction
or grip whatsoever on the grass. On my third attempt, I
took a run at the slope but, despite this, I was about to
slide back down again when, to my considerable relief and
great amusement, President Robinson reached down and
held out her hand to me; I accepted her offer, took her
hand firmly in mine, and she pulled me up the slope.

This incident was a wonderful cameo symbolising the
hand of peace and reconciliation, and Wendy and I
were tremendously impressed by the President's informality and friendliness, encapsulated in this single act
of kindness . . . and pity? It was a great shame that
we were not able to include this in the programme's
transmission.

Once we were back inside the house, the President asked
John to stop the filming because she wanted to have a
quiet private discussion with Wendy and me, so the crew

withdrew while tea, coffee and biscuits were brought in for the three of us.

We sat on a settee, informally, while we chatted. She asked us about our plans for the remainder of our time in Ireland and told us how much she believed our efforts and words were helping to bring some good out of Tim's death. She wanted to know about Dominic and Abbi and who was looking after them while we were away. She also asked us to tell her about Tim as he was in life. Realising that we could not expect to take up too much of the President's time, we tried our best to capture Tim's personality and his life in as short a time as possible, without making it meaningless. The President's interest was very touching and sincere and she confirmed that the Warrington bombing had had a devastating effect upon attitudes in the Republic. She believed that this had given us a solid platform upon which to carry a message of peace and reconciliation. Her final message to Wendy and me struck a chord. 'No side can win,' she said, 'but finding the middle ground is very difficult, and this is why contact, communication and face-to-face meetings are so important.'

After this meeting, we had a two-day break from filming and went home to be with Dominic and Abbi. But even then we had a couple of engagements to fulfil. Wendy's boss, Jane Coleman, had begun a major fundraising effort in local Cheshire schools in support of Warrington's hospital scanner. She called it 'The Tim Parry Appeal'. One school with just 180 pupils, all of whom were disabled to some degree, had raised over £700 in a very short space of time through various sponsorships. The children and teachers told Jane of their keenness to present the cheque to Wendy and me in person.

At a special school assembly, the head teacher called us forward to receive the cheque from two of the children, and I then said some words of thanks to everyone who had worked so hard. However, my words soon began to falter, so I kept them brief, not wanting to stand before the school with tears in my eyes and upset the children on their great day of achievement.

The next day we went to Warrington Town Hall to collect a book of condolences from the people of Roscommon in Ireland. Two Roscommon men, who had lived and worked in Warrington for many years before retiring and returning to their original home, had been so horrified by the deaths of Tim and Johnathan and the many other injuries that they wanted to express their revulsion for the act and their support for our families, through the book of condolences.

Early in the afternoon, we were taken to Manchester Airport to catch our flight to Belfast City Airport. This is Belfast's second and much smaller airport. It took quite a while to get a taxi, but when one finally arrived we settled back for what we expected would be a comfortable journey to our hotel. After a couple of miles, however, we entered an area where a huge bonfire was under construction. I estimated that it stood forty to fifty feet high; it was built entirely of wooden pallets and rubber tyres and, like every other bonfire we were to see over the next two days, it had the Irish tricolour flag fluttering at the very top. As we came alongside the bonfire, where we could see lots of young men milling around, our driver locked the car doors. I asked him why he had done this. He replied, 'I'm taking no chances around here.' Not knowing precisely what he meant, I asked him to explain. From what I could understand of his reply, I gathered that he did not want to risk any of us being pulled from the car or having his car commandeered for a bonfire. His answers made us rather uneasy about what to expect over the coming days. The timetable we had received from Julie had us filming at a midnight bonfire on 11 July, and then on 12 July we were to witness the Orange Day parades followed by a visit to 'the field' outside Belfast city centre where the marchers relaxed before returning home. Wendy, too, was nervous about the next leg of our journey of discovery.

There were a couple of other interviews to conduct before our trip to the bonfire, and the first of these was with a Catholic family living off the New Lodge Road, in the Falls Road area. Sandy and Colleen Patterson live in a small, modern house with their five daughters and one son. Three of their daughters were at home when we arrived and they sat, dressed in their black T-shirts, on the arms of the settee and chairs to watch the filming. Their behaviour was impeccable throughout. Sandy told us that he had been unemployed since leaving school, and he was now thirty years old.

My questions were directed at how they, as an ordinary Catholic family, could see the troubles ending, and what their opinions were about the men of violence. Sandy told us that the New Lodge area comprised 80 per cent Sinn Fein voters. This support, he went on to say, was based on Sinn Fein being an effective party at local level, particularly through its network of advice centres to which constituents could go with their everyday problems concerning housing, paying bills, receiving benefits, and so on.

Sandy and Colleen both stressed that their support for Sinn Fein had nothing to do with the IRA and its terrorist activities. They were similarly unequivocal in wanting the British Army out of Northern Ireland. While we were with them, they catalogued several incidents in which they had been on the receiving end of some mistreatment by British soldiers. However, I was more than a little bemused by their desire to see the British Army out when they acknowledged that sectarian violence would escalate appreciably if that were to happen. They argued that the

RUC and the recently formed regiment, the Royal Irish Rangers, should be made capable of 'holding the line'.

When I had concluded my direct questions, Sandy, Colleen and their three little daughters took us to a local memorial garden. This was a small area behind a railing fence and comprised two grey headstones. One contained the names of local people who had been killed during the troubles by the police, Army or Loyalist paramilitaries, and the other was headed 'IRA Volunteers'. Staring at this headstone I felt quite incapable of asking questions which were free of bias and that wouldn't have betrayed my personal distaste. Thankfully, Wendy came to my rescue and asked how local people, decent, ordinary and hopefully law-abiding people, could erect a headstone to terrorists who are capable of killing young and innocent children like our son Tim.

Needless to say, there was no answer to this question that would have satisfied Wendy and me. I continued to hold my tongue. I had no wish to be rude to Sandy and Colleen, who had been courteous in allowing us into their home where they had shown us considerable hospitality. I knew that had I begun to probe into the ambivalence about the IRA which I felt sure was within them, it would not have been possible to continue the interview. My silence, I felt, said it all.

We moved away from the garden to a road junction where a Catholic teenager had been killed by a British soldier. A plaque on the wall marked the spot, and as Colleen was telling us the background to the incident, a British Army foot patrol appeared and made its way towards us.

Having felt like an interloper for the previous half-hour, I was keen to show that the British Army was made up of ordinary men, carrying out their duty. So I stepped to the edge of the road as the first squaddie drew close. I was sure that he would recognise an English accent and respond favourably to my request. I called out, 'Excuse me, can I speak to you for a moment, please?' The soldier looked at me and said simply, but firmly, 'No', and then, 'And put that thing away!' He was of course referring to the camera.

Disappointed but not giving up, I put the same question to the second soldier walking by. To my relief, he at least had the good manners to say, 'I'm sorry, we're not allowed to stop and talk.' This incident left me with the curious feeling before filming ended that it was an alien army and not the British army on the streets of Belfast. Several more incidents were to leave me with similar mixed emotions.

Towards the end of our time with Sandy and Colleen I asked them, 'How do we break down the barriers standing in the way of peace?' Colleen replied, 'Ordinary Catholics and Protestants must make the effort and not sit back waiting for the politicians to deliver.' Wendy and I then suggested that they join Alfie and Gina McCrory and us for dinner at a neutral venue; there we could try to find some common ground. We felt that this was a positive suggestion but, to our great surprise and disappointment, and without any hesitation, Colleen said, 'No.' She went on to explain that 'The Loyalists would start criticising Catholics and the IRA and we would be forced to retaliate and so it wouldn't work.'

We realised there was no possibility of getting them to change their minds, and so we left it at that. As on previous occasions, our despair was acute by the time we left. It was very hard to see how the ordinary people living in their segregated areas and never meeting people from 'the other side' could ever break out. In this context I mean 'break out' not only in the physical sense of mixing outside their own kind, but also in the mental and psychological sense of thinking laterally. There was a recognition that it would

take the ordinary people from both communities to make
the all-important moves towards peace and reconciliation,
and yet, when it came to making the first moves, there
was an unwillingness to take risks. It seemed that peace
overtures were a riskier business than staying in your
fox-hole, perhaps having calculated that there was a
greater than even chance that the violence would not
touch you directly. This attitude amounted to a fatalistic
acceptance that this was the way life must be in Northern
Ireland. Perhaps the people there have grown accustomed
to things being the way they are, and they've learned to
live with it.

By the time we left the Pattersons' house everyone was
hungry, and so we stopped at a city-centre McDonald's for
burgers and chips. Feeling grossly inflated, as I always do
after eating this kind of food, I was now ready to meet the
Reverend Roy Magee, a Presbyterian minister who had
been conducting private talks over several months with
the outlawed UDA.

Our meeting with Roy took us back to a traditional
Loyalist area, and as we stood in front of the gable-end
of a house boasting a huge mural of King William astride
his white horse, he answered my questions very frankly
and openly. He told us that he took some satisfaction
in persuading the Loyalist paramilitaries to suspend their
violence during Easter, but he was under no illusions
about how entrenched the two sides were and how
institutionalised the violence had become. Roy saw his
main role as one of imploring the leaders of groups such
as the UDA to remember their Christian teaching and to
accept that the taking of life was wrong and could never
be justified.

Like every other Protestant we met, Roy subscribed to
the view that if the IRA laid down its weapons, the UDA,
UVF, and UFF would do so too. The converse, however,

was that if the Loyalist paramilitaries ended their campaign of violence first, the IRA would not reciprocate because they have a different agenda. Roy's efforts were obviously worthwhile, as were those of several Catholic priests whom he knew were talking with the IRA.

As our filmed interview progressed, a large group of young children began to gather around us asking for money. The manner in which they asked was quite insistent, and a couple of times they were asked to let us get on with our business without interruption. This was to no avail, and in the end John Bridcut, belying his physical slightness, had to gently push the group of children away. This was merely a temporary respite, however, as not only did they return, but this time several adults came with them.

We were subjected to a fusillade of questions from all sides which made it impossible to continue with the interview. One enormously fat but very short woman demanded to know, 'What are yous doing here?' Roy Magee replied that we were trying to film an interview for a BBC television documentary, but this wasn't sufficient to satisfy this indomitable lady, who then lapsed into street talk. 'What the fuck are yous doing here?' Wendy and I were taken aback by this language, more so because it was uttered within earshot of so many young children. It was clearly time to be a little more frank with her. She was told who we were and why we were there, and she then yelled to all the other adults nearby, 'This is the people from Warrington who lost their wee boy.' She pushed her way through the crowd in front of her – frankly, they stood no chance of preventing her – to embrace us both in her stout arms. Her sympathy seemed genuine enough. As she stood alongside us, she pulled her small son to her and announced proudly, 'This is my wee little shite!' It struck me as a curious way of expressing pride in her offspring, but then it summed up the tough, no-nonsense environment in which people within the ghetto areas live.

John Bridcut promised we would all make a contribution to the bonfire collection just as soon as the interview was finished, and this seemed to satisfy the crowd, which withdrew far enough to let us conclude the interview without further interference.

Over the next few hours, everyone got some rest back at the hotel before we prepared to go and witness the Tigers Bay bonfire first hand. It was a chilly night and one could never be sure of the Irish weather, for as Paul Smyth said to us at his Coleraine peace camp when we first met, 'If you don't like the weather in Ireland, just wait a minute.' We all put on warm clothes and left the hotel at a little after 11.00 p.m.

We parked the two cars in a narrow street of terraced houses and walked down through the crowds of people already settling into their vantage points from where they could get a good view of the huge bonfire. Frankly, the bonfire was so high, it could have been seen from half a mile away.

Whole families huddled together in groups. Bottles, cans and crates of beer were everywhere. Clearly nothing was going to stop the fun.

John, Simon and Jonathan kept on the move, constantly on the look-out for a good position from which to film. Julie, Gwynneth, Wendy and I followed them as best we could. Several times we lost sight of them, but each time, just as concern was about to set in, we would spot the camera. A number of people enquired in a slightly menacing way why we were there and who we were filming. As a rule, smiling and emphasising that we were not a news team helped to defuse potentially unpleasant confrontations.

Shortly before midnight, the bonfire was lit and the fire

caught hold quickly, so quickly in fact that the heat from it was quite intense and we all backed away to a safe distance. Amazingly, very young children, some of whom looked as young as three years old, were allowed to run up to the fire completely unsupervised by any adult to throw objects into the blaze.

At the top of the street older children began to fire rockets, but instead of firing them upwards into the night sky they fired them almost horizontally so that they screamed by just feet above the heads of hundreds of revellers. One or two actually exploded very close by, with the result that pieces of burning firework rained down on people and could easily have caused serious injury.

It was at this moment that our misgivings about just what kind of party this was increased. From then on, we kept a careful eye trained along the street so that we would see if any more rockets were coming our way.

All the houses near to the fire had their windows boarded up, presumably to prevent accidental or deliberate damage. Meanwhile, the heavy drinking continued apace with people becoming more and more boisterous. Several came very close to us, staring in that hard, defiant 'I dare you to say anything' way, while others told us to switch the camera off and go home – for our own good.

By now, it was close to 1.00 a.m. on the morning of 12 July and the party atmosphere was turning decidedly aggressive and ominous. Wendy and I agreed that this was quite unlike any bonfire celebration we had ever been to before.

The camera was attracting more and more attention and our English accents seemed to be adding to the hostile looks we were getting. I kept thinking there was no good reason to outstay our welcome, but trying to communicate this to the others who were spread out across a fairly wide area was impossible. It was almost as if John and his crew were oblivious to the growing feeling of menace that was becoming palpable wherever you looked.

Every time I spotted them along the crowded street, they were darting here and there to get one more good shot of the fire. It had toppled over some time ago, and on impact with the ground had sent burning embers flying high into the air, air which was already thick with pungent, choking black smoke from the burning rubber tyres. We moved about to avoid being downwind of the blinding smoke which made it very hard to breathe. The houses for a considerable area around the fire must have retained the smell of the fire for many days afterwards. It seemed irresponsible and foolish to us to build fires on such a scale in the heart of a built-up area of such closely packed houses, but I doubt there would have been any effective way of preventing them without causing civil unrest among people determined to proclaim their historical integrity.

It was now 1.30 a.m. and at long last John Bridcut decided there was enough film of Wendy and me near the bonfire and we could leave. We walked back up the street and away from the fire, and when we got back to the cars I felt a sense of relief that we were about to return to comparative safety.

No sooner had this thought entered my mind than from a very dark, narrow alleyway between two terraced houses on the opposite side of the road three men appeared. They immediately formed a half-circle around Simon, pinning him to the side of the Montego estate car. I was alongside Simon to his left and Jonathan was to his right, but it was Simon, with the recording equipment suspended from his neck, who attracted the attention of these men. Julie was on the other side of the car and Wendy was by the tailgate. John and Gwynneth were sitting in Gwynneth's car which was parked on the opposite side of the road, ready to leave.

It was instantly obvious, even before any of the men spoke a word, that we were in a dangerous situation. There was something about the way they materialised from nowhere, the way they moved and, most of all, the way they looked at us which had all our instincts ringing alarm bells.

The men were all wearing zip-up jackets, though the one nearest to Jonathan had his zipped only a little way up and his right hand was inside his jacket in an attitude reminiscent of Napoleon. I kept my gaze on him because he fidgeted rather a lot, and after a few moments I understood why. He was carrying a gun. He didn't speak a word. He didn't need to. Simply moving his right hand inside his jacket had the exact effect that I am sure he intended.

The man in the middle spat his words at Simon. 'What's that you're carrying? What's it for?' I have no clear recollection of Simon's answers as I was too mesmerised by the situation, and particularly by the farthest man with the gun. Simon managed to conjure up a diplomatically low-key and completely unprovocative reply.

His questioner cut across the answer, which was apparently taking too long, and snapped again, 'What the fuck is that? Take it off . . . take it off, I said!' Simon was doing an amazing job of stonewalling while we all considered our options. I noticed that Wendy had somehow spread herself against the tailgate to try to conceal the camera, Jonathan's pride and joy.

As Simon was prevaricating yet again, the guy in the middle was becoming more and more agitated every second. This time, with growing impatience and anger, he demanded to know where the camera was. It then occurred to me that the most obvious way out of this very dangerous situation was for me to explain who we were and why we were filming, so I began, 'Excuse me, can I . . .' I was abruptly cut off by the man

standing nearest to me who had not said a word up to
that point.

'Shut your fucking mouth,' he snapped. I waited just a
second or two, before trying again. 'Can I just explain who
we are and why we're here?' I said. To no avail. The same
man turned to me a second time and said, with as much
venom as he could muster, and this was considerable, 'I
told you to shut your fucking mouth, now do as you're
fucking told, and shut it!' The words 'or else' were not
spoken; they didn't need to be. I realised it was going to
be impossible to get them to listen. At the very least we
would be robbed of our equipment and film, and at the
worst . . . My mind switched off at this point.

Meanwhile I became aware of Jonathan trying to explain
that we were not a news crew, but he too was told in no
uncertain terms to keep his mouth shut.

Just as all seemed lost, and with a large crowd of
onlookers gathering around, no doubt sensing that severe
lessons were about to be administered to the outsiders, a
voice nearby called out, 'The RUC are letting off baton
rounds against ten-year-olds in the street.' This declaration
had a galvanizing effect on our three would-be assailants,
and as quickly as they had arrived, they disappeared. The
gathering crowd quickly dissipated too, and we all jumped
into the cars to beat the hastiest possible retreat.

In a state of complete and total confusion, I drove
up the street and away from the bonfire because my
instincts told me that safety was away from the fire. My
instincts were to prove wrong, however, for the top of
the street ended in a T-junction which led on to other
streets which ran down from it parallel to the one we
had parked on. A further bout of mild panic entered
my mind, along with confusion as to which way to go.
Gwynneth drove her car alongside and signalled for me to
follow her. This involved going back towards the bonfire

in order to find the way out of this maze of small side streets.

Once we were some distance away from the Tigers Bay area, and beginning to relax a little, Gwynneth pulled off the main road that led into Belfast city centre. Not knowing where we were, I turned off too and stopped behind her car. John jumped out and declared that he wanted to shoot some more film of a bonfire we had just passed a few hundred yards back along the road.

I could hardly believe it. Wendy and I were now so tired and ill at ease that it was all we could do not to get straight back into one of the cars and find our own way back to the hotel. We badly wanted the comfort and familiarity of natural surroundings, instead of feeling that we were in a war zone. Yet there was no way of registering our protest at that exact time, as John, Jonathan and Simon had sped off up the road for more filming, oblivious to the fact that we were desperate to get as far away from this area as possible.

Julie and Gwynneth didn't seem to know whether they should stay with us or follow the crew, but eventually they just drifted off in the direction in which the others had gone, but with no apparent sense of purpose.

When John and the crew returned thirty minutes later, John finally uttered the words we most wanted to hear. 'Let's go back to the hotel and relax.' We followed his instructions without comment. All our drive and energy had deserted us, and we just wanted to sit down without feeling in imminent danger of being attacked, or worse.

Back in the hotel lounge, at the ungodly hour of 2.30 a.m., most of the conversation was basic and largely monosyllabic, but the one thing that we did discuss over our nightcap was our experience with the three men who had confronted us. I freely admitted that I could not recall ever being in such a frightening situation in the whole of my

life. We discussed whether we would have been robbed by
these three men, or suffered a worse fate, had we continued
to resist their demands, and we all agreed that they would
not have been able to accept the loss of face involved in
letting us or the equipment go free in front of the gathering
crowd.

What convinced us that this had not been an elaborate
hoax was Jonathan and Simon admitting that they had
never been so scared before, even though they had worked
in places such as Afghanistan, Somalia and Yugoslavia.
They had been in very violent and dangerous situations
where they had been at considerable risk, and still they
felt that our experience in Tigers Bay was the worst they
had ever faced. We sat quietly for a few minutes after
this discussion, each silently thanking the unknown and
unwitting samaritan in the crowd whose words had taken
our would-be assailants away.

Despite the desperately unsettling events of the previous
few hours, we still managed to sleep soundly until our
alarm call at 7.45 a.m. Then, in something of a zombie-like
state, we snatched a light breakfast before departing into
the city centre reasonably early to find a place to film the
Orange lodges parading.

Helpful though the RUC police officers were, there were
many additional checkpoints to control traffic and allow
the Orange parade to pass along its appointed route. We
were directed several ways but in the end managed to find
parking spaces in the BBC Northern Ireland compound.

Everyone hurried to get back to the main road where the
parade would pass. John, as meticulous as ever, eventually
chose a place for the crew, and we mingled with the crowds
on the pavements as we waited. In some places, the crowd
was three or four deep and yet at other points it was still
possible to stand at the kerbside.

The weather was untypically sunny and quite warm,

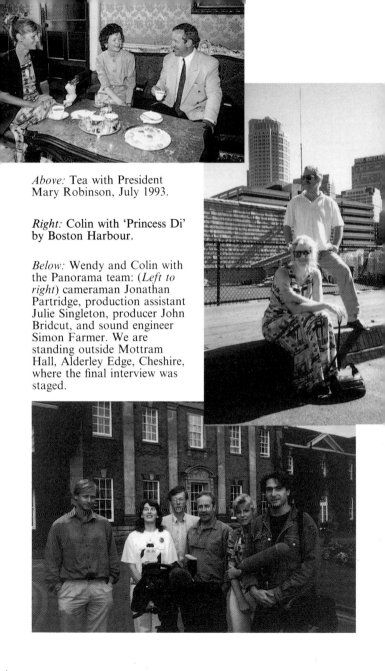

Above: Tea with President Mary Robinson, July 1993.

Right: Colin with 'Princess Di' by Boston Harbour.

Below: Wendy and Colin with the Panorama team: (*Left to right*) cameraman Jonathan Partridge, production assistant Julie Singleton, producer John Bridcut, and sound engineer Simon Farmer. We are standing outside Mottram Hall, Alderley Edge, Cheshire, where the final interview was staged.

Mary Robinson and her husband Nicholas at the launch of the
Warrington Project in October 1993. Warrington's Mayor, John
Taylor looks on.

HRH The Prince of Wales greeting Colin and Wendy at the
launch. Paul Vickers and John Gartside, Leader of Warrington
Council, are in the background.

HRH The Duchess of Kent on a private visit to our home, February 1994.

Wilf Ball, Johnathan's father, (*left*) with Albert Spiby at a fundraising event in Adlington, Lancashire, 27th June 1993.

Tim's headstone.

Forever In Our Hearts
TIM PARRY "TIMBO"
BORN 1.9.1980 DIED 25.3.1993
OUR LIVES WERE ENRICHED BY THE BEAUTY
IN YOUR HEART AND IN YOUR SMILE.
YOU TOUCHED THE WORLD
WE WILL LOVE YOU ALWAYS.
MUM, DAD, DOM, ABBI.

IN REMEMBRANCE OF
JOHNATHAN BALL
TIM PARRY
20th MARCH 1993

The plaque on the wall of Boots in Bridge Street, Warrington, unveiled by Wendy and Marie, Johnathan Ball's mother, on Sunday 10th October 1993. (Photograph courtesy of Tony Hall).

making a welcome change from the rain and wind to which we had grown accustomed. The vast majority of the people who gathered to watch the parade go by were in light summer clothes and looking as if they were out to enjoy themselves, though it was surprising to see people drinking as early as 10.30 in the morning.

Finally, the distant sound of flutes and drums reached us, as the bands began to come into view. Each band was led by a man beating on a big bass drum which proudly bore the name of the band, or by a man tossing a baton. So many bands went by that it was impossible to count them, but I did note that most of the marchers favoured brightly coloured outfits rather than the dark grey suits, bowler hats and the broad orange sash of the more traditional lodges. These I remembered well from my own younger days in Liverpool, when the Orange Day parades were an even bigger spectacle than in Belfast. I looked out for bands from Liverpool, but apart from the bands from Scotland and one from Manchester the remainder came only from Northern Ireland.

During the course of the parade, John and the crew changed their vantage point for filming several times without any problem. The weather continued to be bright and sunny, and the mood of the watching crowd was light-hearted. The only nasty moment occurred with the appearance of a band named after the UVF. Remembering that the UVF was a proscribed organisation, John, Simon and Jonathan set off along the road to get ahead of the band to film them marching towards the camera. They found a suitable position for this purpose and began to film, but as the band drew alongside one of the bandsmen swung his stick and hit Jonathan's camera and then Jonathan himself was given a nasty blow across the ribs by the same man. Thankfully the blow didn't cause any serious damage, though it left Jonathan sore for a couple of days.

After an hour or so, John and the crew returned to tell us that we were going to another point further along the parade's route where we had a pre-arranged meeting with Alfie and Gina McCrory. Parking our vehicles near to where we wanted to be was no easy matter because, quite apart from there being so little space in the side streets, the RUC were operating very strict controls. Eventually we did find spaces and our chief tracker, Gwynneth, located the spot where Alfie, Gina and their children were.

Alfie and Gina were in fine form, and looked genuinely pleased to see us. We settled back to watch many of the same bands we had seen earlier. I remarked quietly to Wendy that it was more than a little ironic that many banners displayed the word 'temperance', considering the amount of alcohol we'd seen being consumed since early morning.

As the conversation with Alfie developed, I asked him whether he could see that parades such as this were intimidating to Catholics and nationalists. 'Not at all,' he told me. 'July 12th is a carnival atmosphere; lots of these people watching the parade will be Catholics.' I asked him whether the same was true of Protestants and Loyalists watching nationalist parades during their marching season in August. 'No,' he said to me firmly. He then told me, presumably as part of his reply to my previous question, that Loyalist violence was not the same as Republican violence. 'We only shoot the IRA, whereas they shoot anyone,' he stated emphatically.

This did not seem to me to be either the time or the place to debate the point further, as I could see that Alfie had been drinking. He was being far more clannish than he had been when we'd met him at home. In other circumstances, I might have asked him to explain his use of the word 'we' in his reference to shooting the IRA, even though

I harboured no serious thoughts that Alfie was involved in paramilitary violence.

As the last of the bands passed us, we again said our goodbyes to Alfie and Gina before setting off to find the field where the bands finally ended their parade. By the time we got there, it was awash with colour; the bands were scattered widely, giving the impression of a painting with wonderfully contrasting colours against the background of a clear blue sky and rolling green slopes. At the bottom of this huge field there was a covered stand where leading Orangemen were making speeches to the sober-suited traditional lodge members.

Elsewhere across the field, thousands of tired, bedraggled marchers stood or lay around, clutching their beer cans to their chests. Broken tunes and musical notes drifted across on the breeze.

John Bridcut and I discussed how we would try to arrange interviews. We agreed to select people at random and then John would quietly approach them, explain who I was, and then ask if they would agree to answer my questions.

A representative cross-section of people were chosen – young, old, men, women, happy, sombre, and so on. Most of the young people were so drunk that interviewing them would have been pointless, but at least they all expressed their regrets about Tim. In another group, several women gathered around Wendy and me to embrace us and wish us well. They were a good crowd, humorous and obviously enjoying themselves. A couple of young men drifted across and expressed their condolences too, but then they descended into loud and abusive language about the IRA and what they had coming to them.

I was beginning to despair of finding anyone with whom I could talk about the purpose of the Orange movement when one very spritely and respectable old chap came into

view. Dressed in a grey suit and bowler hat, he was the
kind of man I would have expected to see marching past
the Cenotaph on Remembrance Sunday. John primed him
and signalled me to come over.

I held out my right hand to shake his and introduced
Wendy and myself. After a few inconsequential exchanges
to get used to each other's accents, I asked him the direct
question: 'Why do people choose to belong to the Orange
Order?'

'To respect and honour our dead,' he told me.

To be sure that I understood him correctly, I asked
him, 'Do you mean those who died at the Battle of the
Boyne?'

'I do,' he said. 'They fought and died and we should
remember them.'

'But that was 303 years ago,' I reminded him, 'in
1690.'

'I know that,' he replied.

'But what is the relevance today of a battle fought 303
years ago?' I asked him, and before he could answer, I
added, 'Isn't it because Northern Ireland is locked into
ancient history that the troubles are still with us today?'

By now, he was showing obvious signs of irritation with
me and my questions.

'You English have no sense of history,' he told me
sharply. 'We remember our forefathers who fought and
died.'

Thoughts of my own father came to mind. 'I was
born after World War II,' I said, 'and I completely
understand that those who fought in both world wars
would want to remember the friends and family they
lost in those wars. But I can no more comprehend
the need to remember those who fell at the Battle
of the Boyne than I can those who fell at the Battle of Edge Hill in the English Civil War, or those

who fell much more recently at the Battle of Waterloo in 1815!'

He no longer seemed interested in continuing this conversation with me, but before moving on I asked him one final question. 'Do you like the English?' His reply was short and to the point. 'Not much,' he said.

If this man's stated reason for belonging to the Orange Order was entirely truthful then, as I remarked to Wendy afterwards, I despair. We must place our faith in the next generation of adults in Northern Ireland, and hope that they will live in the 1990s instead of the 1690s!

However, my belief is that his membership of the Orange Order had nothing to do with those who fell in battle three centuries earlier, but was part of his need to belong to an exclusive club that was striving to maintain its religious purity. Membership of the club meant belonging to something that provided a clear identity and distinguished its members from Republicans and Roman Catholics.

The comment that we heard time and again on the field that day was that the British government was not doing what it should – killing the IRA leaders! Another of the older members of the Orange Order who said this to me was equally scathing about the Loyalist paramilitaries. 'The British should kill them as well as the IRA leadership,' he said, 'because both sides are criminals and gangsters now, nothing more and nothing less!'

Trying to conduct worthwhile interviews on the field was not a success despite scouring most of it in search of people who looked as though they might make an interesting contribution. At one point we came across a Scottish band whose members were extremely abusive and threatening when they saw the camera. I intervened between them and the crew just as I had attempted to do the previous evening, only this time I was successful because several of them recognised Wendy and me and began calling their colleagues, telling them who we were. With many of them gathering around us, we were subjected to hearty backslapping and generous eulogies, though they were mostly uttered with considerably slurred speech.

July 12 was very colourful, very loud and very interesting, but we had learned nothing new. It merely confirmed the powerful sense of tribal pride, symbolised by the Orange clans parading under the gaze of such vast numbers. But for all the colour and music, we did not share the feeling that this was a carnival of fun or a Mardi Gras. It seemed to us that it was one community beating its chest and telling the other community, and particularly the British and Irish governments, 'We are strong, and we are united, so don't take us lightly.'

By the time we were ready to leave, many of the bands were making their way home too. I commented to John that the sight of so many exhausted men trudging off the field, uniforms unbuttoned, collars open, instruments hanging at their sides rather like the weapons of war, created the illusion of soldiers leaving the battlefield at the time of the English Civil War. The feeling became even stronger on hearing the occasional drumbeat or flute being played. The imagery of an ancient battlefield was entirely appropriate, of course, in view of the fact that it is a three-hundred-year-old battle which is commemorated on 12 July.

For the remainder of the day we all unwound back at the hotel. Jonathan, Julie and I decided that before dinner we would play squash and work off some of the stress that had built up during this rather frustrating day. Each of us played with the same determination that had so far characterised our approach to making the programme.

Playing squash always makes me think of Tim, and playing in Belfast brought him back to me very strongly.

I remembered the effort he used to put in to try to beat me, but I also remembered his frailty when he was so tired from chasing every shot that he would become dispirited and fed up. When this happened, just like any other parent, I would play some poor shots to let him pull the score back and encourage him to keep going and try hard again.

In my games with Julie and Jonathan, there were no concessions to tiredness. I played to win and so did they, and by the time we came off court honours were pretty even. Quite what Tim would have made of the kit I wore I do not know; it comprised Julie's knee-length Lycra shorts and her T-shirt, though I wore the T-shirt outside the shorts.

The next morning, after John, Simon and I had recorded an audio interview to get a voice-over commentary for the programme, Wendy and I went on a photo shoot with Mike Day and a local freelance photographer. This took us into hardline Republican and Loyalist areas to be photographed outside Sinn Fein headquarters and then alongside burned-out cars in the Shankill Road.

In the afternoon we went back to the Shankill and Falls Road areas to resume the tour previously conducted by Brian Feeney, only this time our 'driver' was Chris McGimpskey, a Unionist councillor.

Wendy and I had little enthusiasm for this second tour, as it was largely a repeat of what we had seen with Brian Feeney. Chris, like Brian, had a PhD in Irish history, but there the similarity ended. Though they had many things in common, their politics were diametrically opposed, with one supporting a united Ireland and the other supporting the union with Britain.

During our photographic session earlier in the day, the weather had been predominantly dry with the sun breaking through every now and again, but by the time Chris was driving us through the hardline areas the weather had

turned decidedly worse. By the time we left the Falls Road,
and drove on to the Glencairn estate, it was dismal, with
steady drizzling rain, slate-grey skies and a high wind, all
of which combined to make our mood very sombre. Chris
stopped the car and John announced that we were going
to visit a young unmarried mother named Nicola. She was
a seventeen-and-a-half-year-old constituent of Chris's who
had been given a flat by the council, largely thanks to
Chris's efforts, it seemed.

Nicola was a bright and cheerful youngster whose
home was spotlessly clean. While we were with her she
demonstrated a fierce determination to make a success
of her life and that of her young child. Similarly, Chris
was determined to help her all he could. Nicola and Chris
had lots to talk about, whereas I wondered to myself what
I was supposed to question Nicola about. I was lost in
thought and in a sombre mood when my silent reflection
was punctured as Wendy whispered to me, 'What are we
doing here, what has any of this got to do with Tim?' Her
words brought my mind back into focus and I conjured up
the only questions that had any relevance to this situation. I
asked Nicola, 'Have the Northern Ireland troubles touched
you directly?'

'No, they haven't,' she replied.

I then asked her whether she thought peace could be
achieved in Northern Ireland. She answered truthfully
that she did not know. I realised then that Wendy was
right and that this might have been worthwhile for Chris,
responding to his constituent's needs, but it had nothing
to do with Wendy and me learning about how peace and
reconciliation might come about.

We left the Glencairn estate and were taken to the
leafy, attractive suburban area of Belfast where Chris
lived. He showed us around his very pleasant house
and our interview was recorded as we strolled across his

garden. His views were expressed very coherently, but gave me little cause for hope. He stuck entirely to the established Unionist position and said nothing to persuade me that there was room for compromise. I liked Chris on a personal level – he was a lively and interesting man – but I looked to him as one of the next generation of leading Unionist politicians, and I desperately hoped to hear some original ideas from him which would enable Unionists and Nationalists to form a bridgehead for peace and mutual accommodation. I didn't hear any. What I did hear was what so many of us in Britain have heard for a generation now – an unyielding statement that the other side must alter its position if a lasting peace is to be found.

There are stark choices facing the people of Northern Ireland. They must decide whether they are prepared to give a little to win a lot; whether they are prepared to give up some of their sacred doctrine in order to give their children the legacy of peace. The one thing that became abundantly clear to Wendy and me during our travels around Ireland was that the two extreme positions of Nationalism and Unionism are mutually irreconcilable for as long as they remain as absolutes and incapable of change. Too many politicians in the province seem to regard loss of face as a higher political principle than loss of life. They espouse their position as if it were sacrosanct; they maintain the status quo in the belief that the other side will eventually weaken. The consequent political inertia that has resulted at local level is compounded by the apparent passivity of the middle classes. It's as if those living outside the ghettos have concluded that, on the balance of probabilities, they won't be directly affected by the violence and therefore they can live their lives tolerably, right in the heart of their divided society.

Another manifestation of the division in Northern Ireland society was to confront us when we travelled

to Armagh to meet the head of the Roman Catholic
Church in Ireland, Cardinal Cahal Daly. It was 10.00
a.m. on 14 July when we pulled up outside the Cardinal's
official home, Cathedral House, in the grounds of the
splendid Armagh cathedral. We looked out over miles
of rolling countryside from the cathedral which enjoys
an uninterrupted view from its hill-top position. The
view was truly breathtaking, but as we turned back to
the Cardinal's house we noticed that the ground-floor
windows were made of bullet-proof glass.

The Cardinal appeared in the doorway with his arm in
a sling from a recent motoring accident. He is quite a
small man who, though he wears spectacles, has eyes that
sparkle with vitality and give the immediate impression of
great energy and passion. We went inside the house and
into a large drawing room, which was simply but tastefully
furnished.

The Cardinal conveyed his great sympathy to us over the
death of Tim and asked after Dominic and Abbi. He told
us unequivocally of his bitter condemnation of all violent
organisations. He was equally outspoken in his opposition
to any of them having a place at the negotiating table for
as long as they used violence as a means of trying to secure
their end.

I asked him for his views on internment, and he said
that he did not believe its objectivity and fairness could be
guaranteed. He feared that it might serve as a recruiting
agent for the organisations concerned, particularly as
they were very astute at creating martyrs of the men
imprisoned. When I suggested to him that internment
introduced simultaneously by both the British and Irish
governments might be effective, he seemed less opposed
to the idea.

I then put the following question to the Cardinal. 'Why
does the Catholic Church oppose integrated education

when it seems self-evident that children from all religions would grow up with a better understanding of each other's tradition if they went to school together?' He was in something of a quandary, taking several seconds to deal with my question. His answer sought not to decry integrated education, but to explain the strengths and benefits gained by children who receive an undiluted Catholic education. Astutely, he put it back to me that education was not fully integrated in Britain either. My reply was simple. I said, 'In Britain, we're not killing each other.' He acknowledged my reply and we moved on.

I asked him whether he would comment on the question of the Republic giving up its constitutional claim on the six counties of the North. He replied, 'It is not out of the question, all things are possible, but there are people in the South who would find it hard to desert the nationalists in the North.' I observed that some things may be worth striving for, but never worth murdering for.

Next I turned my attention to exploring why it was that the Catholic Church gave the same Christian burial and service to known terrorists who have committed murder as it gave to the innocent victims. Again, he struggled with his answer, but finally he said it could not be assumed that the terrorist has not made a deathbed conversion back to the teachings of Christ. 'Then let his coffin be in the church on its own with the parish priest,' I argued. 'This would allow for the possibility of a deathbed repentance.' The Cardinal answered me by saying that this would penalise the man's family and deny them the opportunity of witnessing a Christian service.

Many times after the *Panorama* programme was broadcast, people remarked in their letters to us and in conversations that the Cardinal looked very uneasy at this question, and some even applauded me for appearing to catch him on the wrong foot. However, my intention was not to cause him discomfort or to score a point. I merely wanted to ask the questions that were in my head and my heart, and to the best of my ability replicate the questions that so many other people in my position would have asked.

We came away from what had been, for us, a very worthwhile experience. We had a very high regard for the Cardinal's integrity, compassion and total opposition to all forms of violence and coercion. My own personal theory on his dilemma with some of my questions is that, firstly, he had not anticipated the fact that I would use the opportunity of meeting him to pose difficult questions; secondly, and this is entirely speculative on my part, that his personal opinion on these issues may well have been at variance with his Church's theological view, hence his real struggle to give my questions convincing answers.

We then had a short but welcome break at home in Warrington before we set off for Boston in the United States. Boston had been selected for the programme because it has the highest percentage of Americans of Irish descent of any city in America.

As we waited in the international departure lounge at Gatwick, Julie gave us the good news that she had managed to have our seats upgraded to mid-class on the Virgin Atlantic flight. However, just as we were about to descend the walkway to the Boeing 747, the steward checking boarding cards took us to one side and altered ours to enable us to travel in first-class seats. Julie and 'the boys' were also upgraded to mid-class from economy, so everyone was happy.

This was our first trip to America and certainly our first flight anywhere in the first-class section. The seats were huge with acres of leg-room, as well as having footrests that sprang out from the bottom of the seat when it was reclined. Miniature television sets were provided with a choice of current films. Drinks were provided free.

We really knew we were travelling first class when the stewardess handed us the menu to choose dinner! We settled down to our six-hour flight with all the creature comforts we could have wished for.

On landing at Boston, there was a plentiful supply of baggage handlers to help John, Simon and Jonathan transport the equipment outside. The only problem was that the van, which was supposed to be waiting on our arrival, had not turned up. Julie gave Wendy and me fifty dollars and suggested we take a cab to the hotel in Cambridge, rather than wait around for the van. When we got to the hotel, Wendy decided to go to bed, but I was feeling hungry and so I set off in search of somewhere to get a bite to eat. I discovered that the ground floor of the hotel had a restaurant which served snacks, so I ordered the curiously named 'blackened chicken' sandwich. When it came, it was huge, and covered with lots of onion rings. As I began to eat, Mike Day joined me and we had a beer together.

An hour later, there was still no sign of any of the production team. Just as Mike and I finished our snacks, Julie appeared, looking tired and sounding very out of sorts. She told us that she had been blamed for the van being late.

Eventually everyone apart from Wendy, who was still catching up on her sleep, gathered in the bar. The team announced that they were going to a nearby fish restaurant, but I declined the offer, having just consumed my monstrous sandwich, and instead I went back to our hotel room for the night.

Breakfast the next morning brought my second pleasant surprise. It consisted of a mind-boggling selection of delicious dishes, including waffles and syrup! After just twelve hours in Boston, I was already several pounds heavier than when I had stepped off the plane.

On our first morning in Boston, we were taken in the van by our driver and researcher to the Roxbury district where we met a civil rights activist, Jean Maguire, and a colleague, Jim Smith. Jim is the communications director of an organisation with the innocuous-sounding name 'The Political Education Committee'. The PEC monitors the alleged human rights excesses of the British government in Northern Ireland.

Jean is a black woman of mixed-race parentage, one of whom was Irish, whereas, quite ironically, Jim Smith's father was from Bootle, just a few miles away from where I'd grown up in Liverpool. We travelled to a public park and our meeting was filmed at a picnic bench and table. It immediately became obvious that both Jean and Jim were completely unsympathetic to the British presence in Northern Ireland. Jim handed me a small leaflet which set out his organisation's position on the province. I read its main points, which began with the assertion that Britain was a colonial power in Northern Ireland and went on to accuse British troops of systematic brutality and breaches of human rights against ordinary Nationalists going about their everyday business. Beatings and shootings were commonplace, the leaflet stated.

I did not know whether to laugh or cry, reading such blatant propaganda. I asked him to justify it and he set about giving me a tortuous, meandering diatribe on the history of British abuse in Ireland going back centuries. When the interview was over, I remarked to John Bridcut that I was sure Jim Smith belonged to Noraid. John told me that he too had been concerned about this and had asked Jim the question himself. Needless to say, Jim had denied any link with Noraid.

Meanwhile, Jean Maguire spoke at length about the many forms that violence takes and how violence was not just physical but, for instance, included a ban on learning

Gaelic! This was her reply to my question as to whether she opposed the use of violence in seeking to further one's political goals.

Jim Smith had not been told beforehand who Wendy and I were, and had assumed that we were teachers. After he had been informed about Tim, his tone was rather less 'gung ho' for the remainder of the time we were with him. On the other hand, Jean Maguire did know who we were and yet, despite this, she said that she didn't know whether we had lost a son or a daughter! She also believed that Warrington was near London. Both of them were very strong on the theme of 'Brits out' and supported the idea that President Clinton had pushed during his election campaign of appointing a US envoy to help broker a peace settlement in Northern Ireland.

When we left Jean and Jim, I commented to Wendy that it had been the least productive meeting we had had to date, because they simply blamed the British for everything. They would not accept that the IRA was a terrorist organisation, but were scathing in their condemnation of the Unionists. The way they rationalised the violence of the IRA was very disturbing and offensive. Neither of them had been able to produce and sustain a balanced presentation of their case because their complete prejudice blinded them from reality. As we drove away from Roxbury, I uttered the silent hope that Jean Maguire and Jim Smith were not going to be typical of all Irish Americans we would meet. Fortunately, our very next meeting proved to be in complete contrast. Our next stop was the offices of the city's premier newspaper, the *Boston Globe*, to meet Kevin Cullen, the correspondent who covered Irish affairs. Kevin joined us in the van and directed us to the south side of Boston, where the major concentration of Irish Americans live. He took us to see several displays of wall graffiti, the prime example

being a large green map of Ireland with a padlock and
chain across the centre, which we had seen so often in
Belfast. However, it will come as no surprise to learn
that, quite unlike Belfast, there was a complete absence
of any gable-end walls showing King William astride his
white horse.

On average, Kevin spent one month in Ireland every
year and, as a result, he was very well informed about
Irish affairs. He told us that the vast majority of Irish
Americans had little idea what life was like in either
Northern Ireland or the Republic. As he put it, 'They
mostly talk crap!' He pointed to the side of the large
green gable-end map of Ireland and said, 'That tells you
the extent of the knowledge most Irish Americans have
about Ireland.' In small letters, someone had scrawled
'Ireland 5 Rumania 4', a reference, I presumed, to an
international football match.

Kevin told us he had written countless articles on Northern Ireland condemning both sides. He actually believed
that if Ireland were ever united, the IRA would turn its
attacks upon the government of all Ireland, because the
IRA wanted to govern Ireland itself. I decided not to
challenge Kevin on this as he said he based his remarks
on statements the IRA leadership had made in the past.

As well as being very well informed about Ireland,
Kevin also had a refreshingly even-handed disdain for
mainstream and radical Irish political groups. The feeling
that we'd had ever since the Warrington bombing, that
the media in America had given the deaths of Tim
and Johnathan very little coverage, was also confirmed
by Kevin.

It was confirmed yet again when we spent several hours
in the home of Mike and Nancy O'Hara on Sunday
morning. We sat on their back porch, bathed in warm
sunshine, with several of their closest friends. Mike is

in personnel management like myself and was born in Ipswich, then raised in Kettering until he was ten years old, when his family emigrated to Boston. Both Nancy's and Mike's parents were Irish, though neither had ever lived in or visited Ireland. Their home is in a beautiful suburb of Boston, a few miles from Harvard University. Interestingly, Mike had created his own bar within a large room filled mainly with memorabilia from England – British Rail station name-plates, Ipswich Town Football Club programmes and beer mats. Another little irony is that on the cover of one of the football programmes was a picture of Paul Mariner, former Ipswich Town and England centre forward. Paul's mother Peggy had worked for me some twenty years ago when Paul had still been trying to break through to the big time. Despite all Mike's connections, I sensed an underlying hostility towards Britain, rather more because of the tone of his voice than any actual words he used.

Nancy sat next to me on the porch and she wept openly as Wendy and I, at their request, gave everyone an account of the days from the bombing on 20 March to Tim's death on the 25th. We passed around several photographs of Tim so that they could all see what a lovely, lively boy he had been.

Wendy and I spoke about the troubles in Northern Ireland, explaining many of the things we had seen and heard during our time there while making the programme. As the discussion progressed, one of the O'Haras' guests, a middle-aged, well-educated woman, leaned forward in the manner of someone about to make a particularly important point and said, 'Of course, when you consider that Catholics don't have the vote in Northern Ireland, you can understand why there is trouble and they resent British rule.'

Quickly but politely, I disabused her of this misconception, and she was genuinely surprised that her information

was so wrong. For my part, I reflected ruefully on the level
of ignorance which clearly exists among Irish Americans.
It brought home to me just how out of touch Americans
are, and how susceptible the vast majority of them would
be to the kind of propaganda that Jean Maguire and Jim
Smith peddled. If an intelligent woman, such as Nancy's
guest, was so ill informed, I shuddered to think what less
educated Americans must believe.

Another of Nancy's guests, though she was a Catholic,
was critical of the presence of priests at Irish American
political gatherings. She asserts that as she had never
known Protestant ministers to be invited to such events,
Catholic priests should not be there either. It was all about
creating balance to prevent the dominance of only one
strand of Irish culture in America, she asserted. It was a
good point.

Towards the end of our long and enlightening discussion,
it was very significant that Nancy and the other three
women present wanted to know what they could do to
help stop the violence in Northern Ireland. They had all
been deeply affected by our account of Tim's death and
meeting us had brought them face to face with the reality
of Irish terrorism in a way they had never expected.

They said that they could never have prepared for an
encounter such as this and, more to the point, they could
never be the same again having met us and learned about
Tim. Their keenness to make some good come of our
meeting was very heartening indeed. Clearly, they were
good, decent people who now wanted to learn more about
the reality of Northern Ireland.

In answer to the pleading question, What can we do to
help?, Wendy and I told them to spread the word to as
many people as they could that putting dollars, nickels and
dimes into Noraid's collection tins was not giving money
to the families of convicted prisoners who had fought

honourably for freedom from oppression and tyranny. It was funding the purchase of Semtex and automatic weapons to bomb and shoot innocent children, civilians, policemen and soldiers. They listened intently, and by the time we left we felt sure that our get-together had been very positive in that attitudes around that table had definitely changed. They were no longer ignorant of the facts and they would never again be so easily duped by blatant propaganda.

It was a great pity that none of this discussion at the O'Haras' was included in the *Panorama* programme. We asked John Bridcut and Nick Robinson about this at the time of the final editing, and they told us that the whole morning had been seamless in the sense that there had been no obvious place where the film could be cut to include even a short part of it, at least not without doing it an injustice. Just as with President Robinson's helping hand to pull me up the slope, the omission of the whole of the O'Haras' group discussion was a shame, as it denied the viewer the chance of seeing well-meaning Irish Americans discovering, probably for the first time, the painful truth about the real Ireland.

On our way to meet the O'Haras, we had an experience that confirmed just how isolated the ordinary American is. As we stopped for petrol John Bridcut stepped down from the van and asked the attendant to fill it up. The attendant looked straight back at John and in a completely serious tone enquired, 'Hey, buddy, what language is that you're speaking?' John looked incredulous and replied emphatically, 'English!' There was a brief pause while the attendant appeared to be considering John's answer before, in a very laconic way, he stated, 'Jeez, I thought I recognised it.' As we pulled away from the filling station, I couldn't help replaying this little cultural exchange over and over. The words and the facial expressions of John and the attendant certainly gave us all something to smile about.

By way of relaxing in the afternoon, we took a Boston Harbor boat ride. The weather was delightfully warm, and the view from the boat of the city skyline was magnificent. Jonathan filmed Wendy and me leaning against the rail looking out towards the city, and an American woman called out to us both, 'Are you two famous?' We both barely had time to smile, let alone answer her question, when she followed up with a second question, this time directed at Wendy. 'Are you Lady Diana?' she asked. Wendy was greatly amused by this. She assured the lady that she was not Lady Diana, and, to give her denial the ultimate confirmation, I added, 'And I'm not Prince Charles either!'

When our trip around the harbour was over, I carried out a pre-arranged interview at the water's edge with Frank Costello, a Democrat who was seeking election as a city councillor. This turned out to be another of those interviews that left me feeling as if I had been talking to a machine. Although not as extreme in his language as Jean Maguire and Jim Smith, Frank Costello still regarded British troops as the manifestation of state terror and in effect no different from the IRA and Loyalist paramilitaries. He belonged to yet another group whose purpose was to monitor British injustices in Northern Ireland. He said he totally opposed all forms of violence, which included the British Army's terrorising of the Catholic population.

My attempts to remind him that the religious inequality that had existed in Northern Ireland in 1969, when the civil rights campaign first began, had now been removed, were met with cynicism on his part. This became an uncomfortable and increasingly pointless meeting, made all the more difficult by ships' horns blasting just yards away from us, and by aircraft landing and taking off from the city's airport across the harbour.

Frank trotted out all the usual criticism of British policy in Northern Ireland. He typified much of what we had come to expect in this city, an articulate, polished and well-prepared condemnation of everything British.

The evening was set aside for us to spend time in an Irish bar to sample the flavour of the Irish American scene. We visited The Black Rose in the busy Quincy Market area of the city centre, and settled down with our drinks to listen to the band. Mike O'Hara was due to join us, but he was a little late, and by the time he did arrive I'd had enough of the endless stream of patriotic songs, immortalising and sanctifying men who were killers, men like the murderers of Tim. To hear them sung of as martyrs was more than I could take. I told Wendy and John Bridcut I was not staying. Wendy left with me, but before we left we thanked Mike O'Hara for his and Nancy's great hospitality earlier that day.

And so our final day in Boston arrived. It was to be our day off, when we could do what we wanted with our time. Dominic and Abbi had already extracted unbreakable promises from us that we would buy them trainers while we were in America, but I awoke to find Wendy feeling unwell. She told me that she had been awake most of the night with severe stomach pains. I rang the hotel reception to ask whether there was a doctor on call, but I was informed that I would need to take Wendy to Massachusetts General Hospital, a few miles away. Julie drove us there and dropped us off, saying she would call back in an hour. Unfortunately, we sat and waited in a crowded room just as we would have done in an NHS hospital back home. I had assumed that an American hospital would be much better organised than its British counterpart, and it came as a real surprise that, if anything, the opposite was true.

Eventually Wendy was examined, given a prescription and we went to find a chemist's shop. After a little while she felt much better, and we set off on our shopping expedition with Mike Day, whom we'd met back in the hotel lobby after being dropped off by Julie.

We went by bus to an out-of-town shopping mall which had lots of sports shops. After checking out several of them, we made our choice of trainers for Dom and Abbi. Needless to say, when we got them home, Dom didn't like his, but although we still had the receipt there was no chance of taking them back for a refund!

When we returned to the hotel, Kevin Cullen interviewed us for a story in his paper, and the local Boston TV channel interviewed us both in the hotel and then at the airport as we waited to catch the flight home to England.

Wendy and I had our fingers crossed that Virgin would upgrade our seats as they had done on the outward journey, but sadly it was not to be. However, the local representative of Virgin Airlines did invite us all into the airline's first-class lounge, where delicious little pastries were on offer. After Simon and I had had our fill, there were very few left by the time our flight was called. Everyone slept soundly on the flight home, except for me. I tried every way I possibly could to get to sleep but failed miserably. Consequently, I didn't relish the second flight from Heathrow to Manchester. We finally arrived back at the house at 1.30 p.m. on Tuesday, having set off at 8.00 p.m. Boston time on the Monday evening.

The next morning, the production team arrived bright and early to film the family going about the usual morning routines. It was a complete shock to Abbi when Jonathan crept into her room to film her as she woke up. To say she was not amused would be an understatement. She was profoundly upset, but it was my fault and not Jonathan's as I had authorised him to do it.

The production team left us to go to Dom and Abbi's school to film a sixth-form discussion, as well as the presentation of two sports awards in Tim's name. Much to our delight, Gareth Bouldsworth, Tim's closest friend at school, won the boy's award, although none of this was shown in the final programme.

The last piece of filming took place at Mottram Hall Hotel, in Alderley Edge, Cheshire. Steve Bradshaw, an established member of the *Panorama* team, interviewed me in a straight one-to-one. Although his father had died just a couple of days earlier, he conducted himself very professionally. Towards the end, he put it to me that some people might accuse me of being naive in making the programme. I told him that no one had the right to call me naive ever again, after what we had gone through. We had earned the right to investigate and speak our minds on the Northern Ireland problem, and I intended making it my business to see that Tim had not died in vain.

When the interview was over, Wendy and I and the whole crew had dinner together for the final time. There was a feeling of sadness that we had come to the end of a very exhausting but fulfilling experience. Over three and a half gruelling weeks together, we had all become very used to each other's company. Indeed, we felt the kind of kinship that inevitably grows when people join together to achieve a specific and worthy goal.

Our role was, for the time being at least, finished, while John Bridcut set about the monumental task of reducing thirty hours of film down to a rough-cut version of sixty-five minutes. This would be the first point at which Wendy and I would see the programme and have a chance to comment.

The date for this was set, giving John just three weeks to the first deadline.

Even at this stage, however, there were setbacks in the editing process. None of the section filmed on the Shankill Road with Alfie could not be used because, to our great amusement, Alfie's flies were undone. So in early August, Wendy and I had to return to Belfast to refilm the walk with Alfie along the Shankill.

During the week leading up to this unexpected return to Belfast, John Bridcut had telephoned me several times to discuss the possibility of meeting Gerry Adams, the Sinn Fein President. John had received word that Gerry Adams, who had previously declined an interview with Wendy and me, was now prepared to meet us, although not on film. John wanted to know whether we would agree to meet the Sinn Fein President, and subject to our saying 'Yes' he would then try to persuade Gerry Adams to appear on film, even though broadcasting restrictions would prevent his voice being heard.

For several days, I had long phone conversations with John during which he updated me about the on–off meeting with Gerry Adams. In the end, the meeting did not take place. The final comment made by a Sinn Fein official to explain why it could not go ahead was that appearing on film with Colin and Wendy Parry would be the height of voyeurism!

This remark incensed me. It elevated voyeurism to the status of being a more heinous sin than murdering our son. The truth of the matter was obvious: Gerry Adams did not wish to be faced with the task of answering the unanswerable question 'How do you justify the murder of our innocent son?' This, and the other questions I would have put to him, he would have found impossible to answer credibly. But I must say that it would also have been immensely difficult for me to talk to the man who heads up the political wing of the IRA.

I had always known that a face-to-face meeting with Gerry Adams would be terribly difficult for me. Conflicting emotions would have pulled me in many directions. I knew, for instance, that it would be essential to remain calm and composed, even though the instinct to yell at the man might have been overpowering. I also knew that, like most other politicians I have met, he would try to close me down by delivering long-winded statements. Faced with such tactics, I was not at all sure how I would have reacted. Another of my worries was that my questions may have been entirely emotional and lacking in any real coherent structure. As I have said before, I did not prepare written questions at any time during the programme, preferring to trust my instincts, which had served me well in my professional interviewing career over twenty-five years. To have departed from my natural style and written my questions beforehand might have made them seem wooden and contrived. Yet to have met Gerry Adams and have trusted myself to keep a clear head and remain focused on asking pertinent, probing questions would have placed an intolerable burden on me and might possibly have been beyond me.

These were just some of the considerations I weighed up between and during my phone calls with John. By the time John said the meeting was not going ahead, I honestly did not know whether I was relieved or disappointed – in truth, I think I was both, if that's possible.

I underwent further soul-searching when John was also trying to arrange a meeting with the Reverend Ian Paisley for the day we were to return to Belfast. When he first mentioned the possibility of this meeting, I had very mixed feelings. Interviewing a leading Ulster politician like Ian Paisley would have meant that a political heavyweight

would have been in the programme when it was intended
to be about Wendy and me, an ordinary British couple,
meeting ordinary Irish and Irish-American people. Had
the Ian Paisley interview taken place, it would have been
counter-balanced by the Gerry Adams interview, or so
John argued. I told John that Ian Paisley would have
been deeply offended to be seen as a counter-balance to
the President of Sinn Fein, and John agreed. Even when
we knew the Adams interview was not taking place, John
was still in contact with Ian Paisley's son, trying to firm up
the meeting. Only when Wendy and I met John and the
rest of the team in Belfast on 6 August did the news come
through from Paisley junior that his father would not be
back in Northern Ireland from a European trip until very
late on the Saturday night. It was claimed that he would
have been too tired to have made an interview worthwhile.
Frankly, although I never said so at the time, I think a tired
Ian Paisley might have been an easier prospect for me to
interview than an upbeat Ian Paisley.

So in the end our final trip to Belfast for the *Panorama*
programme was for one thing only, to make amends for
Alfie's state of undress. The balance of the programme
was not altered after all.

There remained just one more item for inclusion in the
final programme, and that was our home video film of
Tim. Julie was entrusted with the video after we had
agreed with John which scenes we most wanted to be
used in the programme.

We felt it would have been all too easy for people watching to lose track of why we had made the programme in the
first place had Tim not been seen in the film, in life, enjoying himself, as he had always done. Tim was the reason we
made the programme and we wanted all those who watched
it to take him to their hearts and to remember the awful
events of 20 March 1993 and the days that followed.

Tim had so looked forward to becoming a teenager, but it wasn't to be, and instead of celebrating his thirteenth birthday on 1 September we wept at his graveside with our closest family members. Just five days later, on 6 September, nearly six million people watched the BBC *Panorama* film about our ordinary boy.

9

In the weeks following the end of filming for *Panorama*, we remained very busy with interviews and functions, but the major event in our lives was our annual two-week holiday. In the end we decided for the third year running to have a camping holiday in France, even though Wendy was unconvinced at first.

Her misgivings were based on her natural fear that we would be constantly reminded of Tim, but as I told her, wherever we chose to go, we would always be aware of Tim's absence. In any event, Dominic and Abbi had always enjoyed campsites. Generally they were lively and active places with lots of other children of the same age. Our week in Spain in June had been so quiet with Dom and Abbi not being able to make friends, so it was desperately important for them to have an enjoyable holiday.

Wendy and Abbi had never enjoyed the long hours of driving from the north of England to France, so this time we booked the car on to the French rail link to take us from Calais to Avignon. We travelled on the sleeper service and awoke to find ourselves a comparatively short hop from Port Grimaud, near St Tropez, where we were staying. The family in the next berth to ourselves were a lively quartet from Newport on the Isle of Wight, and as the father's name was Tim we found as many reasons as we could for using it – it was good to have a Tim so close again.

The fortnight passed relatively uneventfully, but we did experience the occasional light-hearted moment and share some laughter together, a little like we used to do on previous family holidays. These moments were special to us, but there was still no escape from the guilt of trying to enjoy ourselves and then, when we did, feeling guilty that we had.

During the daytime, Dom and Abbi mainly concentrated on playing in the pool, whereas in the evenings they were attracted by the bar area which featured table tennis, bar billiards, pinball machines and discos. The sounds of high-pitched children's voices playing noisily, shouting each other's names and protesting about something and nothing, were the familiar sounds of a family holiday. Children all live their lives at high speed, like there's no tomorrow, and of course there is no tomorrow ever again for Tim. Time and again throughout the holiday, and usually without warning, desperate sadness and emptiness engulfed us at the recurring realisation that never again would we hear Tim's voice calling a friend's name, or yelling at Dom or Abbi over something and nothing, or just having great fun as children are meant to do.

Tim has been robbed of these essentially simple pleasures and that is what hurts so much. To try to convey the deep pain and despair caused by the loss of our son and to do it effectively is a skill perhaps beyond my reach. Everyone can recall the pain of losing a loved one but for most of us, if our lives follow the natural order, it will be the loss of our parents. Naturally we feel a terrible sense of loss and sadness when that happens, just as I did myself when my mother died. But the pain felt at the death of one's parents is quite unlike the pain experienced at the death of one's child. The empty longing you feel inside is so acute that you are beyond consoling, because the loss of a child is the ultimate nightmare: it offends nature's way.

There are bound to be other bereaved parents reading this account of Tim who know personally the way it affects you. They know only too well what it means to be robbed of a life you have created. They know the deep longing ache to have them back again; they know the primitive human desire to switch places with them, for it to be your life that was taken and not theirs.

Holidays are now bitter-sweet affairs. As a family, we always enjoyed going away together, especially abroad, but then there were five of us. Now, although we do our best to make our holidays enjoyable for Dom and Abbi's sake, we can't pretend that life is the way it was, no matter how hard we try.

This was brought home to me particularly poignantly when Dom and Abbi asked if they might try paragliding at the beach. I was proud of their courage for wanting to try it, and even more proud when they did it, but I could not stop thinking about Tim from the moment they were strapped into their harnesses. They were pulled down the beach and into the shallow water before the boat's speed lifted the parachute high into the clear blue sky. This was exactly the type of challenge that Tim would have loved. Dom and Abbi criss-crossed the bay at speed, though Wendy and I watched with concern when Abbi slipped from her harness and was hanging, instead of sitting. It occurred to me at that point that, had it been Tim up there, he would have shouted, 'Don't worry, I'm OK, this is great!'

One day, towards the end of the holiday, the young receptionist from the campsite office brought a note asking me to call Mike Day at the BBC, and when I eventually made contact with Mike he informed me that the *Mail on Sunday* were very keen to interview Wendy and me for their Sunday edition preceding the *Panorama* screening.

So keen were they on the interview that their reporter, a young Australian called Mike Robotham, was flown from London to Nice to meet us. The poor chap was tired and damp when he arrived, being dressed for London and not the South of France. He interviewed us in the shade

outside the mobile home, before very kindly offering to
buy us dinner at the camp restaurant. We spent a relaxing
evening with him before he left to write what he said would
be a long and detailed article.

Subsequently, despite all Mike's efforts, the *Mail* decided
not to use the piece because the *Daily Telegraph*, which
had interviewed us before our holiday, had run a similar
article in their Saturday edition. So much for the spirit of
competition among British newspapers!

We returned from France a few days before 1 September, a significant date in that it would have been Tim's
thirteenth birthday. The family gathered at our house
before visiting the cemetery. As we stood at Tim's grave,
his five-year-old cousin Penny asked Wendy, 'Will Timmy
be having a big party up in heaven?'

'Yes, Penny, he will,' Wendy replied, 'and he'll also be
looking down at us all visiting him.'

We all stood in silent prayer for several minutes until
each of us was ready to leave, and then, returning to the
cars, Wendy noticed Penny looking up as she walked along.
'Why are you looking up?' Wendy asked her.

'I'm looking for Timmy but I can't see him looking
down,' said Penny softly. Wendy stopped, bent down and
picked Penny up and held her especially close.

The weekend before *Panorama* was televised, Wendy
and I were invited down to London to give a press
conference on the Sunday morning. We decided to travel
on Saturday morning, to give Wendy time to look at the
shops in Oxford Street. Fortunately, the trip was less
damaging to our bank balance than I feared it might be!

In the evening, we had planned to have dinner with Mike
Day and his girlfriend Sue, but they had been to a wedding
in Lincolnshire and were unable to get back to London in
time. In the event Wendy and I ate on our own and had
an early night.

Mike collected us from the hotel on Sunday morning and, as the weather was so good, we walked to Broadcasting House. The press conference was fairly quiet and so I took the opportunity, when the questions were finished, to issue our thanks to the press for their consistently sensitive handling of our family's tragedy. Some of them actually looked a little embarrassed.

Lunch was a grand affair in the Hilton Hotel thanks to the generosity of Nick Robinson, who said that everyone at *Panorama* was confident that the programme would be well received and they all felt it had been a challenging and worthwhile project. It was late afternoon before our elaborate lunch ended, and we were then collected by a chauffeur-driven Jaguar and taken to Sky Television for an interview on the Sky News channel.

Back at the hotel, there was a message for me to ring the Irish radio station, RTE. This I did, and an early-morning telephone interview was arranged for 6.30 a.m. on Monday, 6 September. Immediately after that interview, we were collected and taken to Broadcasting House, where I was interviewed by Brian Redhead.

Now this interview was very special for me, as I had been an avid, regular listener to Brian on Radio 4's *Today* programme for more years than I care to remember. It was always a pleasure to drive to work listening to Brian and John Timpson when they were teamed together in the early 1980s, and even after John Timpson no longer co-presented *Today* I still tuned in daily to Brian.

I had been interviewed twice before on *Today* by Sue McGregor, the lady with the beautiful voice, and she had questioned me very sympathetically on both occasions. However, for me, Brian was the master! Like many others, I believed that he had been blessed with the wonderful ability to pose probing questions without ever becoming strident or hectoring.

My admiration of Brian came up in conversation with Nick Robinson and Bob Strange during one of their earliest visits to Warrington, and it was a great surprise to learn that Nick had been the only survivor of an awful road accident twelve years earlier which had taken, among others, the life of Brian Redhead's son.

Consequently, Nick and Brian were well acquainted, and though nothing was ever said, I think that Nick must have spoken to Brian and told him how much it would mean to me to be interviewed by him. I knew that Brian did not normally co-present *Today* on Mondays, but to my delight he chose to do so on this particular Monday morning.

Wendy and I arrived at 6.55 a.m. and were taken up to the fourth floor to the *Today* studio. Inside the waiting room, sitting huddled together, were Peter Hobday and Rabbi Lionel Blue. They were deep in discussion and neither looked up as we sat down. Unlike me, Wendy is not a Radio 4 fan and did not know why the rabbi was there, so I quietly explained about 'Thought for the Day', which the rabbi regularly presents, always with that unique brand of self-deprecating humour that has made him so popular. Peter Hobday returned to the studio, and when the rabbi and I exchanged glances I said 'Good morning' to him. He smiled warmly and returned the greeting, though I got the impression that he did not know who we were.

Brian Redhead came into the waiting room walking with a very pronounced limp. He said, 'I'm so very sorry about the loss of Tim; he sounded like he was quite a character!' Wendy and I smiled in acknowledgement of how accurate his observation was. Brian then said to us, 'I gather you know Nick Robinson? Did he tell you that he was in the same traffic accident in which my son was killed twelve years ago?' We confirmed that Nick had told us, at which point Brian retorted, 'I have to tell you, the pain doesn't go away, but then you already know that, don't you?' I found myself giving simple 'Yes' and 'No' answers, almost as if I were incapable of saying anything more complex. Looking back, I can only put my temporary loss of voice down to some form of stage fright, being in the company of a person I had always admired.

Eventually, I did manage a question and asked Brian about his leg. He told us that he was due to retire shortly from the *Today* programme, whereupon he was to have hip replacement surgery at Wrightington Hospital, near Wigan. Wendy and I had lived in Wigan for twelve years, but never knew, until Brian told us, that Wrightington Hospital had been the first to pioneer the hip replacement technique in Britain. Brian was also to become Vice-Chancellor of Manchester University. It was easy to warm to this gentle man and to see that he would continue to give sterling service to whichever field of activity he devoted himself to, after he retired from the BBC.

The sad irony is that Brian was to die within six months of our meeting, and on the day before he died in Macclesfield Hospital I finally wrote him a get-well letter after weeks of meaning to do so. I wrote with my best wishes on the Saturday and Brian died on the Sunday. I felt so very sorry that my timing had been so inopportune. I do hope that Brian's family, and in particular his wife, were not hurt by the timing of my letter. Thinking about these events, they were so like the experience we had when we continued to receive similar goodwill letters from people for several days after Tim had died. They said encouraging things like 'We know Tim is going to make it' and 'Don't give up, Tim will pull through, your love will give him the strength to survive.' These were heartfelt, yet heartbreaking things to read so soon after we had lost Tim. Naturally, the support of so many people right up to the end meant a very great deal to us, and we knew how great their sense of disappointment was when Tim lost his fight for life.

When Brian interviewed me, he was the complete professional. His questions and observations were skilful but tactful, as for example when he asked me the following:

'Why didn't you choose to stay at home and nurse your grief? Why did you feel the need to go across to Ireland?'

'Who did you want to meet, and talk to?'

'Did you want to find out how the ordinary people feel about the killing, the politics, about everything?'

'Did you meet some of the people there who had also lost some of their loved ones?'

'Did you get the feeling that there were people who were almost magnificent in their grief?'

'Do you feel the best way to cope is to keep talking about Tim, not only as a memory, but as a presence?'

He finished with, 'I'm sure everyone in the nation will send their love to you and Wendy and think about young Tim.'

Without wishing to be maudlin, maybe Brian has now met Tim, and has told him of our meeting and of all we have tried to do to keep his name alive. It would be comforting to think that Brian has carried our message to Tim.

Immediately the interview with Brian ended, we were taken to the Radio 1 studio where a young woman reporter interviewed me for the midday news round-up. From there it was on to a BBC Radio Ulster telephone interview and then, as we were about to leave for Euston to catch the Warrington train, we were given a message to ring Andy Gill, a Granada TV reporter.

Andy asked us to divert to Manchester and do a live 6.30 p.m. interview with Lucy Meacock at the Granada studios. Granada promised to get us home to Warrington in good time to see the *Panorama* programme. Lucy sat and talked to us in the hospitality room, checking her facts before the interview went out on the regional news. We eventually arrived home at a little before 8.00 p.m. and just prior to the BBC Nine o'Clock News, we saw the trailer previewing *Panorama* for the final time. This was a thirty-second-long series of photographs of Tim from babyhood to the time of his senior school photograph. The actor Michael Jayston provided the voice-over, accompanied by very moving background music. Though it was just a short sequence, the trailer was for Wendy and me a very moving and powerful way of presenting the programme, capturing, as it did, Tim's life in just six photographs.

Dominic, Abbi, Wendy and I settled down to watch the programme, though I must admit I felt strangely nervous about how the final edited version would appear. We'd been offered the opportunity to see the final cut but preferred to see it at home with the children. During the transmission, none of us spoke more than the occasional word, so intent were we on studying it closely to see how effectively it maintained its balance and impartiality. When the closing music played, no one said a word for several seconds before I asked Dom and Abbi for their honest opinions.

Dominic said, 'It was good', and then they both said, almost simultaneously, 'Tim would have liked it.' Typical of me, I wanted to know what they meant by the word 'liked'. Their opinions were more likely to have matched Tim's than mine, and that was why I was curious about their comments. They paused to consider my question, and then Abbi said, 'I think Tim would say that you made a good programme.' Dominic agreed. I pressed them no further, but their comments meant a great deal to us.

Over the next weeks, we received several hundred letters full of support for what we had done. Again, the proportion from Ireland was high, even though BBC programmes cannot be seen in all parts of the Republic.

During the days that followed, several more interviews took place, including Radio Kerry in Ireland, the BBC World Service and Radio Canada. The Radio Kerry interview was particularly notable for me, because Del O'Sullivan, our dear friend from Listowel, was linked up by telephone with the interviewer and me. Graham Bell of the *Sunday Express* asked me to write the 'Comment' column which is given over to a guest each week. This presented me with another opportunity to speak about the prospects for peace and reconciliation.

Meanwhile, on Saturday, 25 September, a very special event took place at Everton Football Club. A trophy called 'The Tim Parry Fair Play Trophy' was kindly presented to us by the Warrington Referee's Society. Two teams of under-12s from the Warrington League in which Tim's team, Penketh United, had played, were to compete for the prize.

The game was played before the Premier League match between Everton and Norwich City. Sadly for Everton supporters, the result from the boy's match, a 1–0 victory for Beechfield over Eagle, was infinitely better than the Premier League result which saw Norwich win 5–1.

Everyone involved with the boys' game had a marvellous day out, but I must single out for special praise Dave Maltby, the Warrington referee whose idea it was to create the trophy. My family were treated very well by the Everton club, by directors and players alike. The Everton captain, Dave Watson, whom we have come to know quite well, was obviously disappointed with the Everton result. In the players' lounge after the game, I moved among the Everton and Norwich players, getting as many autographs as I could for Abbi, who had suddenly decided that football wasn't so bad after all! Mind you, she has developed a disturbing fondness for Manchester United, I think because Ryan Giggs is so popular with girls of her age group. Dom and I certainly do not approve of this treachery and, needless to say, neither would Tim!

On Saturday, 9 October, the culmination of many months of hard work and painstaking preparation came to fruition with the official launch of the Warrington Project. The Project was formed initially by Warrington Borough Council to make sure that some good came out of the tragedy that took Tim's and Johnathan's lives. Its objective is to enable people from Warrington, Northern Ireland and the Republic of Ireland to spend time together in each other's communities and thereby break down distrust and prejudice, and in their place build friendship and understanding.

The concept was originated by the town's civic and political leaders. Soon after its inception, a committee comprising local councillors, two professors and myself as a representative of Tim's family was established to begin the process of fundraising. At an early meeting it was decided that an official launch would be a good way of getting media coverage. A date in October was set to allow sufficient time for all the details to be worked out.

Professor Patrick Buckland, head of Irish Studies at the University of Liverpool, and Professor Paul Wilkinson, head of International Relations at the University of St Andrews, recommended many of the guest speakers for the Project's launch, which was to take the form of a weekend seminar in Warrington Town Hall.

The President of Ireland, Mary Robinson, was invited to give the keynote speech at the start of the seminar, and much to everyone's delight she agreed to do so. With this in mind, I proposed at the final committee meeting just a few weeks before the launch that Prince Charles be invited too. Most of my colleagues on the committee were sure that we had left it too late to stand any chance of there being space in the Prince's diary, but we decided to issue the invitation regardless. To our great delight, Prince Charles sent official confirmation that he would attend, and in the meantime it had also been confirmed that Sir Patrick Mayhew, Secretary of State for Northern Ireland, would be able to be there as well.

Everyone was excited at the support being given to the Project's launch. Warrington's local MPs, Doug Hoyle and Mike Hall, as well as the town's MEP, Brian Simpson, were also to attend the seminar. Leo Enright, the BBC's Irish correspondent in Dublin, and Denis Murray, the BBC Northern Ireland correspondent, also confirmed their attendance. Above all, Wendy and I were especially delighted with the news that Senator Gordon Wilson was attending and would be giving a speech.

On Saturday morning, we arrived at the town hall early, ready for the arrival of Sir Patrick Mayhew. At 10.00 a.m. he was greeted by the Mayor and Mayoress, John and Cath Taylor, before meeting the town's chief executive, Mike Sanders, the leader of the council, John Gartside, and the Project Committee's chairman, Councillor Mary Greenslade. Also there to greet Sir Patrick were the local MPs and MEP, along with John Donlan, the Co-ordinator of the Project, Wilf Ball, Wendy and me.

With the single exception of John Taylor, the mayor, who is six foot four inches tall, Sir Patrick towered over everyone. At first, I found his aristocratic manner a little forbidding but since the launch I have met him on a number of occasions and found him to be a charming man.

A little later, we were summoned from the mayor's chamber, where we had spoken with Sir Patrick privately, to meet the Irish President, Mary Robinson, and her husband Nicholas. Wendy and I felt as if we were meeting a very special friend when she shook our hands, only this time it was our turn to thank her for coming to Warrington. I said to her, 'You may recall telling Wendy and me, when we met last in Dublin, that it was symbolically important for us to be in Ireland. Well, we regard it as symbolically important that you are here with us in Warrington at the launch of our Project.' The President smiled and told us how pleased she was to be able to show her support for the aims of the Warrington Project.

In her keynote speech, passages of which I have reproduced below, she spoke candidly about the realities of Northern Ireland, but also about the hopes of ordinary people:

> Ordinary people – in Belfast, in Dublin, in Warrington – have begun to put into words and demonstrations the revulsion and sense of injustice they rightly felt at the taking of lives for political ends – whether Irish or British, Nationalist or Unionist, Catholic or Protestant.
>
> At the time, I expressed the hope that the grief and outrage felt over the deaths of Johnathan and Tim, and of all who have died by violence in the last twenty-five years, could be harnessed in a constructive way to promote peace and reconciliation on the island of Ireland and between these islands.
>
> It is clear to me that there is at community level in Ireland and Britain a strong awareness of the futility and injustice of violence and a burning desire for peace.
>
> It seems to me that the people of Warrington have in this Project the great moral authority which such a community can draw upon when they make a common possession of their suffering and a common purpose of their healing. I have been deeply impressed – as have so many people in Ireland –

by the compassion and the authority of the people of Warrington. But we must understand that there are many people in housing estates and rural areas throughout Northern Ireland, Catholic and Protestant, who are deeply hurt and pained that the attention so rightly given to the tragic deaths and injuries in Warrington has not been matched by similar attention to their loss and suffering.

There are places in Northern Ireland . . . where the death of children and the destruction of homes and families are a nightmare, and yet such a regular occurrence that they no longer attract major attention or outrage. Places where individuals, as well as having to bear the suffering of violence, have to endure the indifference that the routine version of it attracts. I think we would be insensitive here if we did not realise that, while community action after a shared suffering is something nobody would have chosen, it is also – as you have structured it – a deep dignity and a method of self-expression which communities locked in the midst of recurrent, brutalising violence cannot hope for and cannot achieve. In all humility, the spirit of Warrington should pay tribute to their endurance, should include their suffering and understand their pain.

I hope the Warrington Project will serve as a model for community-based efforts to promote mutual understanding between the people on the island of Ireland, North and South, and between the peoples of Ireland and Britain, and that it may also serve to further enhance relations between the Irish community in Britain and their neighbours.

Schools in Northern Ireland have introduced a course entitled 'Education for Mutual Understanding'. I have in the past raised the question as to whether this course should be introduced . . . throughout Ireland. I would suggest that the Warrington Project may wish to consider a similar approach. Tolerance, as we all know, stems from knowledge, and tolerance is the key to mutual respect and mutual understanding, where differences in outlook and tradition can be accommodated and valued. These requirements apply with particular force to the complex relationships between Britain and Ireland. All of us must learn from past mistakes, we must be determined to avoid becoming trapped in the dead ends of historical antagonisms or comfortable prejudices. We must redouble our efforts to listen to each other, to understand the causes of those antagonisms and to ensure that at the level of neighbour and community, the mistakes and injustices of the past are never repeated.

The way in which peoples, communities and individuals are bound together is often a mystery. Barriers and divisions which seem age-old and implacable can melt away in a moment of common pain and common understanding. Out of the scars of Warrington, the Warrington Project has been born and that is its great strength and its great hope.

From my place alongside her on the platform, I could see in the faces of all the delegates that her speech was being listened to and, more importantly, heeded.

It fell to me to respond to the President on behalf of the Project, the town of Warrington and my family. I spoke as follows, after first thanking her and Sir Patrick Mayhew for gracing us with their presence.

Your presence with us here today shows the friendship and compassion that you and your fellow

countrymen have for us in Warrington. You share
and understand our pain so well because you have
had so much of your own.

Your presence also states clearly, from the highest
office in your country, that which we the ordinary
people demand, that the violence must stop.

Today is another day of symbolic importance.
Through this seminar we are founding a lasting,
community-based project. Our achievements and
progress won't be spectacular but they will be worthwhile. We won't be in the news very often but that
won't mean we are not doing all we can to bring our
communities closer together.

Friendship, understanding and co-operation will
come from this joint effort. However, our efforts
at community level on their own cannot bring about
peace. Politicians, Church leaders and community
leaders must not rest between atrocities. They must
tackle the causes of the violence. I challenge them
all to search their hearts and souls and consider
their own positions, many of which have remained
unchanged for so long. I tell you this, that the
ordinary people not only expect, but demand a
lead from you. You have been placed in high
positions in society because you have it within
you to bring about change and improve the lives
of ordinary people. You do not have the luxury of
putting the problem to one side because it seems
insoluble.

Tim, Johnathan, the other 120 children and the
3000 adult victims of these terrible twenty-five years
demand through those of us they left behind that
you leave no stone unturned and that you consider
anything and everything which will prevent other
families from losing their Tim or their Johnathan.

> For what it's worth, I shall continue to do every-
> thing in my power to bring about a lasting and
> honourable peace.

I sat down, relieved that I had not deviated too much
from what I had set out to say. For me, public speaking
was and still is a nerve-racking experience. I find that I
sometimes crank myself up as I am speaking and generate
more force and feeling than perhaps I should. On such
occasions, it would not surprise me too much to be
heckled or challenged by someone whose views I have
offended. This in fact has never happened, though I do
occasionally wonder why. I know that by nature I am
outspoken and opinionated and could quite easily upset
others. It's not that I deliberately or consciously set out
to be provocative – indeed, I almost always set out to be
the very opposite, as I dislike confrontation. But there
is something about public speaking which awakens in
me the wish to be thought-provoking in my words and
challenging in my tone. Add to this the nervous energy that
is adrenalin-generated and the natural desire to avoid being
dull, and you will understand why occasionally I worry that
I will make the audience very uncomfortable.

Set against all this, though, is the fact that, as Tim's
father, I am probably given rather more latitude than
others. People's natural sympathy means that they make
allowances for my occasional intemperance.

After my response to the President's speech, we had a
coffee break and were then treated to a wonderful Irish
speech, a delightful blend of rich humour and common
sense, from James 'Jimmy' Hawthorne, ex-head of the
BBC in Northern Ireland, and now chairman of the
Community Relations Council.

After the morning session, most of the delegates
adjourned to the huge marquee for lunch, while those

of us due to meet the Prince of Wales returned to the reception area. The President and her husband awaited a private audience with Prince Charles in the mayor's chamber.

At 12.30 p.m. the Prince arrived and was greeted by a small but enthusiastic group of Warrington people waiting outside. He stopped and talked with them for a couple of minutes before coming inside the town hall with the Lord Lieutenant of Cheshire. The mayor and mayoress showed Prince Charles into the mayor's chamber.

The same people who had been introduced to Sir Patrick Mayhew and President Robinson were introduced to Prince Charles, with the addition of Bronwen and Paul Vickers, who had arrived after the seminar had started. The Prince made his way slowly along the line, talking to everyone in turn. He was clearly in good spirits for the occasion, and was extremely friendly to us all.

'I've followed with interest all you've been doing since your terrible loss,' he told Wendy and me. 'You've been extremely busy, I know, and I hope you'll be able to keep going. It matters such a lot.'

We thanked him for the personal letter he had sent us soon after Tim had died, and we also explained that Tim had been a good son whom we could not just allow to slip into oblivion. He seemed to understand our motives.

As Prince Charles came to the end of the line, he walked to a table in the centre of the reception area, and there he signed the official visitors' book as Sir Patrick Mayhew and Mary Robinson had done before him. As he got to his feet after the signing, I approached him again, in order to ask whether he would consider becoming a patron of the Warrington Project. He said he would consider it and asked that the request be put to him in writing.

Prince Charles was taken to the marquee to meet as many of the other delegates as time allowed before he had to leave. Everyone was pleased to see him eating sandwiches because we had been told beforehand that he never ate anything offered to him in circumstances such as this. So much for rumours!

Prince Charles, President Robinson and Sir Patrick Mayhew all made a very favourable impression upon everyone they met, and it was very gratifying to see how warm and friendly the greeting between Prince Charles and President Robinson had been at what, we were told, was their first-ever meeting.

After lunch, the seminar resumed with a variety of speakers, clerical and secular, from both sides of the Irish Sea, covering the key topics of education and religion.

Dinner that evening was in the marquee and was a light-hearted affair, particularly as sitting on my right-hand side was Denis Murray, the BBC's Northern Ireland spokesman. Denis was great company and a keen family man. We talked of the love our respective daughters had for the pop group Take That. Denis chatted to Abbi about the group for quite a while and asked her whether she'd been to any of their concerts, and whether she had met them personally. This was a sore point with Abbi, as she had been promised the chance to go back-stage to meet her idols a couple of months earlier, but on the night had been told at the very last minute that it couldn't be arranged. That news was just about bearable, but when she discovered that other fans had been allowed back-stage, she was extremely upset.

As if to make up for her disappointment, Denis reckoned he could probably organise the group's autographs for Abbi, though it might take a while, he said. Abbi was delighted. Denis struck up a good rapport with Dominic too on Dom's favourite subject, football. It gave me great pleasure to see Denis so at ease with our children and more importantly taking the time to talk to them.

Doug Hoyle, MP, was the first speaker after dinner, and befitting the occasion his remarks were serious. He was followed by Leo Enright, the BBC's Dublin correspondent. Leo judged that a little levity was required and I think his judgement was probably right. As with so many of his countrymen, Leo could tell a good story, liberally tinged with a touch of the blarney. It was very entertaining stuff and it brought the day to a suitable, enjoyable close.

The Sunday morning session was most notable for the moving and emotional address given by Gordon Wilson. Gordon talked of his loss when Marie was killed at Enniskillen. He spoke with power of a father's love for his lost child, and he did so in a way that had Wendy and me in tears. Gordon cried too as he spoke of how the Warrington bombing had made him relive his own horror in 1987. He appealed to all men and women to find ways of settling their ancient disputes without resorting to violence and murder. When he finished he was applauded loudly, and he richly deserved it. He is a man who inspires others through his unshakeable commitment to peace.

The Project's launch proved to be a wonderful weekend in more ways than one, but it ended for Wendy and me with the most testing and upsetting event that we had had to face since Tim's birthday. The delegates to the seminar were joined by our family, and together we all walked, in glorious sunshine, from the town hall to Bridge Street for the unveiling by Wendy and Marie Comerford, Johnathan Ball's mother, of a plaque on the wall of Boots the Chemist.

The plaque says 'In remembrance of Johnathan Ball and Tim Parry, 20 March 1993'. It was secured to the wall immediately alongside the spot where the bin containing the bomb had been placed.

Apart from the one brief moment when Wendy and I laid flowers at the place where Tim had been fatally injured,

I had been back to Bridge Street only once. Even then I did not go any closer than perhaps twenty yards away, but Wendy had not set foot in Bridge Street at all. I lost count of how many times she had told me that she could not go near the spot where Tim had fallen.

But on this day she had to go there. The unveiling ceremony had been arranged as the final part of the Project launch weekend. As we arrived at the top of the street, we could see quite a large crowd of people gathered for the unveiling. Their numbers were swelled by the people who had walked from the town hall and by the presence of television cameras and newspaper journalists and photographers. A number of simple and brief speeches were made by members of the Warrington town centre clergy and then by the mayor. Wilf Ball took the stand and thanked everyone and, finally, I did the same.

The moment then arrived for Wendy and Marie to jointly pull the curtain back to unveil the plaque which showed Tim's and Johnathan's smiling faces. Wendy and Marie were both deeply upset, and both sobbed into their handkerchiefs.

What followed then was one of those unexpected but very moving events. It seemed that just about everyone in the crowd filed past the plaque, one by one, shaking our hands or embracing us. I found this a humbling experience, as I have done in several similar situations since. People smiled or wept or said wonderfully kind things to us, and, frankly, they left us speechless.

Wendy gradually recovered her composure and after most of the well-wishers had slowly drifted away we rejoined our family to return to the town hall where tea, sandwiches and cake were provided in the marquee.

Not all the delegates from Ireland were able to stay beyond lunchtime, and only a few of them walked along Bridge Street for the unveiling, but one of those who did,

whom I could pick out in the crowd of faces looking back
at me as I said my words of thanks, was Gordon Wilson.
Wendy and I were touched that Gordon came to the
spot where the evil deed that had taken Tim had been
perpetrated. Unfortunately, we did not get a chance to
thank him and he left before we saw him again, but his
presence meant a great deal to us.

Looking back on that weekend, the Warrington Project
could not possibly have had a better launch. Everyone
responsible for organising, speaking, attending and par-
ticipating deserved the highest praise.

Since that time, the Project Committee has applied for
charitable status, and has written to major fundholders in
the hope of gaining significant support in order to finance
and facilitate its educational programme and the exchange
visits we so desperately want to see happen. I find this a
frustrating process because progress is inevitably slow. I
always fear that the impetus the launch gave us shall be
lost and with it that window of opportunity which all too
briefly opens. Everyone continues to strive as best they
can, but as with all committees there are always going
to be differences of view, not on the main principles and
aims perhaps, but as often as not on matters of detail.

Not having come into contact with councillors before,
and having to adjust to the way they do business, even to
the extent of the language they use in meetings, is an alien
situation for me. My outspokenness has sometimes been
out of place, not always making the process of moving
forward as smooth as it might otherwise be.

People with the best of intentions who come together
for a common purpose do not necessarily gel, no matter
how hard they try to do so. So it is on occasions with the
Project, but the committee has stuck to its goals and has
been able to set aside any personal difficulties to achieve
progress. At the time of writing, it has agreed to fund a

peripatetic teacher to introduce Irish Studies into three Warrington secondary schools, a project which we feel sure would meet with the approval of President Robinson.

A further cause running parallel to the Warrington Project has been undertaken more recently, but this time with Wendy making all the running. When the Warrington Project seminar was under way, Wendy expressed the view that the Project needed a base from which to operate. Periodically, during the months since October, she has raised the subject whenever it seemed opportune to do so and, in Councillor John Gartside, she has found another who shares her enthusiasm. John was with Wendy and me one evening discussing matters in general when he mentioned that there was a thirteenth-century Grade II listed building in Warrington known as Bewsey Old Hall. The more he talked about it, the more we all became convinced that it would make the perfect base. At the end of the evening, John promised to speak to the Commission for New Towns (CNT) which owned the Hall.

The next time we met, John was very confident that the CNT would transfer ownership of the Hall to Warrington Council provided the Hall was to be refurbished and developed as an international youth centre, suitable for accommodating young people from Ireland and elsewhere in the world.

This process, we are happy to say, is now under way, with a trustee board appointed to try to bring the Hall to its finished state by the second anniversary of the bombing in Bridge Street. The Hall will not be directly part of the Warrington Project, but it will provide the perfect base for youngsters when they visit Warrington. The nickname given to the Hall amongst the trustees is the 'Wendy House'. Two eminent, locally based businessmen, Peter Greenall, head of Greenall Breweries, and Peter Waterman, record producer and pop group manager, are

among the trustees aiming to raise the £500,000 needed
to restore and equip the Hall. Peter Waterman's wife
Denise, also a trustee, is leading the fundraising activities
with Wendy.

Part of the means by which we have held on to our
sanity after losing Tim is by immersing ourselves in what
we consider to be worthwhile activities. My involvement
with both the Warrington Project and Wendy's extremely
active involvement in the youth centre have given us goals
to try to achieve. There is certainly no limit to Wendy's
commitment and enthusiasm for the project to restore the
Old Hall. With terrific help and support from life-long
friends like Mick and Sandra Ambler, and new friends
like Albert Spiby and Denise Waterman, she really has
made great progress in a very short time. Wendy is in
her element when she is involved in practical, hands-on
activities. This is the way she has always been, and it is
good for her to have something like Bewsey Old Hall to
pour her heart and soul into, all in the cause of keeping
Tim's and Johnathan's names alive.

When it is finished, the Bewsey International Youth
Centre will be a living memorial to Tim and Johnathan and
an everlasting reminder of the need for co-operation and
friendship across national borders. Inside the youth centre,
we intend to give a pictorial and narrative account of the
tragic consequences of the bombing for those families in
the town that were affected, but above all we want our
son's name to be synonymous with reconciliation and to
carry a message of peace and hope – just as I said I wished
it to be on the day of Tim's funeral.

10

In the period between October and Christmas, the extra effort required for peace in Northern Ireland to become a realisable dream suddenly seemed to be forthcoming. On 15 December, Prime Minister John Major and the Irish Premier, Albert Reynolds, produced the Downing Street Declaration after many weeks of careful negotiation.

There were those who claimed that it was a kneejerk response to the revelation that the British government had been holding secret talks with the IRA. For my part, I think the Declaration was a skilful, even-handed document regardless of its timing. It represented both governments' positions in a way that was to be welcomed. Britain no longer claimed any right to retain Northern Ireland in perpetuity, and the Republic recognised the Unionists' position. At first, I was disappointed that the Republic did not also unilaterally give up its constitutional claim to the six counties, but I understood the need to ensure that the IRA and Sinn Fein were not given an immediate pretext for distancing themselves from the results of the Anglo-Irish talks.

The much-publicised discussions held during the summer between SDLP leader John Hume and Gerry Adams appeared to be dead in the water because of government unease, particularly on the part of the British government. Yet the very fact that such a dialogue had been taking place at all was encouraging, for it appeared to signify that Gerry Adams was exploring political solutions at least as seriously as terrorist activity.

Disheartening throughout the whole process, of course, was the IRA's unwillingness to forego violence and terrorism as a means of pursuing its ends, and in October the terrible carnage in the Shankill Road occurred. Innocent people, and particularly innocent children again, paid the ultimate price for the failure to find a political solution. One knew immediately that a retaliatory terrorist act would take place as vengeance for the Shankill bomb. So it did in the small community of Greysteel, when Loyalist terrorists calmly walked into the Rising Sun bar on Halloween and sprayed the people inside with bullets, killing young and old, Catholic and Protestant alike. Once again it took acts of appalling barbarity to increase the tempo of political activity, but one must say that at times governments and politicians such as these are damned if they do something and damned if they don't.

Predictable hardline opposition to the Declaration came from the Reverend Ian Paisley while we suffered. We also saw the endless prevarication of Sinn Fein leader Gerry Adams. He claimed that clarification of the Declaration was needed but, if this was the case, I couldn't help wondering why, he did not simply submit the points requiring clarification in writing. The British government might then have been able to explain any areas considered unclear by the Republican movement. I know I will be open to the usual charge of naivety, because there will be those who say that I know too little for my views to be valid, but in my opinion the Declaration was a balanced and realistic attempt to close the seemingly unbridgeable divide separating Unionists from Nationalists. The proponents of these two polarised positions ought to be able to discuss the options and choices before them without resorting to violence. However, instead of making serious efforts to achieve lasting progress, we watched Gerry Adams being fêted by certain sections of American society. The media fell over themselves to interview him, and a New York Police pipe band gave him a reception more befitting a visiting head of state. I was asked many times by the British press what I thought of the treatment accorded to Gerry Adams in America. My answer was that it seriously undermined my confidence in those Americans who are apparently unable to distinguish between a saint and a sinner.

At the time, several British newspapers offered to take Wendy and me over to America to put us on the same television programmes as Gerry Adams had appeared on just a few days earlier, no doubt hoping we would be the antidote to Sinn Fein mania. Unfortunately, each of the offers required an immediate departure, which was simply not possible given family and job commitments. Nevertheless, it was a considerable compliment to be seen as the right people to set the record straight as far as IRA propaganda was concerned. Gerry Adams had groomed and prepared himself very professionally for his US trip and had scored what appeared to be a notable PR success, judging by the coverage the British media gave to his visit. Newspapers in Britain were quick to ask us to put the victim's case and thereby restore some balance, in so far as we were able, to the American public.

Again, it was interesting to reflect on the impact an ordinary family in extraordinary circumstances was capable of having on the political stage. We could never have foreseen in those dark and desperate days after 20 March that we would be invited to represent the British position on the Northern Ireland situation, albeit from a non-political point of view.

Claims were made at the time of his visit to the States that Gerry Adams would make a positive move on the peace process, and that at the very least he would deliver a ceasefire lasting long enough for it to be of real value to the diplomatic moves that were taking place. Regrettably this did not come about, and it was believed by many that Gerry Adams had reneged on promises made at the time he was granted an entry visa.

There is no doubt in my mind that the deaths of Tim and Johnathan did trigger a renewed vigour in the search for a peaceful solution. John Major had told Wendy and me at the town's memorial service in Warrington that he would do all he could to end the violence, and despite his many critics both within and outside his party, we cannot fault the serious efforts he has made since our son died.

Having considered the Downing Street Declaration from the perspective of a victim of the troubles and with no political axe to grind one way or the other, I take the view that together the British and Irish governments have moved quickly to find an accommodation that skilfully gives neither the Unionists nor the Nationalists any legitimate reason for opposing the peace process. However, the dimension that is lacking, and which for me is so important for lasting progress to be achieved, is the determination of the silent majority to voice their demands for peace to their political leaders. I am convinced that this group, made up of Protestants and Catholics alike, supports the peace efforts, because it recognises that peace can only be achieved through an accommodation such as the Downing Street Declaration. The exact form of words may not yet have been found, but when it has, the ordinary people on both sides of the divide must give their unconditional support. This support, along with the Republic's renunciation of its constitutional claim to the North, are surely the crucial missing pieces in the jigsaw.

In contrast to South Africa, the economic and social differences between opposing groups within Northern Ireland are very small. Unemployment is high regardless of religious or political affiliation. Housing standards are similar for all, and the prosperous middle classes are a mix of both religious and political groups.

Contrast this with South Africa under apartheid, where the overwhelming black majority had few, if any, democratic rights. They stood to gain so much, and the white minority to lose so much, and yet both knew that the status quo was unsustainable. The inevitability of change was widely recognised, but it took a statesman free from bigotry and hatred, to lead from the front. Nelson Mandela, despite twenty-seven years in prison, emerged as a visionary to be the catalyst for change in South Africa.

Where is the visionary for Northern Ireland? How are Unionism and Nationalism to be reconciled? How do you make Protestants trust Catholics and vice versa? How do you stop people questioning their neighbours' religion? So many questions but so few answers. The one certainty is that if violence ends, trust and collaboration will begin and a pathway to lasting peace and reconciliation will emerge. But as long as violence continues, people will be afraid to speak out. It is fear which stops the vitally needed but simple acts of human decency, like saying 'hello' or holding out a hand of friendship. While violence reigns, friendly acts are portrayed as treachery, punishable by knee-capping or a bullet in the back of the head.

It is difficult to imagine any rational person choosing to live in a society riven by extremes of politics and religion, where outrages on the scale seen over the past twenty-five years are tolerated. It seems that too few people in Northern Ireland have the will to change things. But why is this? Could it be that when outrages are not being committed, life is quite normal, despite soldiers on foot patrol and army checkpoints? After all, people know that soldiers aren't likely to shoot law-abiding citizens and that checkpoints are more an inconvenience than a threat.

Too many citizens of Northern Ireland may now have

settled for the uneasy status quo. The British government ploughs billions of pounds of taxpayers' money into the province every year to maintain its normality. There is no Soweto, no townships or homelands here. No, this is part of the United Kingdom, where everyone speaks English and everyone has the vote. Culturally, the people from both sides of the sectarian divide do the same things, like the same things, buy and eat the same things, live in similar houses in familiar streets and drive the same cars. So what is it that stands in the way of peace?

The answer is violence, which is the extreme manifestation of the deep-rooted distrust of one community for the other.

Many people now fear that if the violence does not end soon, there is a serious possibility that it will become completely criminalised. The violence will no longer have a political goal to give it respectability. It will exist simply to extort money to give the terrorist godfathers a comfortable lifestyle and the power to control their own group of enforcers at street and community level. To all intents and purposes the IRA, UVF, UFF and others will be little more than a form of Mafia. They differ from the Mafia now only in that they claim allegiance to a political cause. And yet these organisations must know that their violence cannot be allowed to secure a political victory. No government can be seen to bend the knee to terrorism, otherwise where will it all end? Will Scottish, Welsh or Cornish nationalists be next to try violence and terrorism to achieve their goals?

A united Ireland, or a Northern Ireland within the UK? This question depends entirely on the will of the people of Northern Ireland, we are told. But what of the views of the people of the Republic? Are they not allowed to say where they stand, at least on the question of whether they actually want the six counties within a united Ireland?

Joe Dalrymple, eldest son of Gerry Dalrymple, murdered

in Castlerock on the day Tim died, commented to me, 'I don't care whether we are ruled from London, Belfast, Dublin or even Moscow, all I want is the right to bring my children up in peace.' It's quite remarkable, but every time without fail that a bereaved parent, child, husband or wife is asked to comment upon their loss, they all say the same thing. That they don't want retribution, they want the killing to stop. We don't want others to suffer as we have. If only everyone could try to imagine how we feel, and imagine how they too would feel, then perhaps . . .

One of the subjects in which the press showed a lot of interest was the amount of compensation paid to Wendy and me by the Criminal Injuries Compensation Board (CICB) for the unlawful killing of Tim.

The sum concerned was £7500. We were asked by several newspapers to comment, and in the end, with some reluctance, we decided that we would. It was an awkward subject to air publicly because criticism of compensation can be construed as a means of seeking more. Public opinion is a fickle thing, and thus far we had been fortunate enough to have remained on the right side of it. When we considered some of the press treatment of Wilf Ball and the comments people made to us about Wilf's relationship with Michelle, his young companion, we were relieved not to be facing the same.

After considering the risks of speaking out, we decided that the sense of injustice we felt about the sum paid was something that we should comment on. The sense of injustice came from the fact that I am aware, by the very nature of my job, of the levels of compensation paid in damages for industrial accidents. Sums very similar to the £7500 we received are paid as out-of-court settlements where employers' insurance companies consider it less expensive to settle in this way than to fight the claim in

court. Even larger sums are awarded by judges in court
for comparatively minor injuries.

A *Sunday Mirror* reporter researched the typical level
of personal injury compensation settlements, and in her
article listed the fact that the loss of an index finger would
be compensated by the same amount as we had been paid
for the loss of Tim. This information, together with the
£350,000 damages paid to Elton John after he succeeded
in his libel case against a Sunday newspaper which alleged
that he chewed his food and then vomited it in order to
lose weight, magnified our sense of injustice. If society
estimates Elton John's outrage at £350,000, but the brutal
murder of our child at just £7500, then, as I said at the time,
there is something desperately wrong with our society.

Wendy and I were not aggrieved about the amount of
compensation per se, but we were upset about the topsy-
turvy values behind it. Personal and industrial injuries
rightly take account of pain and suffering as part of the
process of calculating compensation, but how can the pain
and suffering caused by the loss of an index finger ever
come remotely close to the pain and suffering endured
by losing a child. I wouldn't be at all surprised to learn
that the total compensation paid to all parents of the 120
children killed as a direct result of the Northern Ireland
Troubles does not exceed the amount paid to an already
fabulously rich man like Elton John.

The theme of injustice came up in several different guises
either side of Christmas. On one occasion I can recall
with vivid clarity, I was interviewed by Anne Diamond
and Nick Owen on their mid-morning programme from
BBC's Pebble Mill studios in Birmingham. The interview
progressed along fairly orthodox lines until Anne Diamond
reminded me that I had said that terrorists who are
killed should not be permitted a normal Christian burial
service. 'Won't your views cause a great deal of anger

and resentment?' she asked. Momentarily I was aghast that any level-headed person could possibly consider that my view on this point was unreasonable, but when she put her question, and several times since, I have had to accept that I don't have a monopoly on being right, nor will I always speak for the ordinary man or woman. My instinctive reaction to Anne's question was to feel that it was an unjust challenge. This was the first time during an interview that something I had said was challenged, and I was not used to the experience at that time. However, as time has gone by, I am asked increasingly often to comment on political or ethical questions, as well as on the central question of being a bereaved father. I treat it as a considerable compliment when invited to take part in serious discussions beyond my immediate field of experience, but I do recognise the danger that others may attribute a wider authority to my words than is perhaps warranted or has been earned on merit.

Channel 4's *Right to Reply*, chaired by Jon Snow, debated the broadcasting bans imposed on Sinn Fein by the British and Irish governments in a joint programme with RTE, filmed in Dublin earlier this year. We were invited to take part in the programme, which included among others programme controllers from Channel 4 and RTE, Michael Mates, the ex-Northern Ireland minister, and Ken Maginniss, the Official Unionist party spokesman on defence.

The programme was broadcast just a matter of days before the Irish government lifted its twenty-year-old ban on all broadcasting by Sinn Fein. The panel and the audience were split fairly equally on whether such bans should remain or be lifted. I maintain that if there is to be a ban then it should be total, as the Irish themselves applied it. To my mind the partial ban, favoured by the British, where actors' voices are dubbed over the voices

of the likes of Gerry Adams, exposes the government
to ridicule. On balance, however, I disagree with any
ban, as it is likely to give weight to the charge that
the government is being undemocratic. Such charges are
aimed at Britain from America with unerring accuracy by
the Irish-American propaganda lobby.

Increasing opportunities were beginning to come our
way to participate in public and private debates, and
Wendy was aware that I valued the chance to take part,
though she always felt too nervous to contribute person-
ally. Consequently, when I was invited to participate in
a weekend conference to consider the future of Northern
Ireland, I went alone. The other speakers included Sir
Patrick Mayhew, Joseph Small, the Irish ambassador to
Britain, Senator Gordon Wilson, Sammy Wilson of the
Democratic Unionist Party, Ken Maginniss of the Official
Unionists, Sir John Hermon, ex-Chief Constable of the
RUC, John Alderdice of the Alliance Party, and Mark
Durkan of the SDLP. Dr David Starkey, Professor of
History from the London School of Economics, chaired
the discussion. I admit to being both flattered and a little
nervous at the prospect of addressing such distinguished
and experienced delegates. I suppose it was this which
induced in me a state of mild anxiety after I had arrived
at the conference, and caused me to depart from my usual
practice of either speaking on an entirely ad hoc basis, or
of preparing the very briefest of notes just moments before
being called upon to speak.

According to the conference programme, I was sched-
uled to speak on Sunday, and consequently I'd planned to
work on what I would say early Sunday morning. However,
after waking early on Saturday morning, the outline of
what I might use in my speech quite unexpectedly began
to take shape. I have a notoriously poor memory as a
rule, and so rather than run the risk of forgetting my

ideas, I quickly transmitted them to paper. I then set off for breakfast feeling rather satisfied with myself about the fact that I now had a day to spare to fine-tune what I would say to the conference on Sunday.

During the morning break for coffee, one of the organisers approached me to tell me of a change of plan. He asked whether I would mind presenting my speech immediately following lunch on the Saturday rather than on the Sunday morning. Somehow it felt less like a request and more like a polite notification of a change, but thanks to my brain having begun to operate at a much earlier time in the morning than it usually did, I was able to agree to his request.

It was a relief that I had jotted down the broad outline of what I wanted to say. I am not a politician and neither am I party-political, but the gist of what I said in my speech was intended to pose direct and straightforward questions to all the politicians involved in the Northern Ireland question. What I said is reproduced below:

> I represent no group or organisation. I represent only my family and perhaps the bemused, the ill informed and the largely disinterested British public. My comments are personal, honest and, I hope, straightforward. Whether they are accurate and of any use to this debate (on the future of Northern Ireland) is, of course, for you to decide.
>
> I have characterised the search for peace in Northern Ireland as a battle of WILLS.
> - Will people of all sides accept that the status quo will not end the violence?
> - Will everyone accept that there must be change?
> - Will everyone realise that change begins inside each and every one of us?
> - Will those who kill look inside themselves and change?

- Will those who give encouragement, support and shelter to those who kill understand that they are equally culpable?
- Will those who don't kill but nevertheless hold extreme views which induce fear in others and represent an obstacle in the way of change also re-examine their consciences?
- Will the elderly hardline Orangeman who told me that he was honouring his war dead live in the 1990s and not the 1690s?
- Will the Loyalists who claim they want to remain 'British' accept that their Britain no longer exists?
- Will hardline Republicans understand that 75 per cent of Northern Ireland's population want Northern Ireland to remain within the UK? This includes the majority of Catholics.
- Will Republicans understand that a reunited Ireland can only come about if the majority in Northern Ireland wants it?
- Will the Irish Catholic Church reconsider its policy on integrated education?
- Will the British government worry less about the semantics of whether clarification equals negotiations and instead urgently pursue peace in every way it can?
- Will the middle-class population of Northern Ireland, which has the highest disposable income in the UK, end their passive attitude and actively work for peace?
- Will ordinary people living in ghetto areas behind the so-called 'peace lines' make the effort to meet their neighbours from the other side again?
- Will Irish Americans take the trouble to find out what the Ireland of today is like?
- Will all parties consider a third-party neutral, who

could begin to broker a peace, much as Norway
did with Israel and the PLO?

No one pretends that there are easy answers,
but if everyone opens their hearts and minds to
work in a spirit of co-operation, then peace can
be achieved and the bereaved parents club that
Gordon and Joan Wilson and Wendy and Colin
Parry belong to will grow no further and will, in
the end, die with us.

The reaction to my speech from the audience was very
favourable and complimentary, with several delegates
shaking me warmly by the hand as they told me that I
had asked a lot of pertinent questions. I felt very relieved
that it had been well received.

The two-day conference reminded me once again that
there are rather more opinions than there are solutions
to the Northern Ireland problem, and as one speaker
observed, 'Every time the English solve the Irish question,
the Irish change the question.'

In March I was invited to be a 'witness' on the BBC
Radio 4 programme *The Moral Maze*. The subject under
discussion was the British government's invitation to the
German government to take part in the VE Day celebra-
tions. The debate centred on the question of forgiveness,
and I was asked to contribute from the perspective of
whether or not I could forgive the IRA. I was also
aware that I would be invited to comment on the main
question, and so the day before I asked my father for his
view, hoping it would be the same as my own. My father
was a chief petty officer in the Royal Navy throughout
World War II, and for as long as I can remember he
has always held strong views about the experiences that
he and thousands of his comrades shared between 1939
and 1945. I was pleased that his view echoed my own,

and I felt a little more comfortable espousing the view in favour of reconciliation. Given the adversarial nature of the programme, it was put to me that I should forgive the IRA in the same way as it was being assumed I forgave Germany. In fact I did not say that I forgave Germany, but in any event I saw a huge difference between German forces fighting for their country, even when its government was evil, and terrorists planting bombs in litter bins in Warrington. I also reiterated that neither Wendy nor I can ever forgive the callous, inhuman people who took our son's life after hideously injuring him.

During the year since Tim was taken from us, there have been three especially difficult times when our sense of loss has been overwhelmingly strong. The first was 1 September when he would not only have celebrated his birthday but would also have become a teenager. This is a big milestone in a child's life, ranking alongside their eighteenth and twenty-first birthdays, but instead of celebrating with Tim at a normal happy family party we stood in silent prayer at his graveside, remembering the magnitude of our loss.

Christmas, we always knew, would be particularly hard on us. Every other Christmas I could recall, we had put up decorations and the tree two weeks or so before Christmas Day. But this Christmas was not like any other. We had no sense of joy or happy expectation. There was very little discussion about what to buy for whom, which is usually part of the exciting build-up to the day. It had always been one of Tim's most endearing traits that he regularly put down markers about what he hoped to receive at Christmas or his birthday, months before the event. I lost count of how many times he would then change his mind as the time got closer. This habit always drove Wendy to distraction, since it generally fell to her to take care of this side of our domestic routines. How we would both have welcomed back any of Tim's irritating habits!

Christmas was saved from being unbearably empty and painful by the many invitations we received from our family and friends. Without our ever saying so, being out of the house was what we needed most. The house felt and looked empty no matter how hard we tried. Decorations and our tree were brought down from the loft and put up a day or two before Christmas, along with the scores and scores of cards, not only from family and friends but also from many well-wishers. In any other circumstances, the scene would have appeared festive and colourful, but in our hearts there was nothing but sadness.

For sixteen years, Wendy and I had always invited her parents, my father and her brother and sister to our house on Christmas Day, but this time Phil, Wendy's brother, and Karen, his wife, insisted that we go to stay with them at their home near Leek in Staffordshire, and we were pleased to do so. Coming downstairs on Christmas morning to open Dom's and Abbi's presents without Tim was a nightmare prospect for us. But being away and watching our young nieces, Penny and Alice, opening their presents with Dom and Abbi meant that the heartache was a little less severe.

Inexorably, the sadness had been building up over many days. On Boxing Day we all met at Wendy's sister's house, and the dam burst, with Wendy crying her heart out in Carol's kitchen. We all, in turn, tried to console her, but her heartbreak and her feeling of loss swept over the rest of us like a tidal wave. We all cried with her until a kind of exhausted calm fell over everybody. Tim had been the only topic of conversation during the afternoon in the kitchen. Friends of Carol and Terry wisely remained in the other rooms, realising that private family grief was being poured out in the kitchen. The trouble was that the food and drink were in the kitchen too!

I think we all felt a little better after this outpouring,

almost as if we had all been cleansed and relieved at the
same time. Memories of Tim were recounted with great
feeling and occasional humour throughout the afternoon.
In every way, apart from his physical presence, Tim had
been with us all that day. His life and the abject pain of
his death had permeated every fibre and nerve-end in an
intense assault, leaving a kind of lightness in the heart and
soul afterwards.

The third and perhaps the most difficult time of all
was from the first anniversary of the bombing to the
first anniversary of Tim's death. Cards and letters began
to arrive in the week before 20 March, expressing kind
feelings for us, recalling the senders' own feelings of one
year earlier. On Sunday, 20 March, the four of us went
back to Bridge Street to lay flowers at the place where
Tim had fallen so desperately injured. As we laid our
flowers, Johnathan Ball's mother, Marie, also arrived to
lay flowers. I put tape on the stems of two white carnations
so that Wendy and Marie could stick them to the plaque
on the wall.

Media interest in the victims of the bombing and in the
town itself was quite intense over the week. Timed to
coincide with the first anniversary of the bombing was
a special edition of the programme *40 Minutes* on BBC 1,
featuring Bronwen and Paul Vickers' brave fight to overcome Bronwen's terrible injuries. What most viewers did
not know was that, having done so well to adjust to her
artificial leg in such a short time, Bronwen was then struck
down by a recurrence of the malignant cancer she had
suffered some years earlier. In a way which typified her
courageous qualities, Bronwen fought against this further
terrible setback and throughout the early part of 1994,
despite the advance of the disease, she continued to play
her part in supporting the good things to come out of
Warrington.

Sadly, on July 7, Bronwen's fight for life ended when the cancer reached her brain. As Paul, her husband, told me when he rang me with the dreadful news, "Bronwen would not have wanted to live like that, (a reference to the terrible final effects of cancer) it is better that she has gone to where there is no more pain." When I was asked in an interview to comment on Bronwen, my reply was, "If I know Bronwen, she'll be sitting with her arm around Tim, smoking one of her rolled up cigarettes, with a half pint of bitter, telling him all about the past fifteen months and all that we have been doing to keep his and Johnathan's names alive."

The day after the first anniversary of Tim's death, Gordon Edwards and Liz Antrobus got married. Gordon and Liz suffered very nasty leg injuries, but like Bronwen, both showed a single-minded determination to make it down the aisle on their wedding day and they succeeded in doing so.

Wilf Ball and Marie Comerford, Johnathan Ball's parents, are putting their lives back together, but separately. Wilf met and planned to marry a young lady called Michelle Smith, but the relationship broke up. Marie is rebuilding her life with her husband and sons. She is a woman who seems more than capable of coming to terms with her loss. Wilf, too, has the character to adjust to his new circumstances and although we know he misses little Johnathan terribly, he is made of strong enough stuff to get his life back together.

All the other victims of the Warrington bombing are slowly but surely mending their bodies and their minds. They will never forget what they felt and what they saw on 20 March 1993. It has changed them and the rest of us in very fundamental ways.

As for Wendy and me, there were other events in our lives which, in their own way, helped us to rebuild and

find the strength to go on. Memorable among these were
a trip to Northern Ireland as guests of the British Army
in November and a private visit by Her Royal Highness,
the Duchess of Kent to our home in February.

The visit to Northern Ireland followed an invitation
from Brigadier Irwin, commander-in-chief of land forces
in Belfast. In his letter, the Brigadier apologised for the
soldier on foot patrol in the Falls Road area who had rudely
brushed aside my attempt to speak to him when we were
filming for the *Panorama* programme. He also suggested
that we might find it useful to talk to ordinary British
soldiers stationed in the province. We had in fact already
seen the other side of the British Army when we had been
filming our *Panorama* programme. The opportunity had
arisen when John Bridcut wanted to film us together with
some soldiers, and to this end we had travelled to the Turf
Lodge area of the city.

Soon after we arrived, several foot patrols from the
Devonshire Regiment arrived on the scene. As one drew
near, I bid him 'Good day.'

Noting my accent, he remarked, 'You're not from
around here, are you?'

'We're from Warrington,' I told him.

'So what are you doing here, then?' he asked me. When I
had told him, he said, 'I thought your face was familiar.'

'Hey, boys,' he said to his mates, 'this is the couple who
lost their young lad in the Warrington bombing.' Several
of his colleagues called out their 'hellos' and their sympathy
as they carried on walking. But what impressed me most
was when I saw several of the soldiers chatting in a very
relaxed and friendly fashion with teenagers from the estate.
There were no signs whatsoever of any ill feeling or friction
between them.

The Brigadier was pleased to hear that our experience
of the Army had not been entirely negative. During the

course of a very interesting day, we visited Girdwood Barracks, Woodburn Barracks, Musgrave Park Hospital and North Howard Mill, where the Marines are based.

Lunch was at Army Headquarters in Lisburn, where we were joined by Colonel Mick Hill and Assistant Chief Constable Ronnie Flanaghan of the RUC, together with the wives of the Brigadier and the Colonel.

On our visits to the barracks, we could see that life was quite obviously anything but normal for soldiers doing their tour of duty. Living quarters were generally very cramped, though everyone's spirits seemed high, and Wendy and I received a very warm welcome everywhere we went. This had been a tiring but worthwhile trip back to Belfast, as it gave us yet another perspective on Northern Ireland.

The following February we also spent a marvellous twenty-four hours in Ireland as the guests of the Limerick Peace Initiative. We were invited to present the prizes to youngsters in a number of age groups from four-year-olds to twelve-year-olds for a painting competition on the theme of peace.

We were greeted at Shannon Airport by the airport manager, who escorted us to a private lounge to meet Una Heaton and Valerie Quigley from the Peace Initiative.

RTE Radio and Television interviewed me, and then Wendy and I were taken to a civic reception at the city hall to meet the mayor, her fellow councillors and the local members of parliament. The mayor, Jan O'Sullivan, together with Noel Flannery, the chairman of the Limerick Peace Initiative which was formed in the wake of the Warrington bombing, presented us with a framed poem and a Peace 2000 print.

We then travelled to the University of Limerick where Wendy and I were to present the thirty awards. The room was crowded with excited children and their parents. Noel Flannery made a very moving speech welcoming Wendy

and me and then I replied, but in view of the age of many
of the children I kept my response brief.

It fell to me to call out the names of all the winners, but
because many names were Gaelic and totally unfamiliar
to me I required constant assistance from Valerie. When
the presentations were over, I was completely submerged
by children wanting their certificates signed and their
photographs taken with Wendy and me. The children
made the whole awards ceremony an exhausting but truly
gratifying experience.

Later that evening, we enjoyed a lively dinner in the
hotel with our many new friends, and on Saturday morning
Una and her husband John took us to Dromoland Castle
for coffee. At midday, Noel and his wife drove us all the
way from Limerick to Dublin, a journey of two and a half
hours, to catch our flight back to Liverpool.

As we approached the end of our first year without Tim,
Wendy and I felt we had experienced Ireland from every
conceivable angle. We could not imagine what else we
could have seen or who else we could have met to complete
our intensive education. We still do not pretend that we are
experts on Ireland, far from it in fact, but there will not be
too many other ordinary English couples who have been
pitched into Irish life quite as sharply as we have.

The Duchess of Kent's personal secretary had written
to us some months previously to inform us that as
the Duchess was fulfilling official engagements in the
north-west of England, she would be particularly pleased
if she could pay us a private visit on the same day. We
were only too happy to agree. The Duchess is one of
the members of the Royal Family whom both Wendy and
I have long admired. She always looks so relaxed and
genuinely interested in everyone she meets. I must admit
that her recent, and very public conversion to Roman
Catholicism also interested me, though Wendy warned

me that it would be far too personal an issue for us to mention it.

On the day, the Duchess called with her lady-in-waiting and her personal detective. The detective chose to wait in the kitchen, while the Duchess and her lady sat with us in the lounge. There the Duchess showed a very keen interest in our family and our well-being since, as she put it, 'the dreadful events which took Tim from you'. I must say that we found talking to the Duchess a great pleasure. It reminded us of our chat with Prince Charles. She was both interested and interesting. She told us of the many times she had visited Northern Ireland and of the times she had spent visiting the troops stationed over there. We told the Duchess about our visits to Northern Ireland, including the recent trip as guests of the British Army.

The Duchess complimented Wendy on her coffee, but that was the only time I thought she was being too kind! Her one-hour visit simply flew by and, as she departed, she expressed the hope that we would meet again soon. She also told us to let her know if she could be of any help whatsoever in the future.

One of the more distressing loose ends to be resolved before the first year ended was the matter of a legal verdict to account for the deaths of Tim and Johnathan. On 16 February, in the coroner's court in Warrington, we gathered to listen to the Cheshire County Coroner, Mr Hibbert, deliver his verdict. He declared that the inquest had been opened last year and would now reach its judgement.

Documentary evidence from the two Home Office pathologists was read out, and we winced in the expectation that all our efforts throughout the year to avoid hearing lurid details of Tim's injuries were about to be wasted. However, to our eternal relief, the Coroner simply read out that the pathologist, James Burns, had written in his official report that Tim had remained 'unconscious throughout' the time from the bomb blast to his death, and that he had sustained 'head and facial injuries'.

Under oath, I was required to confirm my identity, the fact that I had made a written statement following Tim's death, and that I was his father. As my statement was read out by the Coroner, I became quite upset without warning. Hearing my own words read out in a court of law hurt me in a way I could not have foreseen. As I sat in the witness stand, I fought to keep my emotions in check, but was unable to do so. I felt deeply uncomfortable, breaking down in such a place. The fact that it hit me without warning did not make me feel any less awkward.

Chief Inspector Mick Holland of Cheshire CID was requested to take the witness stand and read out his prepared statement which confirmed the place and times of the bombs and the property and human damage that resulted. Mick Holland stated that Johnathan Ball had died almost immediately and Tim had sustained very serious injuries. He added that responsibility for the bombing had been admitted by the Provisional IRA in Dublin. Mick went on to give more background information, keeping his tone of voice steady and his gaze directed at the Coroner.

Once Mick Holland had completed his evidence, the Coroner summed up by saying that the court could now release the boys' death certificates. He added that both deaths were caused by shrapnel due to an explosive device, planted with the clear intention to kill or maim. His official verdict was 'unlawful killing'. The whole court proceedings took just thirty-five minutes from start to finish.

Mick Holland and his senior officer, Chief Superintendent Les Lee, had shown considerable sensitivity to our family throughout the months since the bombing. Their team worked tirelessly to try to get a conviction, but to this day that goal has eluded them. However, Wendy and I have formed the greatest possible respect and admiration for many people in the Cheshire force from chief constable down through the ranks to constable. All of them did everything they could in what was for them the most shocking and upsetting case they had ever had to deal with. Les Lee told Wendy and me that he would never forget the grief he felt personally on becoming involved in the investigation.

March 25 marked the commemoration of the Tim Parry Memorial Garden at Great Sankey High School. A considerable amount of money was raised in a variety of ways by many kind people locally, but none more so than Albert Spiby who raised £1500 through a twenty-three-mile sponsored walk from Chorley to Warrington. The school's annual Fun Run also raised a considerable amount, and John Britton, the head teacher, consulted Wendy and me fully about the location and style of the garden.

Exactly one year after Tim's death, and on the last day of term before the Easter break, the vast majority of the school's pupils turned out to hear the Bishop of Warrington and the vicar from St Mary's, where Tim's funeral service had been held, give their blessings to the school for its fine efforts in commemorating Tim. During the Bishop's sermon, it seemed as if Tim had personally intervened. Throughout the day, intermittent heavy rain had fallen and the temperature had been cold owing to a strong blustery wind. At the exact moment the Bishop called upon Dominic and Abbi to lift the velvet material from the memorial stone, the clouds parted, and the most brilliant shaft of sunlight illuminated the whole area. It was such a moving moment that even the Bishop himself felt compelled to remark on it.

The ceremony included the school band playing several pieces of music, but when they played Michael Jackson's 'Heal the World', which had been played as Tim's coffin was carried from St Mary's on the day of his funeral, Wendy and I squeezed each other's hands tightly. Along with several hundred of Tim's friends and schoolmates, we wept openly at the memories that came flooding back.

When the singing and music ended, the children of Tim's school year filed past the memorial to plant ceramic flowers they had made personally. The children behaved perfectly and with great dignity, and did themselves, the school and Tim proud.

The day had ended in a most appropriate way, with many children who had known Tim personally remembering their friend in their own way. We, for our part, stood proudly as Tim's mother and father, having survived this most traumatic year.

If we had been asked on 20 March 1993, 'How well will you come through the year ahead?', I doubt very much that we would have had any confidence whatsoever that we had the emotional and psychological strength to survive one week, let alone one year. That we did, both individually and collectively, I credit entirely to Tim. The fierce determination that gradually took its place alongside our sense of desperate loss gave us the will and the strength to keep his dear memory alive and to link his life and death with the turning point in the search for peace and reconciliation in Ireland.

Our total commitment to keeping Tim in our lives and hearts will never diminish. On the morning of the first anniversary of Tim's death I was privileged to be given the 'Thought for the Day' slot on Radio 4's *Today* programme, which gave me the opportunity to tell listeners again of our beautiful son and his untimely death.

THOUGHT FOR THE DAY
25 MARCH 1994

It was exactly one year ago today that I lay down beside my son to hold him close for the final time before his life-support machine was switched off.

I held his hand as he died from the injuries caused by the IRA bombs placed in Bridge Street, Warrington.

At the time, I could never have imagined that Tim's death would affect so many people, or that Warrington could be the turning point in the search for peace in Northern Ireland.

Sadly, there have been more atrocities since Warrington, and I recall the outrages at Greysteel and in the Shankill Road, which left more families with the heartache of losing a loved one.

It's a chilling thought that there are people living among us who choose to kill other human beings. Who they kill is of no consequence to them, because they kill people they don't know and then rationalise what they've done – by proclaiming that the end justifies the means.

Two weeks ago I listened to Ronnie Flanaghan, assistant chief constable of the RUC, speaking about a fellow officer killed by an IRA gunman. He said the IRA had not murdered an anonymous member of the security forces, they'd murdered Jackie Hagan, the father of six-year-old Jason and five-year-old Terri. They'd murdered Jackie Hagan, husband of Kim, who is expecting their third child in August. It was right that Ronnie said these things. Because the victims of violence are real people and by talking about them we not only keep their memories alive but also make the murderers face up to what they have done.

Those who kill must not be allowed to ever forget

that they murdered a real person who had a name, and a family, had friends, and enjoyed life, and above all, had a God-given right to that life.

I believe that the people who kill do have a conscience and that it can be reached by seeing Tim's happy face and by reading of the impact his murder had on his family. If I'm right, then it's still not too late for those people to renounce violence.

They can be true to their cause without killing their opponents or innocent children, and in place of violence, they can use quiet persuasion or impassioned argument. They can even shout and scream if they wish to – but they can never justify taking the life of my twelve-year-old son, whatever their cause.

Ending the violence will allow trust and goodwill to return to Northern Ireland where people have the right to live free from the fear of being shot or blown apart. Understandably, violence makes people afraid to speak to those with different religious or political beliefs. Violence also forces good people apart, but in my experience good people are also brave people, and if enough of them tell the men of violence to stop and at the same time tell their politicians to set aside their seemingly unshakeable dogma, then peace can be built where it matters most – at community level.

Our son died one year ago today – and now he lies cold in the ground, denied his right to a long and happy future. Our hope now is that his life has been given to help bring about peace in Ireland so that all Irish people can enjoy the long and happy future that Tim had snatched from him, in that final moment of terror in Bridge Street last year.

Epilogue

All parents, regardless of differences in race, religion or sex, share an innate sense of personal responsibility for their children's welfare. Concern for your child's well-being is a constant feature of your life not only during the years when they are dependent on you, but also long after they have become adults.

It is because of this instinct to protect our children that we recoil in horror at the sight of the terrible tragedies that befall children the world over. Whether through war, starvation or just terrible misfortune, it is always the death of children which affects us most. When their innocent lives are cut short, we feel it deeply. We also feel the parent's pain and shudder at the thought of it ever being our own child.

Sometimes the tragic scenes on our television screens are so harrowing and so shocking that it is too much to bear and we look away. But when we do watch, our feelings of sympathy are occasionally tinged with the feeling of 'there, but for the grace of God, go I'.

Until 20 March 1993, Wendy and I had only ever felt the pain and suffering of other parents who had lost their children, whether they were black or white, Catholic or Protestant, boy or girl. When the scenes on television became too much for us to bear, we too could turn away. But not any more. Not since we became members of an exclusive club; a club that no one ever asks to join; a club that never has a waiting list.

We belong to the bereaved parents' club. It has a worldwide membership. Its members include people who

have lost a child at birth, and people who have lost a child
through ill health. It also has members whose children have
been killed, perhaps in a road accident or through a freak
sporting injury. There are members whose children have
been murdered, and there are members whose children
have been murdered in random acts of terrorism. There
are very few indeed of these, and within the British Isles
these few have mostly lived and died in Northern Ireland.
Mercifully, in mainland Britain, there have been very few
child victims of terrorism other than Tim and Johnathan
and Danielle Carter, killed in the Baltic Exchange bombing
in 1992.

It was the sudden, unexpected brutality of the bombings
in an obscure town like Warrington, where the deaths were
of two young innocent boys, which so moved Britain and
Ireland. The IRA bombing of Warrington, occurring as
it did on the day before Mothers' Day, was like the
brutal carnage that has occurred frequently in Northern
Ireland over many years. What Warrington demonstrated
beyond all doubt, however, was that terrorist violence can
be perpetrated with impunity at any time in any British
town or city. This stark realisation, and the loss of two
young, innocent lives, was what shocked the British and
Irish people. For the Irish, news of Warrington was all
the more sickening, coming as it did on the day when Ireland defeated England in the Rugby Union international
game at Lansdowne Road. Feelings of national pride and
celebration were replaced by feelings of national shame.

Losing a child is the most devastating and bitter experience any parent can ever face, but when your able-bodied,
fine-looking, fit and healthy twelve-year-old waves you
goodbye and never comes home again because a terrorist
takes him from you and you don't know why, then at the
very least you search for answers.

We feel, no matter how irrational it may be, that because

Tim was murdered we failed in our primary duty as parents to protect him when he needed it most. Where were we when he didn't know which way to run after the first bomb exploded? Had we been there with him, we might have kept him away from the second bomb. Of course, on the balance of probabilities, our presence would have made no difference whatsoever; in fact, we too may have been hurt or even killed. But whatever the consequences may have been for ourselves, at least we would have been consoled by the fact that we were with our son, when he needed us most, instead of which we will always live with the anguished knowledge that he was alone and terrified. In a life-threatening situation, the instinct for survival takes over, and naturally everyone looks out for themselves and their own family. In those final moments of blind panic and terror, Tim had no one to help him; he was completely alone at the moment when his life was snuffed out by flying shrapnel. I've often wondered what his last thoughts might have been. Did he think of his mum and dad? Did he call out to us for help?

Had we been there and had the same fate still befallen Tim, we would at least have been able to hold him, love him and talk to him in his final moments as his life ebbed away.

We know that it makes no sense to admonish ourselves over matters completely beyond our control. But as Tim's parents, we relive those dark moments when the life we created faced its final desperate moments alone. Our son's fateful decision on which way to run proved to be his last-ever decision, as he chose the wrong way. Had I been with him, would I have grabbed his hand and run the right way, the way to safety? I'll never know, but that won't stop me taking the question with me to my grave unanswered, and when Tim is there to greet me, as I pray to God that he will be, I still won't know the answer. Still, I hope he will forgive me for not being there when he needed me most.

There was a powerful and emotionally disturbing dream that came to me one night. It was so vivid and so clear that when I awoke, my conscious mind was in a state of extreme confusion and shock. In the dream, I visited Tim's grave every week to clip his fingernails. His hands, which were sticking out of the ground in front of his headstone, were white and still perfect, and it seemed the most natural thing in the world for me to clip his nails, since this had always been my job when all three of our children were very young.

I knelt down facing Tim's headstone, talking to him silently inside my head as I always do, and I began clipping his nails, though his fingers were rigid and very cold. When I had nearly finished, his fingers moved and began to feel warm. I was startled and rocked back on my feet, when suddenly the ground in front of me broke open. Tim's head and upper body emerged from the ground so that he was in a seated position, and then slowly he stood before me, perfectly still, and as his eyes opened, a beautiful, kind, angelic smile lit up his face. He looked just as he used to after emerging from the shower before getting ready for bed. He was wearing his green towelling robe. He held out his warm hands to me as I remained in my kneeling position looking up at him. I was beside myself with joy and love for him. To be holding him again like this was a miracle I could never have dared hope for. His voice was strangely calm and soothing when he spoke to me. He said, 'Dad, I know that I'm dead, but I've come to tell you that I don't want you to be upset.' With that, he stepped forward but without any appearance of walking, and he cradled my head to his waist and held me close as I wrapped my arms around him tightly the way I always used to.

We stayed like this for several minutes, me pressing my head and face into the warmth of his body, savouring every precious moment of a father's love for his young son. Then suddenly I woke and he was gone. But all my instincts told me that he had really been there with me, to reassure me that he was free from pain and still loved me. He was telling me not to feel guilt and, though I still do, I do not feel it with quite the same intensity as I did before he visited me. I have longed for the same dream to come again, but it never has, though when Tim is ready to commune with me another time he will. I know that now.

Twice since Tim's death, the film *Ghost* has been on television, and although we had all seen it at the cinema and found it to be a moving film, watching it on the two occasions since Tim died we found it to be even more poignant.

Wendy and I share the hope that at the moment Tim was being called to God, angels encircled him and carried him to Heaven. Patrick Swayze's final words to Demi Moore as she sees him for the last time before he is taken to Heaven, are: 'It's amazing, Molly . . . the love inside, you can take it with you.' Tim had our love inside him and he has taken it with him to Heaven. When his life ended, I told myself that he knew we were all with him and sending him to God with our love.

Wendy has dreamt of Tim too, and she recalls most clearly how in one particular dream Tim had survived the bombing but, despite sustaining less serious brain damage than we feared would be the case had he lived, he was completely blind. In this dream, I took Tim to his first football match at Everton after he had been released from hospital. Throughout the match, I performed the role of commentator, telling Tim everything that was happening on the pitch. Wendy told me that he smiled with pleasure at Everton scoring and winning the game, but it cut her to the heart to contemplate Tim being unable to see, and being unable to play with his friends, doing all the things he had so enjoyed doing. Wendy felt overwhelming sadness that Tim's life was so diminished, being lived through the

eyes and the senses of those around him. Even though Tim
was often cheerful in her dream, Wendy was heartbroken
looking at him when he was unable to look back at her.

She awoke from her dream weeping, as she has done
many times before, with the pain of his suffering and his
loss. It hurts Wendy deeply to see his friends, on the
long summer evenings, playing their games of football,
or just standing together talking. She has often wondered
whether the men who make and plant their bombs ever
stop to think of the consequences of their actions, in real,
everyday human terms. Do they, or indeed can they, ever
comprehend what they have done to us? Can they ever
comprehend Wendy's personal nightmare of wanting so
much for Tim to come back in whatever form he can, to
visit us, and yet being terrified that if he ever did she would
see him as he was after his injuries and not before, when
he was her golden-haired, good-looking boy.

We have pondered whether Tim himself ever had a
premonition that he would not live a long life. One of
the first projects he carried out in English at the High
School was entitled 'Tim's Life'. Within the project, which
covered a number of subject areas, such as friends, pets,
holidays, birthdays and Christmas and football, was a
family tree. Only after he died did we notice that, quite
inexplicably, Tim had omitted any reference to himself in
the diagram. He showed his maternal grandparents, John
and Betty, who produced Carol, Philip and his mum,
Wendy. He showed his paternal grandparents, Eric and
Lucy, who produced only me, his dad. He then showed
how his mum and I produced Dominic on 12 October 1978
and Abbi on 12 October 1981 but he omitted any reference
to himself in the family tree altogether.

The day Wendy noticed this omission, she reminded me
of a very strange and unexpected question that Tim had
asked us just three weeks before the fateful day of the

Bridge Street bombing. It was the Sunday immediately following the IRA bombing of the gasworks in Warrington. A local resident had videotaped the fireball rising into the black night sky and the major news bulletins on BBC and ITN were showing the dramatic film just as we were leaving Wendy's parents' house. We all stopped to watch the news report. Nobody spoke, although I expressed surprise that someone just happened to have their video camera to hand in the early hours of the morning.

Driving back from Manchester to Warrington along the M62 motorway, we were listening to a pop music station on the car radio until Tim punctured the conversational silence by asking, 'What would it be like to die?' There was a short pause before Wendy said, 'Timmy, what a question!' Then we gave him the answer we expect many parents would give to their inquisitive twelve-year-old. 'People who have almost died, but then recovered, have said that at the moment of death you enter a long tunnel, which has an extremely bright light at the end, and this is the sign that you are going to God.'

He asked us no further questions on the subject, which suggested that he was satisfied with the answer he'd been given. We, meanwhile, have been left to ponder his question many times since his death, and we have silently prayed that Tim did see eternal light and eternal life before him as he entered Heaven, and that he is now sure in the knowledge that we will all be reunited one day. These are our constant prayers and, God willing, they will be fulfilled when our time comes.

It was through Tim's friend Gaz that another quite remarkable and seemingly prophetic story came to us. Being as loyal as he was to Tim, and having taken his death so hard, Gaz decided that only he would use Tim's classroom chair and Brenda, his mother, told Wendy and me about it. We were touched by Gaz's decision and to this day he still uses the chair. But it was some time later, in a separate conversation with Gaz, that another angle to this story emerged, and it was this which shook us so much.

We told Gaz that his decision to use Tim's chair was something of which we entirely approved, and indeed understood, but then we asked him, 'Surely all the chairs are the same, so how do you know that you are actually using Tim's chair?'

Gaz's reply made me feel very strange. He said, 'That's no problem, Tim's chair is the one with the cross on it.'

'What kind of cross do you mean?' I asked. 'Do you mean a crucifix, like this?' I found myself making the sign of the crucifix with my fingers, just to be sure that Gaz and I were talking about the same kind of cross.

'Yes, that's right,' he told us.

'Was it you, or one of Tim's other friends, who put the cross on the chair?' I asked him.

'Oh no,' Gaz said. 'Tim put the cross on the chair himself, using a Tippex pen!'

I sat back, stunned by the fact that Tim had done this just a short time before his death. This was another bizarre event which only served to intensify my questioning as to whether Tim's death was meant to be, after all.

The question most commonly asked of us by many people is 'How are you coping?' This is a short question to which there is no short answer. The fact is that slowly we are becoming adjusted to our changed family. We have not all changed in the same way, or at the same pace, but so far the change has been handled as well as could be expected.

Dominic and Abbi were changing physically and mentally from children to young adults anyway, as indeed was Tim at the time of his death, and so we will never know how differently they would have developed had the IRA not targeted Warrington and had Tim lived and developed to full manhood himself. There have, of course, been times when we have considered the 'what if' and the 'if only' questions concerning our children's development. But these periods of reflection are usually inconclusive where Dom and Abbi are concerned, and very upsetting where Tim is concerned.

There was one occasion when I wrote to a particular ITN newsreader who we were told knew an expert in the science of projecting how young people would look at a more advanced age. This skill was generally used for the purposes of finding missing children. I became quite obsessed for a time, wanting to know how Tim might have looked as a man, and eventually I did make contact with the expert concerned, only to have my hopes dashed when I was informed that it was at best a speculative business and likely to be accurate only in the case of very young children. I thanked the person concerned for their time and trouble and became resigned to never satisfying my curiosity. No doubt many people would claim it was a foolish quest, but I cannot deny that I would still like to know how he might have looked as a man. For me it would be rather like having Tim live on, developing with our other children, even though it would be an illusion. But then illusion and reality are both a part of my life now anyway.

What of the Parry family now? Let me begin with Dominic, at fifteen a very big and solidly built young man, standing six foot one inch and over fifteen stone in weight. He talks a great deal, as he always did, and although his comments and questions are not always tactful or well thought out, we know that, at heart, he is a kind and warm-hearted lad who cares far more than he is capable of expressing. His feelings show in his face, in his expressions and, most of all, in his eyes. Dominic can and still does cry . . . in anger, in frustration, and in his love for his 'kid' brother, whom he had every right to argue with, fight with, laugh with and, above all, grow old with, as brothers are meant to do.

When Dominic is older and one day forms a lasting relationship with a woman he loves, we hope he will have children of his own, and we know that when he does he will bring Tim to life in their hearts and minds. Dom and I have already got a 'cast iron' agreement that his first son will be named Tim. It will be good for the next Tim Parry to become the man that our son Tim was never allowed to become. The one and only promise that I shall always expect Dominic to honour is to give me a blond, blue-eyed grandson called Tim, whom I can hold and love.

And what of Abigail, to give her the full name she hardly ever uses? She is not like her brother Dominic, nor is she particularly like her brother Tim. She is Abbi. She is very strong-willed and she is not to be put upon. She is able to see things through and she sticks to her principles and her beliefs. I see her future less clearly than I see Dominic's. I know she thinks often of Tim and I know she too will always keep him in her life. That she loved him is in no doubt, that she misses him is in no doubt, that she has adjusted to his death is, I think, less clear at this stage. Abbi is less obvious than Dom. She thinks more and speaks less. She already believes that she is independent and self-sufficient at just twelve years of age. She may be right. The year she has just lived through is bound to have accelerated her mental development considerably. She is tougher and probably more resilient than her older brother, though, if I put this to him, he would dismiss it out of hand. Nonetheless it is true.

Despite Abbi's apparent strengths, she is much more private about her own thoughts and hopes than Dominic. Without doubt, she has grown away from us both, but from me particularly. The warmth and affection so evident until 19 March 1993 has been replaced by something else, though I'm not yet sure what it is.

Wendy and I want Abbi and Dom to be educated, healthy and well-adjusted people, but above all to be secure and happy. That they would have been, in normal circumstances, I do not doubt. That they still will be is, as yet, less certain. So far as it is within our power and influence to do so, we will keep them close to us and safely guide them through the next crucial years in their lives.

When I look at Wendy, I see someone who has suffered the loss that is every parent's nightmare. That she has real and deep reserves of strength is obvious, for without them she would have never have come this far without the loss of Tim breaking her.

She is exceptionally well balanced and has a practical side to her which has enabled her to continue being a very good mother to Dominic and Abbi. Her pride in the family has never diminished. Despite all the pressures and the new commitments we have chosen to take on, Wendy still works long and hard to maintain a sense of order and pride in each of our lives.

Mostly she keeps her grief inside. It is quite rare for Wendy to articulate her real feelings. I know that last thing at night Wendy closes her eyes, remembering Tim, and when she awakes in the morning it is to thoughts of Tim. I know this, but not because she has told me. Discussing her feelings openly does not come easily to Wendy. The most straightforward way of describing this side of her character might be to say that feelings are for feeling and not for speaking.

She can be hurt, and is hurt, by insensitivity. There have been occasions when people have said, 'Why don't you just get on with your life? Why do you get involved in all these other things?' Though they may not intend to be critical, such questions do hurt because of the implication they carry within them, that we are not doing what's best for each other and for our other children.

People have even hinted that we may have sought publicity for its own sake, presumably forgetting what it was that put us into the public eye in the first place. The few people who have questioned our integrity or sincerity are, we are relieved to say, vastly outnumbered by those who continue to show us great support and encouragement.

Considering that Wendy would never have encouraged the media's intervention in our lives, she has handled it superbly well. I know that she would have preferred, in those early days, to have declined the television and press interviews; they made her feel nervous and uncertain about what she should say. After the event she always believed that she had said something foolish or ill considered, but that was never the case.

It took great courage on her part to make the *Panorama* programme. She used to tell me not to expect her to ask any questions or to take an active part, and yet, often to her own great surprise, she found herself pitching in. The trouble was that, even after taking an active part, she would assume that she had said something wrong.

Wendy's confidence in public has grown. It has had to. Had it not done so, she would probably have confined herself to the house. The attention the family received meant that, even if we had not talked to the press, we would still have had to adjust to the recognition that comes from being involved in a major news item. However, as time goes by, the nature of the public's interest does change. Instead of remembering Tim and your suffering, people begin to judge your behaviour and your actions and, of course, when this happens you are vulnerable to criticism.

We did not choose to have our son's life shattered. We did not seek anything other than to lead a perfectly normal, conventional life. But when Tim was taken from us, it seemed as if the world wanted to know how it felt, how we were coping, and how it affected us. So we told them as honestly as we could.

I freely admit that I could not have dealt with our son's death in any other way. I had to talk about our loss with as many people as I could. Only by talking so much about Tim, and by writing this book, have I managed to maintain my sanity. I could have chosen to say very little and do no more than simply satisfy the media's curiosity about our family and our grief, but that would have left me without a serious long-term purpose. Had I chosen that route, I know that I would soon have become bitter and angry about the terrible injustice of our fate. Such bitterness and anger would then have driven me to total despair. With no goal to strive for, I would have been of little or no use to Wendy, Dominic and Abbi. So the fact that I chose to be public about Tim has at least given me the chance to direct my energies and my questions to some good, in Tim's name.

This does not mean that I have always been fair and reasonable with Wendy or the children. There have been times when I have become irritated and short-tempered over something very minor, the most common example being the occasional moodiness of the children. My tolerance of anything that smacks of self-pity is very limited now, and no matter how unfair it is to remind Dom and Abbi that they have a life and a future that Tim doesn't have, I cannot help myself. Even on the occasions when I don't actually say this openly, I still think it. Perhaps one day when they have children of their own, they will understand better that being a parent does not always make you sympathetic to your child's every whim, particularly when you have far more important matters on your mind than when their next pocket money is due, or whether they can have a friend over to stay.

*   *   *

Tim never came back home – home where he was safe, where he was loved and cherished. I was not about to let him be forgotten, nor let him be just one more victim. He was our son. He was our joy. He was innocent and he was murdered by a faceless coward. So if anyone thinks I am misguided or just plain wrong to talk about Tim constantly, I would ask them to remember this:

On 1 September 1980 at 1.25 p.m. Tim Parry was born, weighing 7lbs 14ozs and measuring 48 cms in length. Wendy gave birth to a healthy, cuddly baby and I was there as he entered the world.

Twelve years, six months and twenty days later we listened in abject disbelief to the most terrible and shattering words any parents could ever hear: 'I am sorry to have to tell you that I don't think your son will survive the night.'

Five days later, following the most monumental fight against all the odds, our son Tim succumbed to his dreadful injuries and died. He died with me holding his hand. His chest stopped rising and falling as I looked on helplessly. His skin turned from healthy pink to cold blue before my eyes and he was gone, gone for ever. His life was over and I looked on helplessly.

When our cherished son entered this world I was there, elated and overjoyed, and when our cherished son left this world I was there, devastated and heartbroken.

No mother or father could have prayed harder or begged to the good Lord more for their son to be given his life back. If prayer, hope and raw pleading produced miracles, then Tim would be up and about and with his family today. But it was not to be.

Wendy and I produced a real gem only to have him snatched from us, and I'm damned if I will ever stop talking about our Tim, an ordinary boy.

Postscript

It was 2.30pm on Sunday, May 22 1994 when I finally laid down my pen having written the epilogue to this book. I confess that what I felt most at that moment was a sense of relief that it was finished. Yet within hours my mood changed to one of emptiness as I came to realise that I would never again face a challenge as worthwhile as the writing of this testimony to our son. Whether this memorial to Tim will prove to be of any consequence to anyone beyond our immediate family does not matter unduly, for the sole purpose in writing it was to create an honest biographical account of an innocent boy's life, and his death in the name of a cause of which he knew nothing.

Since May last year life for our family has been quieter and rather more normal than it had been in the first year following the bombing. It had been the developments across the Irish sea which have brought us most pleasure and a deep sense of satisfaction, and they have certainly served to keep our spirits from flagging.

By far the most notable of these was the announcement that from midnight on August 31 1994 the IRA would cease its campaign of terror. This meant that from September 1, the day which would have been our son's fourteenth birthday, the violence, which took his life and his vitality away from us forever, would be over. For this eagerly awaited deliverance from twenty-five years of evil, to take place on this day of all days, was the most poignant vindication yet of our increasingly strong belief that Tim had not died in vain.

Alongside our own personal joy at the news of the ceasefire, was the joy we felt for all the people of Ireland, north and south, that they may begin to enjoy the normal, everyday, simple things of life.

Some six weeks later, the peace process took another major step forward when the Loyalist paramilitaries declared their own ceasefire. The exact date of this was October 13th – the day after Dominic's and Abbi's sixteenth and thirteenth birthdays. So again it seemed to us that Tim was laying his own hand on events.

When we sit quietly and reflect upon the terrorist attrocities of the past two years; those in Warrington, the Shankill road, Greysteel and at Louchinisland; we cannot help but recall that at the time there seemed little realistic prospect of an end to the violence. And yet, here we are now, on the verge of securing a lasting peace. The question on everyone's mind, of course, is will it hold through the many difficult negotiations that lie ahead? Frankly, I believe the answer is yes, provided sufficient numbers of people from all sections of society demand it, and provided the politicians then obey the will of those people.

Some may say that this is a simplistic view, but it is no less true for that. For as long as people grow used to the simple but wonderful fact that living in peace with one's neighbour is greatly to be preferred to the constant fear of death by bomb or bullet, then the political way through what will undoubtedly be a long and tortuous process can be found. No one believes it will be easy, for there are hundreds of years of bloody history which stand in the way of rapid progress, and people cannot be expected to forget what they, their families and their communities have suffered.

Yet it is precisely because of that suffering that the ordinary citizens of Northern Ireland, the Irish Republic and Great Britain must compel all those with influence in their respective decision-making roles to understand that they must not be allowed to throw away this opportunity. If lost, it may not return for another generation or more.

Earlier in this book I said that Northern Ireland was crying out for a visionary politician, like Nelson Mandela, who could capture the spirit of the new age. Although no one single person may yet have emerged, we can be thankful that there is a recognition that the old guard, who have preached the same unyielding message for so long, are approaching the end of their time. They should stand aside to let the new generation make progress if they are incapable of delivering the dreams of the people.

My dream, Wendy's dream, Dominic's dream and Abbi's dream is that Tim's death made a difference. That his life was blessed and special, we already know, because of the joy and fun and vitality he brought to this little corner of North West England for twelve and a half years. But we yearn that his sacrifice – his supreme sacrifice – was not in vain, and that as a result no more children in Ireland or Britain will lose their lives in the name of a cause which should and could have always been pursued peacefully. We pray that in his new home, free from pain and worry, God is taking good care of him until we are all united again. Until that day, Tim . . .

March 1995